MW00365315

DEDICATION

To My Wife and Best Friend, Mary

Thank you for letting me spend a month at "sea"
and two years writing and editing,
so I could actually finish this book.

THANK YOU !

***With Deepest Thanks and Gratitude
to My Lord and Saviour Jesus Christ***

For giving me the boat and the heart to take this voyage,
and for blessing my trip, my life, and the
production of this book beyond my wildest dreams.

Contents

1. Cruising on (not so) Dry Land 11
2. Refreshment and Rest? 21
3. Miracles, Stop Lights and Rubber Fish 29
4. Crossing into the Promised Land 43
5. Dead in the Water for a Reason 51
6. Up a Canal without a Motor 63
7. I Didn't Know God Made White Pelicans 73
8. The Anchor Holds 81
9. Meaner than a Boat Yard Dog 91
10. Bold Adventurer or Aging Fool? 101
11. The Coast Guard Searches for "God Speed" 111
12. Any Port in a Storm 123
13. Hurricane Ahead of Me–Hurricanes Behind Me 133
14. Lost 139
15. Hunkered Down in a Blow 147
16. Learning to Trust My Compass 155
17. Aground at Four AM 163
18. Singing to the Dolphins, Feeding the Gulls 173
19. Help from an Unlikely Source 183
20. Private First Class US Army Aboard 191
21. Scary Dreams and Scarier Situations 197
22. Monster from the River Bottom 209

23. Twice Aground in Two Days 215
24. A Three Hour Tour. 227
25. Courage in the Darkness. 237
26. The Docks that Were Built Just for Us. 245
27. Buzzed by a Navy Helicopter 255
28. No See Ums and Young Lovers 263
29. "Big Waves Sink Small Sailboat on the Chesapeake" 269
30. In the Wrong Place at the Right Time 277
31. The Royal Treatment in a Hidden Harbor 285
32. His Majesty's Ship Surrenders to the Enemy 297
33. A Bridge Too Low and a Mast Too Tall 307
34. Blessed with a Brand New Engine 323
35. Seven Foot Seas in the North Atlantic 339
36. Guiding Angels on the Hudson 353
37. The New York State Barge Canal. 367

Voyage
Of The Heart

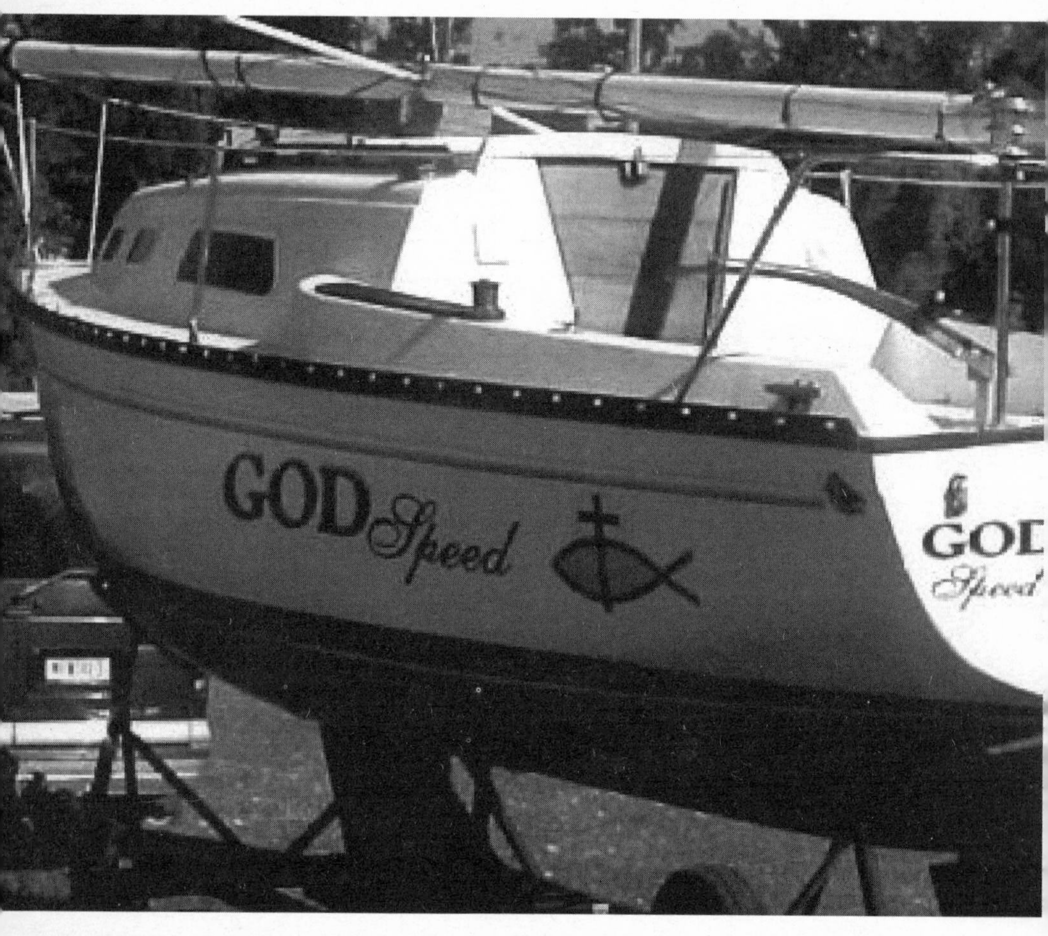
GOD Speed
GOD
Speed

Chapter 1

Cruising on (not so) Dry Land

Vaarrraaauuum!! I cringed as yet another tractor-trailer roared by me sending a wave of water and spray against my windshield. My view of the road was obliterated for a second as my wipers beat furiously to cut through the wall of water that swept over me. My mirrors told me that the suction from the truck had caused the boat trailer to fish tail again. Two tons of sailboat precariously balanced on the small, lightweight, trailer now swayed back and forth behind my van. The large boat on its trailer outweighed and towered above my Astro van making it seem tiny by comparison. I could feel all that weight moving the back of my van and threatening to push me out of control and off the road, or worse yet into the path of the next truck that passed me. I slowed down gradually, trying to steer the straightest course possible, so the trailer would stop swaying. As I did, yet another semi thundered by, again flooding my van and windshield with water. I had been driving south on interstate eighty-one after dark in a torrential downpour. I had learned that the homemade trailer that came with my sailboat was not really adequate to tow the boat a long distance at highway speeds. The small single axle trailer was fine for towing the boat a few miles down the road to our local marina, but it started to sway dangerously at any speed over forty. This was especially true if I didn't steer a straight course or the wind from a passing truck gave it a push. I was forced to crawl along at forty miles per hour keeping my oversized load as far over as I could in the right lane while trucks and other traffic zoomed by me doing seventy. I shuddered as vehicles blew by my wide swaying load, missing it by what seemed like inches and shot by me as though I was standing still. The relentless downpour, the darkness and the poor visibility caused by my worn wiper blades fighting a losing battle with the water, all began to take their toll on me. I felt like I had been driving forever, underwater in a dark endless abyss. My slow speed made the very long drive to Florida seem unbearable. I had accepted the fact that it would take two or three days to make what would normally be a twenty-four hour trip, but the thought of it now seemed overwhelming. Although I was only doing forty, I felt like I was going too fast and my rig was out of control. I was physically and mentally exhausted and emotionally drained. I continued to push through the night with a death grip on the steering wheel. My minds eye saw visions of the van laying on its side in the ditch and the beautiful boat that I carefully cleaned, waxed and polished broken and scattered across the highway in several pieces, like a giant fiberglass egg. *This is crazy, I thought, what am I doing here? Why am I doing this? Lord Jesus, please allow me to arrive safely at my destination so I can take this once in a lifetime trip. Help me to have positive experiences, lasting memories and to touch hearts and lives, as I travel on land and in the water. Please put your angels around me and slow down the rain and the traffic. Help me to remember that I am in your hands and that this is your trip. Please be with me now as I travel, Amen.*

Ever since I got hooked on sailing twenty years ago, I had been infatuated with the idea of traveling a long distance using sails and the wind. I learned to sail by playing around with my Uncle's Sea Snark one summer, and even then I felt a strong desire to do more than just zig zag back and forth across the lake. One windy morning I tied the "Snark" to the top of my car and drove to a boat launch at the south end of the lake. With a stiff south wind and two-foot following waves, I sailed the tiny boat all the way to a park at the north end of the lake, fourteen miles away. That small craft was little more than a shallow Styrofoam bathtub with a sail, but when I stepped out of it three hours later, I felt like a great adventurer and was hooked on sailing for life.

Over the years I had owned several different boats. Most of them had a small cabin that slept three or four, with a sink, a stove, an icebox and a porta potty. I was intrigued by the idea of traveling and exploring by boat and living in the boat. My hopelessly romantic mind told me that a sailboat that was also a floating camper had to be the best thing in the world. What could be better than cruising as far as the wind and the waves would take you by day and then tying up to spend the evening at a different dock each night? Or dropping anchor near a beach or island and wading ashore to rest, explore, swim or fish? You could cook dinner on shore or on the boat, before settling into your bunk for the night. Through the open hatch above your face you would watch the top of the mast swing slowly back and forth as if to point out every constellation in the star-filled summer sky. You would be gently rocked to sleep by the boat and awake to a sunrise over the water. For a sailor who was also a fisherman, dinner might be the catch of the day. The only thing better than owning a water front home, was cruising in a small floating water front "home" with sails that was in a new and different place each morning.

These idealistic dreams of cruising under sail caused me to subject my children, my wife and my friends to many "adventure" trips over the years. I had always been a school band director and having the whole summer off made it easy to plan extended sailing trips to “far away” places. Over the years we had traveled up and down the New York State Barge Canal and through New York’s Finger Lakes. We had been through the Welland Canal beside ocean going ships and had explored the U.S. and Canadian shores of Lake Ontario and Lake Erie, spending a night in each harbor along the way. We had crossed Lake Erie and Lake Ontario several times in small boats fighting big waves. Three summers ago, my son and I sailed a day sailor from New Jersey to Virginia Beach on the Intra Coastal Waterway, surviving eight foot waves on the last day of that trip. Once I sailed a canoe across Lake Ontario, equipped with a homemade sailing rig I had built and was trying to have patented.

There were many experiences, and countless memories, and some of them would last a lifetime. Yes, there were some beautiful times, just like the ones I imagined, but those moments were actually few and far between in the real world of traveling in a sailboat. Many times a good part of the trip would be frustrating, disappointing and a lot of hard work. There were many scary moments when we were lost or fighting big waves, rain and high winds. I shuddered, as I remembered times that I had foolishly placed myself, and worse yet my children, in dangerous, life threatening situations. I continued to drive through the darkness and the rain, reflecting on the highlights of past sailing trips. I smiled as I remembered my children diving off the boat, or happily sitting on the bow with their feet dangling over the side. They loved to feel the boat rise up and then slam down into a wave, sending spray into their faces and splashing their legs and feet. I could still see them huddled together in their pajamas nodding and smiling as a lock operator on the barge canal serenaded them with his accordion on a still summer night. As I weighed all of the fond memories against the negative ones, I knew that something in me really loved doing this. Here I was at age fifty-two, poised on the verge of the longest and most demanding sailing trip I had ever attempted. Ever since I owned my first sailboat, I had dreamed of sailing a boat down the intra coastal waterway from New York to Florida. This always seemed like the ultimate sailing adventure: sailing and camping on the boat for a month or more, passing through nine different states and seeing almost the entire east coast. As a Christian, it was also an excellent way to touch hearts and lives for Jesus Christ. Traveling through that many states, past boats, marinas, yacht clubs and waterfront homes in a boat with a highly visible, thought-provoking Christian name could be a powerful missionary trip. If I flew a Christian flag from the top of my mast, there would be no doubt what I stood for, what I believed, or who I was sailing for. I would meet and have the chance to talk to many people along the way as I tied up or anchored in a different place each night. There was no telling how many lives I might touch; covering most of the east coast on a waterway frequented by up scale, well to do boaters.

As I planned the trip, I remembered sailing south on the Intra Coastal to Virginia Beach with a south wind in my face most of the way. My sailor's instincts told me that if I *started* in Florida, and sailed north to New York, there was a greater chance I would have the wind behind me and could use my sails more often. I was intrigued by the long distance, yet relative safety of this trip. The Intra Coastal Waterway was a system of canals, rivers and bays connected and maintained to allow boaters to travel up and down the coast safely inland, without having to be on the open Atlantic. There was just one short stretch off the New Jersey coast where boats had to venture into the ocean for about thirty miles to get into New York harbor and the Hudson River. That made me a little nervous, but I could always do that stretch when the weather was perfect, and stay close to the Jersey Shore. *Besides, thirty miles was no big deal, I could do that in four hours motoring at full speed if I had to. How bad could it possibly get out there in just four hours?* Having plowed through big waves many times in much smaller boats, I was confident that I could navigate my way through just about anything.

As I drove, I thought about the blessings that led to the purchase of the boat now swaying behind me in the darkness. God must have wanted me to have it, because the amazing chain of events was far too miraculous to have happened by chance. I had sold my last cruising sailboat years ago when my wife and children lost interest in going with me. Three summers ago the Lord blessed me with a small, used day sailor that I picked up for almost nothing. After refurbishing it, I sailed it to Virginia Beach with my son. The trip rekindled my love of sailing and traveling by boat and I soon caught myself looking at and dreaming about, larger sailboats. Although I couldn't really afford one on a Christian school teacher's salary, it was fun to look and to dream. I had learned how to find great deals buying and selling things on eBay. Over the course of two years, I bought, fixed up, sold and traded seven different boats and several motors and trailers. With the Lord's help, a lot of hard work and by being honest with people, I was able to work my way from day sailor to twenty-five foot sailing yacht, spending very little money out of my own pocket. I had to drive to Michigan, Cape Cod and the Jersey Shore towing boats, but now that I owned a boat that was larger and newer than I ever dreamed possible; it all seemed worth it. My twenty-five foot Hunter was larger and heavier than any boat I had ever owned, and it really was like new inside and out. Roomy, clean and loaded with features and equipment; it had a trailer, a shallow draft fixed keel and an almost new Honda four stroke outboard. It was hard to believe that I finally owned a boat big enough to be considered a "yacht" (at least in my own mind) and one that I felt was big enough to sail to Florida. I knew that the good Lord wanted me to have this boat because it was already equipped with everything I would need for this trip, including the shallow water keel. I was to learn only too well how critical it was to have a shallow draft boat on certain sections of the Intra Coastal Waterway. I felt God's hand of blessing on every transaction as several boats sold for much more than I expected. The most dramatic example was when the former owner of my Hunter 25, in Michigan, agreed to accept a small down payment and wait until spring for the balance, even though he had an offer for the full amount from someone in his town! Because the Lord had blessed me with such a beautiful boat so perfect for my needs, I vowed to give it a name that would glorify him and remind people of his presence. "God Speed" was the name I chose, the classic two word blessing people used to wish someone a safe and speedy journey. That name was even more significant, since every sailboat relied on the wind for speed and God controlled all winds and weather. The name also expressed the wish that Jesus would return to the earth soon during these last days of sin, trouble, wars and tragedies. I purchased a custom boat graphic with the words "God Speed" and a large Christian fish emblem for the sides and the back of the boat. The highly visible name and emblem, were now in the face of every motorist who passed me as a reminder that God was real. Perhaps it was even his will that I wasn't able to go any faster. At forty miles per hour, far more people would pass me and see the boat than would have if I was able to cruise along at sixty-five or seventy! I began to realize how many lives I might touch just towing this monster down the road, not to mention sailing it back up the coast of America. It also occurred to me how much the enemy would love to stop me from doing this. He wanted me to get discouraged, lose heart, forget what I came for and give up this "crazy" idea. If I gave up now due to rain, weariness and fear, he would win a major victory. A new desire and focus came over me as I gripped the wheel ever tighter, determined to keep going. *I will make it, I vowed, I can do this. I am going to put this boat in the water and take this trip as long as the van can still pull it and the motor and sails will move me forward. I will make this trip as long as there is a way to keep going and my heart is still beating! I believe the Lord has given me this boat to make this voyage for him. I have waited, planned and prepared for this, and I have invested too much time and hard work to turn back now.* I reminded myself that all I had to do was keep driving, and I would be able to point my bow northward and set sail on the voyage I had dreamed about for so long!

Voyage of the Heart

Chapter 2

Refreshment and Rest?

My fuel gauge told me I would need gas soon, my stomach was starting to call for food and my eyes, brain and jangled nerves badly needed a break. I was somewhere in Maryland and the next exit looked like it was home to a large truck stop, so I signaled, slowed my "rig" and started down the exit ramp. It felt good to be out of the stress and noise of all the traffic. I thought it would be a good idea to get something to eat and then sleep for a while. Maybe if I slept until midnight and then drove in the wee hours of the night, there would be fewer trucks on the road and perhaps the rain would have stopped by then. "It was nice to be out of the driver's seat," I thought, as I stretched my arms and legs. Protected from the rain by a canopy, I gassed up with the boat outside the windows of a truck stop cafeteria, in full view of the truckers and other travelers inside. It looked warm and inviting in there and with each opening of the door the smell of hot food wafted out to tempt me. After paying, I went inside and called my wife to let her know my progress, then I eagerly looked at the food that was available at the stainless steel buffet bar. Staring hungrily through the plate glass shield, I ignored the greasy fingerprints on it, but quickly realized that the food behind it was not as appealing up close as it had looked and smelled from outside. Maybe I had been driving too long, but every thing looked old, runny, dried up or congealed. Some of the items seemed like a guaranteed invitation to heartburn, and the hefty prices would certainly put a dent in my limited food budget. Oh well, when in doubt go with what you know. I had lots of "provisions" stowed away in the storage compartments of the boat, and I was going to be climbing up there now to sleep, so I chose not to dip into the "food money" just yet. As I came back outside, a young man approached me with a friendly smile. "Wow, that sure is a beautiful boat, and I love the name on it! I'm a believer too," he stated proudly. I told him about my trip, and how I hoped to witness to people or at least remind them about God as I traveled. "What a neat trip and a great idea, I wish I could go with you," he said sincerely with admiration in his voice. (Admiration I didn't deserve) "God Speed brother, have a safe trip, I hope you make it, nice meeting you!" He showered me with encouragement and blessings, and shook my hand enthusiastically as we parted company. Lord, was that a chance encounter, or did you put him here to inspire me to keep going? Thanks Lord, for reminding me how visible the large boat with its prominent lettering really was, and the kind of impact it had on other people who saw it. A smile came to my weary face as I kidded myself that perhaps the friendly young man had been an angel, placed in just the right place at the right time to spur me on and lift my sagging spirits. As I opened my van door to climb into the driver's seat, a tall burly man wearing camouflage approached and asked me about the "Outdoor Videos" that were advertised on my van. Besides being the band director at a Christian school, the Lord had allowed me to film and produce eight different "outdoor" videos over the years. Being an avid hunter and wildlife photographer, the videos had come about as the Lord blessed and used one of my hobbies beyond my expectations. I sold and distributed them as part of an outreach ministry to outdoorsmen and nature lovers. I was often asked to show my videos and share my testimony at church game dinners, hunter's banquets and men's breakfasts. To advertise my videos and my availability as a guest speaker, I had lettering on my van. Since it was already lettered for a Christian ministry, it gave me the excuse to also have the words "God Loves You" in large letters on the back door. The words on my van had drawn the attention of this large man who appeared to be a hunter. "What type of outdoor videos do you have?" He asked, with a hearty smile and sincere interest. I dug out one of my brochures from the pocket behind the driver's seat and handed it to him. "Are you the guy that has the Christian radio show for hunters every Saturday morning?" He asked, as he looked eagerly at the brochure. "No, that's not me, but I've heard about the program," I replied. "He's a good man with quite a ministry," the guy said, and then added that he listened to it every week. "These videos you've produced look great," he continued, "It looks like the Lord is using you, too." "Well, I fall short a lot, but I try," I answered, and then went on to tell him about the voyage I was about to attempt. He wished me a safe journey and a blessed trip, as he shook my hand and thanked me for the brochure.

I picked a spot that I could pull out of without backing up, as I eased my rig in among the tractor-trailers behind the truck stop. As I stopped, I noticed several more trucks heading down the exit ramp and pulling into the large parking area. Apparently other drivers had the same idea. Rest for a while, and head out again later to do battle with road and spray at a calmer, quieter time, or in the comfortable safety of daylight. The damp night air was tainted with the smell of diesel fuel from the idling trucks. I didn't know much about diesel engines, but I did know that truckers left their engines running for long periods when they were parked, so they wouldn't have to restart them. As I listened to the rumble of the truck engines, it occurred to me that with all the noise and smell this might not be the best place to take a nap. "Oh well, as worn out as I am, I should be able to sleep through just about anything," I thought.

When the boat sat on its trailer, the lowest entry point to climb aboard was at least ten feet off the ground. I brought an aluminum stepladder with me for getting up into the boat while on the road. The lightweight older ladder had a loose support brace and was not known for its stability. My daughter had broken an arm falling from it as a young girl helping me with a roofing project. To get into the security and comfort of my "floating camper" on land, I had to stand on the very top step (the one that says do not stand on this step) and reach up to pull myself up and over the side. Coming down was even more treacherous, as you had to lower your body and feel for the flimsy top step with your feet. Once you were standing on it, you could gradually relax your death grip on the boat and descend when you were "sure" the ladder wasn't going anywhere. When I was safely aboard, I pulled the ladder up after me and folded it on the deck. More secure than at any marina, I could then rest easy, knowing that no intruder could get into the boat (unless they carried a ladder around with them).

Once inside, the touch of a finger on a ceiling light fixture illuminated the boats cozy interior. The small space that would be my home for the next month seemed safe and appealing. I nodded with approval as I admired the clean carpeting and new looking upholstery. The natural wood grain of the dark teak bulkhead and cabinets had a rich glow in the soft light. Countertops and sink shone with a reflective sparkle and there was a place for everything and everything was in its place. I had spent the last month cleaning, vacuuming, shampooing, caulking, and polishing. I also made several improvements and minor repairs, installing a heavy-duty motor bracket and a new lighted compass to get the boat ready for this once in a lifetime trip. On the main bulkhead was a framed eight by ten print of the famous oil painting "Christ Our Pilot" by Warner Sallman. This painting shows a young man steering a ship through huge crashing waves on a dark stormy night. Standing behind him, with one hand on his shoulder and the other pointing the way through the storm is Jesus. I framed and hung this picture in the cabin as a constant reminder and encouragement for myself during the trip. As my gaze fell on the picture, mixed feelings of awe, thanksgiving, and joy welled up in me as I was overcome by emotion. "Heavenly father, I can't thank you enough for giving me a boat that is this big, this beautiful and this well equipped," I praised. "Lord, it is hard for me to believe that this really is my boat and that I am really here. Please keep it safe and protect me as I travel. Thank you for the work that was accomplished to get it ready and your provision and blessings that have allowed me to make this trip!"

Too excited and worn out to pull out utensils and prepare real food, I dug greedily into my stash of homemade trail mix. The plump juicy raisins mingled with the taste of peanuts in my mouth, as I felt the sweetness from the chocolate chips send a surge of energy through my weary body. I marveled at how good the simplest food always tasted when you were starving or on an "adventure" far from home. I sipped on the straw of a partially frozen drink box relishing how good it also tasted. I had forgotten that the front compartment where I slept was filled with sail bags and the aluminum boom that attached to the mast. They would be on deck when the boat was in the water, but now they made a compact living space even smaller. Moving them out of the way and dousing the lights, I stretched out my tired body on the front berth. The soft cushion felt wonderful beneath me as my knotted muscles and jangled nerves began to relax. My head settled into the cool softness and familiar smell of my pillow as I stared at the white fiberglass ceiling above my face. The streetlights and headlights from moving vehicles lit the now dark cabin and glared into my eyes. The steady rumble of idling truck engines around me seemed louder now as I tried to sleep, and the smell of diesel fuel was sickening. Although my body was relaxed, my mind raced with thoughts and plans as I nervously anticipated what lay ahead and mentally reviewed the day's events.

As I rushed to get an early start that morning, I backed over a Styrofoam ice chest in my driveway with the boat trailer. When I finally got rolling, a noise caused me to pull over and retrieve some tools I had left on top of the van when I made a repair to the mast top antenna. *I didn't get off to a very good start, did I?* I thought, pretty disappointed in myself. I hoped those miscues were not a preview of oversights and mistakes that would occur as I traveled, resulting in damage to the boat or a serious injury. *Was I too old and too absent minded to be doing this? I wondered. Would I have the physical strength and stamina I would need, in a desperate situation when I was alone? Well, I had made it that far, I would just have to remember that God was with me, and continue to rest in his strength.*

It didn't take long for me to realize that with the noise, the smell, the bright lights, and my over active mind, I wasn't going to fall asleep there anytime soon. *It's eleven o'clock and it looks like many of the truckers are pulling in for the night. There shouldn't be as much traffic out there now, I thought, as my mind raced with ideas and plans.* The heavy drumming of rain drops on the cabin had slowed to a light pitter-patter, so I decided that this would be a good time to gain as many miles as I could, while driving conditions were better. I decided to drive until I felt really drowsy and could fall asleep easily. Then I would sleep deep and long; hopefully waking up rested and refreshed.

Out on the highway, things were better than before. The rain had slowed to a drizzle and there were fewer trucks blowing by me. I brought some trail mix and a couple of drink boxes into the van. My short break and the improved driving conditions gave me new confidence and a more positive mental attitude. Having food and drink energized me and helped pass the time as I plugged along in the darkness at my slow, tedious pace. After three and a half hours I was feeling very drowsy. I was now on a stretch of highway that had an occasional stop light. Side roads crossed the main drag occasionally and right and left turns were allowed. Since traffic was very sparse at that hour it was easy to turn left, crossing both sides of the divided highway to pull into a commercial fuel stop with a large truck parking area. Conditions at that parking lot were similar to the last one with noise, diesel smell and bright lights, but by now I was completely mentally and physically exhausted. Once inside the boat and sprawled out on my berth, I drifted into a state of restless sleep. I must have eventually drifted deeper, because I was harshly startled awake by the shriek of an air brake and the roar of acceleration as a big rig pulled out to head for the highway. "Praise the Lord I got some sleep!" I shouted happily. My joy lasted for all of twenty seconds, as I fumbled for my watch in the darkness, and discovered that it was four thirty AM, and that I had only slept for two hours. I knew that it would be a waste of time to try to fall back to sleep, so I encouraged myself with thoughts of how far I could get that day with such an early start and the fact that it would soon be daylight.

As I sat behind the wheel, preparing to pull out of the parking area a prayer came to mind: "Heavenly Father thank you for allowing me to get this far and for keeping the boat and my van safe. Speed me on my way Lord, and travel with me. Please help the remaining miles and hours to pass quickly, and give me the peace that passes all understanding. In Jesus name I pray, Amen."

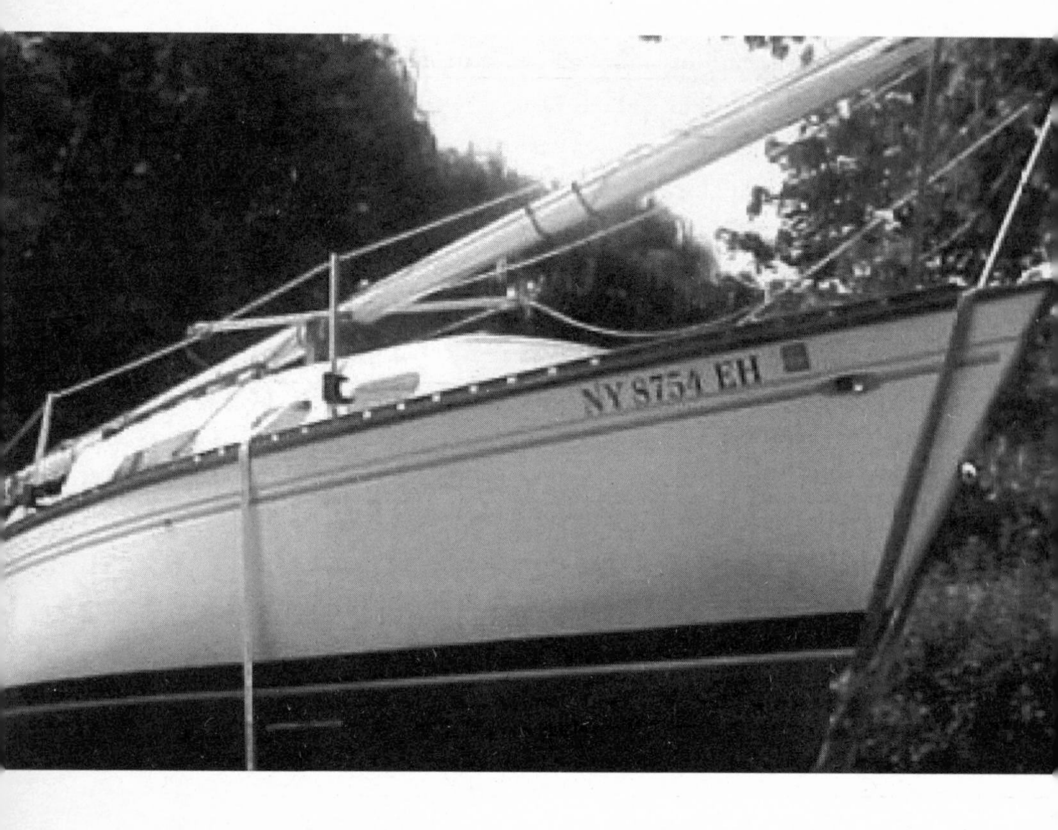
NY 8754 EH

Chapter 3

Miracles, Stop Lights and Rubber Fish

The parking area I was in was on the northbound side of the highway, but I was headed south and there was no light there. With the limited traffic in the dead of night, it had been easy to turn left, cutting across all four lanes to pull in there with my slow moving load. As dawn approached, a steady stream of cars and trucks now flowed in both directions on the busy divided highway. I nosed forward hoping for an opening, only to see an endless wall of traffic whizzing by me in both directions. Turning right and merging to head north would have been hard enough, but pulling out across all four lanes to turn left and head south was out of the question. If I was driving a sports car, I might have had a fighting chance if an opening occurred, but driving a forty-foot long, four ton rig that did zero to forty in three minutes, I was dead meat! At that very moment, something that I believe was the first "miracle" of the trip occurred. As if on cue there was a huge gap in the traffic flow in both directions at once. I couldn't believe it! There were no cars coming for half a mile from the right and for half a mile from the left! What had just been a solid wall of traffic four lanes wide was now an empty highway! It was like the "Red Sea" had parted right in front of me, just so I could get across! Wasting no time, I lumbered my ponderous rig across the north bound lanes, through the opening in the median and safely over to the far right lane on the southbound side. With tears welling up in my eyes I praised the Lord for his faithfulness as I pointed the van and the bow of my ship southward once again.

I now drove with more confidence as the eastern sky began to glow with the first hints of light and the road gradually became more visible beyond the range of my headlights. As I descended one hill after another, I thought about what a blessing it was that I was heading downhill most of the time. Some of the hills were quite steep, and I was glad I wouldn't have to tow the heavy boat back up them on a return trip. I really had to be on my toes, since there were traffic lights and crossroads along that stretch of highway. Because the boat was so heavy, the trailer should have had its own brakes but did not. That made it critical for me to start slowing down gradually, long before I had to come to a stop or make a turn. If I was clipping along coming down a steep hill at full speed and a light turned red just as I reached it, the results could have been disastrous. I found myself playing "chicken" with every light as I approached them, trying to outguess each one: " . . . Okay you've been red for a long time . . . you should be turning green any second now . . . I shouldn't have to slow down for you . . . c'mon baby turn green . . . turn green now I'm not going to slow down . . . yes! I'm through that one I hope there aren't too many more." Or: " . . . I don't know . . . this one's been green for a long time . . . watch out now it's gonna turn red just as I reach it . . . look out, be ready . . . I better start slowing down just in case . . . I'm almost to it and it's still green . . . oh well, full speed ahead green or red! . . . Watch out, guys, wide load coming through! . . . Whew! . . . Thank you, Lord, that was a long light." And so it went, as God's timing helped me to make it through or slow down in time for every light. I was so focused on watching the lights that I missed the first signs for route ninety-five. The busy interstate was America's main north and south highway from New England to Florida. Once on that major expressway, I could cruise steadily all the way to Florida without worrying about lights, crossroads or connecting with other highways. I had been eagerly looking forward to getting on it for a more relaxed drive. Suddenly a sign appeared, showing that I was right at the entrance ramp for interstate ninety-five. I couldn't believe that it had come up so fast, and that I had somehow missed the previous signs. "Oh No," I gasped, I was in the left lane with a solid wall of cars to my right, blocking me from access to the entrance ramp I had waited so long to reach! I slowed and signaled, but if I went another fifty yards, I would miss the ramp, and with my big rig and all the traffic, I could waste a precious hour or more just finding my way back to a spot where I could enter ninety-five south. "Lord, I can't miss this ramp I just can't," I cried, as cars behind me began to honk. A look in my right side view mirror showed me that a car was hanging back behind the boat to hold the right lane open for me. A nice lady was smiling, flashing her lights and waving me in ahead of her. "Thank you Lord," I praised, "for putting the right person, in the right place, at the right time once again." Without hesitation, I pulled into the right lane and headed down the entrance ramp to one of America's most heavily traveled highways.

I was amazed by how much traffic there was on the interstate even at six thirty in the morning. In this busy stretch there were three solid lanes of traffic speeding south toward Richmond and an endless sea of vehicles on the other side racing toward Washington DC. I was now on the "yellow brick road" that would take me all the way to Florida, but I could see that it wasn't going to be a relaxing drive all the way. As a steady stream of traffic roared by me, I reassured myself that once I got beyond the city of Richmond, the number of other vehicles would decrease. My fears about the heavy traffic soon gave way to a sense of adventure, as I thought about God's perfect timing and method to this madness. "Lord, you couldn't have picked a busier time to have me tow my giant "bill board" along this crowded stretch of highway where so many people would see it," I thought, smiling.

I forgot that interstate ninety-five passed right through Richmond, winding its way under overpasses, through narrow concrete tunnels and over bridges. Maneuvering through that city on the expressway was always a challenge, but pulling a slow moving wide load at the peak of morning rush hour traffic may have been foolhardy (even for me). Trying to stay as far to the right as possible without scraping guard rails and concrete walls, my pulse raced as other vehicles seemed to miss the boat and trailer by just inches. It was difficult to keep the trailer tracking straight on a highway that had so many bends in it. The frequent curves forced me to reduce my speed even more, making other drivers that much more frustrated and impatient with me.

Trucks and other vehicles going well above the speed limit flew by me on the sharp curves and in the narrow confines of each concrete underpass. "Keep me going Lord," I whispered under my breath. "If I can just get past Richmond I'll be okay," I kept saying, both audibly and in my mind, as I negotiated each curve with a white-knuckle grip on the wheel. Having driven to Florida before, I knew that beyond Richmond the road was a flat, straight, four-lane highway that passed through the rural sections of North and South Carolina and the woods and swamps of Georgia. If my memory served me right, it didn't pass through a major city again until Jacksonville, Florida and I would be leaving the expressway just before Jacksonville.

Gradually there were fewer bridges and underpasses. Office

buildings and cigarette factories had given way to shopping malls and a look in the side view mirrors told me that the "skyline" of downtown Richmond was now behind me rather than around me. As the last restaurants and stores gave way to fields and farms, the highway narrowed from three lanes to two, and I knew I had made it. "Thank You Lord," I whispered, breathing a sigh of relief, "thank you for keeping me safe and bringing me through that difficult stretch of highway. "Lord, I pray that out of the thousands who saw the boat this morning, at least a few were reminded of your presence. Please continue to travel with me and make the next leg of the journey less stressful and more enjoyable." I prayed, hopefully.

Driving was easier now as I cruised through an area with little traffic, enjoying straight, smooth highway. Around half past nine, my body began to remind me that I had only slept for two hours in the past thirty-seven. I was ready to nod off at any moment, so I took an exit for a fuel stop called "Travel World" about twenty miles into North Carolina. A warm summer rain was falling as I pulled in and parked next to the driveway that led into their lot. By parking there, I wasn't blocking access to the pumps or the store, yet I was in a position where the boat was highly visible to anyone coming or going from the rest stop. I was also somewhat removed from the noise, and activity of that busy facility, which increased my chances of getting some sleep.

At nine thirty a.m. it was already quite warm and muggy on that late July day. The hatch above my head and the cabin door had to be closed because of the rain and with no ventilation the boats interior was like a sauna. As sweat ran down my face it occurred to me that I was much farther south than I had been the last time I stopped. Too exhausted to think about the heat, I soon drifted off to sleep in the oven like interior of the closed cabin.

I awoke to see a fly walking upside down on the hard white

surface above my face. I marveled at God's design in even the smallest insect that equipped them to walk on such a smooth shiny surface (even upside down) without falling off. The suffocating heat inside the closed boat was now unbearable. My clothes were soaked and I could feel the sweat running down my face and forehead. It occurred to me that I had never been in the southern states during the summer, and I hoped this wasn't a preview of what it would be like to sleep in the boat each night once I was on the water. My watch told me that it was almost one o'clock and that I had slept for over three hours. Opening the hatch above my head, I saw that the rain had stopped and that It was almost as hot and muggy outside as it was in the boat. The midday southern sun broiled down on everything not protected by shade, and as it reflected off the polished white surface of the boats exterior it made the deck too hot to touch. "Wow, it really gets hot down here in the summer," I thought. "I better make sure I wear my straw hat and have plenty of water aboard when I'm cruising all day in this heat." Even though I was a mass of sweat, I was thankful that my nap had made me aware of how important it would be to rig for extreme heat on my voyage.

Grabbing toiletries and a change of clothes from the compartment under my berth, I headed into the travel center hoping to find a trucker's shower, but found none. Using the men's room sink I submerged my head, and then I stripped down to my shorts and washed everything not covered by underwear with a wash cloth, soap and ice cold water. As I dried off with a towel and slipped into clean clothes I felt awake, refreshed and invigorated. Feeling like I could drive "forever", I went into the snack shop. My original idea was to fill my travel mug with my usual concoction of coffee, milk and flavored creamers to keep me alert as I drove. But in the stifling heat the only thing that sounded good was a cold drink. After grabbing a large Diet Pepsi with lots of ice, I checked the tie down straps on the trailer by plunking a note on each one. Then I topped off my fuel tank and headed south again at about one thirty.

I cruised easily now, knowing that with each hour that passed I was a little closer to my destination. For the first time I began to believe I would really make it to Florida. It was hard to imagine the joy and excitement I would feel seeing the boat actually in the water, fully rigged with mast and sails. I pictured her gliding through a quiet backwater, cruising slowly northward toward home. I could almost feel the massive hull, so heavy and ponderous on land, gliding lightly and effortlessly beneath me as it responded to the wind, the water and my hand on the tiller. Those pleasant daydreams kept me occupied and motivated as I drove. In my exuberance, I began to sing a song I had heard from one of those wacky rubber fish that are mounted on a plaque. I laughed inwardly as I imitated the singing of "Billy The Bass" who turned his head, moved his rubber mouth and sang: "Take me to the River . . . Put me in the water.. .. Oh yeah."

The famous billboards I passed for "South of the Border" amused me and let me know how far I had to go to reach South Carolina. Some quick calculations told me the mileage and the approximate number of hours I would need to travel to reach my destination from there. As I crossed the border into South Carolina, my heart sank as I saw the first speed limit sign for that state. Speed limit seventy-five, minimum speed forty-five it read, much to my disappointment. I had almost lost control of my rig several times when my speed crept above forty yesterday. The boat had started to sway and fish tail, sending my nerves and brain into a state of panic as I fought to maintain control and slow down. Would I have to exit the expressway and take side roads through stop and go traffic with my oversized, slow moving load? That would add many extra hours or even an extra day to my trip. If I pushed my speed up to forty-five, I would be risking a serious accident that could destroy the boat and my van. I would also be endangering my life and the lives of others. I shuddered as I thought about being responsible for an accident that could involve a young family on their way to Walt Disney World and I knew that speeding up was out of the question. I decided to keep going at forty, and trust God. He had gotten me that far and he would get me the rest of the way in his way and in his time. If I was stopped by the police, I hoped the only thing that would happen would be a warning to either speed up, or get off the expressway at the next exit. I could then worry about it if and when the time came. I turned on my flashers to let other vehicles know that I was traveling at a slower than normal speed, and I prayed earnestly that the Lord would allow me to stay on the expressway and make it through that state without incident. Later that day, I would find to my relief, that I did make it all the way through South Carolina without being stopped or questioned. I even drove right through a radar trap set up to catch speeders, and later a state police car cruised by me patrolling the highway. "Thank You Lord for the small 'miracles' that have kept me safe and allowed me to keep going," I praised, as once again I felt his presence and his covering.

I had some Christian tracts with me, hoping that I could give them to people I met along the way. The Lord began to put it on my heart to leave some in the men's rooms of each rest area when I stopped. For the remainder of the trip, I left them on toilet paper holders and on sinks each time I made a bathroom stop. I even found myself pulling in to a large visitor center when I didn't need to use the facilities. I was excited about this idea, but also disappointed that I hadn't thought of it earlier as I drove through the northern states.

In the pile of tracts I found one that was written by a Christian trucker that was perfect for truck drivers. It had the picture of a "big rig" on the front and as I looked at it I found myself wishing I had a hundred of them with me. Since I only had one, I had to really make it count (like a hunter with a single bullet). As I pulled into the next rest area, I saw a truck driver climb out of his rig and head inside. While he was away from his truck I placed it on the step he used to climb into the cab and put a stone on it to weight it down. "Lord, please let him see this and read it," I said, as I ran inside to use the facilities.

I crossed the state line into Georgia just after eleven and pulled into a visitor center that came up right away to spend the night. Since there were very few cars in the lot at that hour, I parked right in front of the restrooms which put the boat under a security light. I didn't feel it was wrong to do this, since there were so many open parking spaces in the lot and I would be gone at first light. Now that I was only ninety miles from my destination my plan was to spend the night there, and leave to drive the remaining distance at first light.

The marina told me that I could park and lock my van and the empty trailer in their parking lot after launching the boat. My son Dan was going to pick up the van and trailer at the marina. As part of the plan, Dan had already flown down to visit a friend in Jacksonville. Dan and his buddy were going to pick up my rig a few days later and drive it back to our home near Rochester, New York.

I had purposely left the boats fuel tanks empty for the road trip, so their considerable weight (when full) was not added to the weight I was towing. I didn't want to fill them when the boat was in the water where gas usually cost a lot more. I would have to pay marina prices many times on the trip, but I could make every penny count by starting out with two tanks that were filled at "gas station" prices. I wanted to leave early in the morning and stop to fill the tanks and the van, before crossing into Florida where gas cost more. I promised Dan that I would leave the van with a full tank and leave enough cash locked in the glove compartment for the additional gas he would need to get home. My heart raced with excitement as I thought: "If I can get an early start, and the launching and rigging of the boat goes smoothly, I will be on a river in Florida cruising north tomorrow afternoon!"

As I set up the ladder to climb aboard for the night, a man with a heavy New York City / Hispanic accent came over with his son to admire the boat and asked where I was going. After telling them about my plans for the trip, I came on pretty strong, telling them how the Lord had blessed me with this beautiful boat and allowed me to go on this voyage. I told them that they should trust Jesus as their Savior and invite him into their lives if they hadn't already. I felt the man trying to "brush me off" and end the conversation when he heard what I was saying, so I shook hands, gave them a couple of tracts and left them with a sincere "God Bless You." They wished me good luck, and said that maybe they would read about me in the paper or see me on the news if my trip was a success.

I felt safe there in front of the visitor center, and it was relatively quiet now with little traffic. Once inside the cabin and relaxed on my berth I drifted into a state of deep sleep as soon as my head settled into my pillow. My eyes opened naturally, staring blankly at the white fiberglass surface above my face and then my pulse quickened as I remembered where I was and how close I was to Florida. I groped for my watch in the darkness to see how long I had slept and was happy to see that it was almost morning. "Thank you Lord," I praised, pleased that I had finally been relaxed enough to sleep all night. I had gotten a decent amount of sleep, and still woke up early enough to get to the marina that morning. "This is great, I'm getting the early start I hoped for," I thought excitedly as I descended the ladder.

There was very little traffic on that stretch of highway in the predawn darkness. As the roadside markers counted down the miles to Florida, I got more excited with each one I passed. Picking up the strong signal of a Christian station in Atlanta, I focused on the radio intently for inspiration and to pass the time. About half way through Georgia, I took an exit with several gas stations to make the fuel stop I had planned. "This could take a while and be quite an ordeal," I thought, as I pulled up to the last pump under the canopy. As I filled the van I thought about how hard it would be to get at the boat's fuel tanks and bring them up on deck. I did not want to take the chance of spilling any gas below decks where the smallest spark from the battery could trigger a fire or explosion. Even a couple of drops could produce strong toxic fumes in the closed living quarters of the boat that would take a long time to go away. That meant they had to be brought out to be filled. The tanks were stowed in a compartment under the cockpit floor. I had to twist my body like a pretzel to get down into the tight confines of that small area to get them out. After filling the van I pulled forward so the back of the boat was as close to the pump as possible. I placed the ladder in position and carefully climbed it, carrying the gas pump nozzle up with me. Once in the boat, I had to set the nozzle down and wedge it so it couldn't fall to the ground, while I squeezed below to get out the tanks. The cramped space of the fuel compartment was even more limited now as every square inch of storage space was packed with the equipment and supplies I would need to survive on the water for a month. The tanks were wedged in by fishing poles, life jackets and the oars for my inflatable boat. With very little room to move, I was somehow able to muscle things around enough to get the tanks out on deck and fill them. Getting them back underneath was even more difficult, since they were so heavy and hard to maneuver in the tight quarters when full. "Wow, that really took a lot out of me," I moaned, as I looked at my skinned knuckles and the brush burn on my elbow. My day hadn't even started and I was already sweaty and tired. As I descended the ladder and went inside to pay, my confidence fell as I realized how much hard work lay ahead of me on this "dream" trip. The thought of a "simple" chore being that difficult and taking that long caused me to wonder if the trip was really worthwhile. I also questioned whether I had the strength and stamina to do this for a whole month at my age.

As I walked outside, my gaze fell on the boat looking so beautiful and so impressive as it towered above my van at the pumps. The lights from the fuel canopy gave the heavily waxed surface a deep luster as they reflected from it. The first low rays of the morning sun lit the boats east side with an almost "heavenly" radiance, making the large Christian emblem and the words "God Speed" stand out more boldly than ever. I felt foolish that I had such a short memory (like the Israelites in the desert). I couldn't believe that I had allowed myself to get down and have negative thoughts, even after all the blessings and small miracles that had gotten me that far. As I stared at the boat I could almost feel the presence of the Holy Spirit touch my heart and wash away my doubts and fears. "Thank you Father," I whispered with reverent awe. "Thank you for the ways that you remind me about the purpose of this trip, and for always being with me. Please forgive me for having doubts, even for a moment and please continue to travel with me and encourage me along the way." As I climbed into the driver's seat to cover the remaining distance to the marina, I was very sure of three things:

1. God was with me, he had given me a beautiful

boat. I had already witnessed his hand of blessing, encouragement and protection several times in just the past two days. As long as he was, there was no reason to doubt or fear anything.

2. Yes! This trip was absolutely, positively worthwhile!

3. I would have all the strength and stamina I would need for a month, or even for a year if necessary, because his strength would be perfect when my strength was gone.

Chapter 4

Crossing into the Promised Land

As I drove the last fifty miles to Florida I was relaxed and confident yet filled with excitement, as I anticipated the adventure that lay ahead. The last mileage markers counting down the distance came so slowly that it seemed like they were two miles apart and the extra weight in the fuel tanks made the trailer sway back and forth more than ever. I drove conservatively, trying to be even more careful than before. I did not want to risk blowing the whole trip now that I was so close. The marina where I would launch the boat was on a side channel, off the Intra Coastal Waterway north of Jacksonville in Fernandina Beach. This small marina on Amelia Island was the only one in the area that had a travel lift capable of picking a boat up from a trailer and setting it into the water. The directions said to take the very first exit in Florida. Having driven to Florida before, I knew that I would cross a bridge over the St. Mary's river and somewhere on that bridge I would cross the state line. My impatient eyes strained eagerly for the sight of a bridge ahead as I passed the last two mileage markers in Georgia. Finally I saw the road rise up to pass over a long low highway bridge. My heart felt ready to burst as I reminded myself that once I crossed the river I would be in "the promised land." Halfway across the bridge I lost it completely as I passed a sign with a picture of an orange that read: "Welcome To

Florida, the Sunshine State." I honked the horn loudly and shouted "I made it, oh Lord, I really made it!" "Thank you Lord! I praise your name for getting me here!" My view of the road was blurred as an unrestrained flow of tears ran down both cheeks and dripped into my lap. "What's wrong with me, I'm blubbering like a baby," I thought, but then realized what had happened. The release of two days of stress and tension, combined with my excitement and joy, caused my tightly wound, sleep deprived body to be overcome with emotion as I passed that sign. "Well, so much for the bold, unshakeable, adventurer 'Captain Dave'," I laughed, "Apparently he has the heart of a child." Smiling through my tears, I thought: "That may not be such a bad thing. Scripture says that we are to become like little children to enter the kingdom of heaven. "Heavenly father," I prayed. "Please give me the courage of a lion and a child like faith as I face whatever lies ahead of me. Please allow the launch to go smoothly and continue to be with me as I travel, Amen."

As I came off the bridge, an exit sign came up right away. Although my directions told me to take the very first exit in Florida, it didn't look right. There was nothing on the sign that mentioned Fernandina beach or Amelia Island, just a route number that didn't match anything on my directions. Checking the paper again I read aloud: "The first exit in Florida will be for Fernandina Beach." Was it possible that the marina owner had forgotten that there was another exit before the Fernandina Beach exit? A still small voice told me not to take that one, but to wait and see what the next exit sign said. Ten minutes later a sign for the second exit began to materialize in the distance. "Please Lord, let this be it," I prayed, as my eyes strained to read the words on it. As the sign grew larger, the top line of lettering finally focused into the words "Yulee / Fernandina Beach." "Yes! Thank you Lord, for telling me not to take the first exit," I shouted, as I burst into a chorus of: " . . . take me to the river . . . put me in the water . . ."

Once off the expressway, I felt that I had arrived and was just minutes from the marina, but I quickly learned that was not the case. To my disappointment, maneuvering my big, slow moving rig through the lights, turns and morning rush hour traffic in that busy residential area seemed to take more time than driving through the state of Georgia! I had brought an inexpensive cell phone with me that I borrowed from my daughter. Although I wasn't a believer in cell phones, and did not own one myself, I knew that the tiny device would be a necessity on this kind of trip. Getting it out, I called the marina to let them know where I was, and clarify the directions for the last few miles. An older man with a relaxed friendly voice stayed on the line and patiently talked me through each turn, accurately describing the landmarks that I passed. In spite of his guidance, I still wound up in the wrong lane twice when I needed to make a turn. It must have been the "God Speed" name and Christian emblem, or the sheer size of my load that touched the hearts of other drivers, because it seemed like guardian angels were directing traffic for me that morning. Each time I made a mistake, other motorists would hang back and hold up traffic to give me enough space to change lanes or turn where I needed to.

At one point, I crossed a bridge that actually took me over the Intra Coastal Waterway! Looking down, I admired the shimmering watery highway below, neatly framed with marsh grass as it stretched north to my left and south to my right as far as I could see. "There it is!" I sighed in awe. "That is where I will be cruising later today, right down there on that calm green water." I couldn't believe how beautiful and how peaceful it was, with not one boat in sight in either direction. It seemed too good to be true that I would have a whole month of freedom, peace and solitude on the water. I found myself wishing that I could somehow push a button, and be down there right now, gliding effortlessly northward surrounded by marsh grass and birds. Mentally traveling ahead in time, I dreamed that in a few days I would be gliding under a bridge like this, ignoring the cars and trucks above. As I passed under them, perhaps someone in a car would look down and wish they could be aboard the beautiful sailboat cruising on the calm water below, instead of being surrounded by the bustle of every day life and the traffic on the bridge.

At last I made the final turn into the driveway of the marina and my pulse quickened as I asked a young man which fork led to the travel lift and boat ramp. As I wound my way toward the launch area, I passed a fleet of large boats parked under the palm trees. A sense of awe came over me as I drove by one massive hull after another. Those enormous vessels towered above me with an ominous presence that made the beautiful boat rolling behind me seem tiny by comparison. "Well, I guess everything is relative," I murmured, as I thought about how "huge" my boat seemed yesterday and how small it seemed today. "I hope I'm not biting off a trip too big in a boat too small," I thought. But I knew that it would mean more to complete a trip like this in my small boat, than in one of those impressive "giants". I reassured myself that since I couldn't make this trip in a great big boat, the Lord would allow me to do great things in a small boat. Although my boat would not be one of the biggest on the water, it would be the prettiest and the best, because of the time and effort I had put into it, and because of the message it was carrying.

It looked like many of the giant "ships" had not been in the water for several years. I wondered if their owners used to be as excited about using them, as I was about launching my boat today. I felt sad as I thought about how long it had been since someone lovingly scrubbed and waxed every inch of those boats as I had done to prepare for this trip. As I looked at each mammoth hull, now stained with algae and rust, I realized that they were a grim reminder that material possessions, no matter how impressive, are only exciting for a while. What a powerful object lesson that was about storing up treasure on earth where rust and moth will destroy, but instead to build up treasure in heaven by living for God and for others.

As I parked in front of the marina office, I was surprised at how little activity there was. Being used to the busy marinas and crowded boat launches on Lake Ontario, I expected quite a different atmosphere. The launch ramp was deserted and the travel lift sat idle. The sandy boat yard seemed like a ghost town as the intense heat of the midsummer sun beat down on everything in sight. I went into the small cluttered office to let the manager know I had arrived, and was greeted by a tanned middle aged woman with a raspy voice. "Bill will be back in a few minutes," she said. "Back your boat in by the travel lift and start getting it ready to go in the water, he'll come down as soon as he gets back."

I backed in next to a large older sailboat that needed lots of TLC. Working on the deck with a paintbrush was a thin blonde man in his mid thirties. His deeply bronzed leathery skin spoke of many years of boating and outdoor work in the Florida sun. I greeted him with a cheerful good morning, as I began to loosen the trailer straps and remove the bungee cords that secured the mast. I complimented him on the large boat he was working on. He assured me that it was not his and that he was just doing touch up work and minor repairs for the owner. With a quick smile he added that he was a power boater, and wouldn't want a sailboat if I gave him one because they were too much work. I told him about my trip, and asked if he had any tips for "rookies" on the Intra Coastal Waterway.

He said that in order to head north, I needed to turn left as I came out of the canal and be sure to always watch the red and green ICW channel markers carefully.

Across the lot, a young man was sanding a large powerboat that looked like it had been built the same year as the Titanic. He tried to stay within the small patches of shade that were cast by the boat's hull, as he half-heartedly worked at the tedious task in the broiling sun. "I don't envy you doing that kind of work in this heat," I shouted. "I only work on whatever side is in the shade," he replied, forcing a smile. I felt a little guilty that these men were doing such tedious work in the hot sun as I prepared to take a cruise for a month. "What a study in contrasts," I thought. The kind of work they were doing had been a rewarding "labor of love" for me as I prepared my own boat for the trip, but doing that kind of work on someone else's boat seemed like the worst chore imaginable.

One of my concerns about getting the boat "water ready" was being able to lift the outboard eight feet in the air to hang it on the motor bracket. The motor was stored in the van while traveling and weighed over 100 lbs. Once again the good Lord in his faithfulness provided the help I needed. As soon as I asked the man working next to me for help with the motor he climbed right down to give me a hand. Working together and using his sturdy stepladder, (instead of my tippy one) it was an easy matter to lift the heavy motor up onto its bracket and clamp it securely in place. "Thank you Lord," I praised, relieved that a tough job I had dreaded was now done, and done so easily.

As I finished untying things, Bill the marina owner and George his employee came down to check on my progress. Bill, who was well-dressed and professional, appeared to be the hard-nosed businessman type. George, an older man with baggy, paint spattered coveralls and an old flannel shirt, seemed as easy going and down to earth as the clothes he wore. Bill lifted my mast into position with a crane, as George and I attached the stainless steel cables and hardware that secured it to the deck. I praised the Lord for George who seemed to have a knack for attaching the cables easily and called me "captain" as we worked. Two wide straps were then slung beneath the boats hull and she was lifted straight off the trailer and into the air. The boat looked much larger now with her mast up and I watched excitedly with pride and satisfaction as she rolled slowly toward the water suspended beneath the huge machine. Once the travel lift had gone as far out on the docks as possible, the boat was slowly lowered into the water until it floated free of the straps and began to move in the current. Using ropes and a boat hook, George and I guided it out of the launch area and around the corner to an open dock spot, where we cushioned it with fenders and tied it securely.

After going into the office to pay the launch fees, I came back out on the dock, eager to finish the final rigging that was needed to get underway. I noticed that Bill the marina owner hadn't been very warm or friendly toward me, and I wondered if the name and emblem on my boat had turned him off, or made him think I was some kind of religious fanatic. I didn't let it bother me too much, thinking that he might respond that way to all newcomers, or maybe he just didn't like northerners. At any rate, I had no apologies and no regrets that my boat, with its graphics and a Christian flag now flying at the top of the mast, made it clear to everyone what I believed and what I stood for.

GOD Speed
GOD Speed
HONDA

Chapter 5

Dead in the Water for a Reason

I stood on the dock for several minutes just admiring the boat and praising the Lord. It was hard to believe that it was really in the water, tied to a dock in Florida. Getting down to business I climbed aboard to get out sail bags, tools and equipment. Installing the tiller handle and extension I then attached the boom and the mainsail to the mast. I worked eagerly, rigging sails, ropes and pulleys to prepare my vessel for the adventure that lay ahead. The midday Florida summer sun was unbearable. It felt like you could fry an egg on the shiny reflective surface of the deck, and the boats interior was like an oven. I sweated profusely as I worked, and it seemed like the enemy was causing little things to go wrong just to frustrate me. My eagerness to work fast, the extreme heat, and the absent-mindedness of a fifty-two year old, caused me to make small mental mistakes, making the simplest jobs take longer and forcing me to do some things twice. But I kept going and prayed for the strength and composure to complete the time consuming tasks quickly. The thought of finally starting the motor and pulling away from the dock to begin my voyage spurred me on and kept me going as the oppressive heat sapped my strength and my energy. After a couple of hours I sat exhausted on the cockpit seat. My shirt was saturated, and trickles of sweat ran down my face. Looking around, I took a mental inventory of what still had to be done and a smile came to my weary face as I realized that everything was done. I double checked again just to make sure, because it was hard for me to accept the fact that the moment I had dreamed about for so long had finally come.

Putting the tools away, I sat by the motor to start it. "Once I'm moving, there should be some breeze off the water to cool me down," I thought. "I'll cruise until it's almost dark," I decided. "It should get cooler later in the day as the sun goes down. My Honda, four-stroke outboard was almost brand new. That "top of the line" engine was the "Cadillac" of outboard motors, well known for its dependability, longevity and quiet power. Although quite expensive, it had proven itself to be well worth the money over the past two summers. I had only used it a few times, but was thrilled by how quiet it was and by the way it burst into life with just one pull. With a happy heart I squeezed the fuel bulb, set the choke and gave the rope a pull. To my surprise nothing happened. I quickly gave two or three more hard pulls and much to my dismay was greeted only by silence. "What is going on here," I thought. The motor had been stored in my basement since last summer and had not been started yet this year. Since it was so new, I hadn't taken it to a marina for a professional tune up, but had the oil and spark plugs changed by one of my students who was a backyard mechanic instead. I didn't trust mechanics and it always ran great, so I chose to bless a good kid with some money rather than pay marina prices. "Heavenly Father, please allow this motor to start, or show me what I need to do to get it to start," I prayed with all my heart. After six or seven more pulls the only sound I heard was the rubbing of the fenders against the dock. The motor that was to carry me up the East Coast and safely home before Labor Day would not even make a pop or a cough when I pulled it. Squeezing the fuel bulb many times and pushing the choke in and then out, I pulled the rope frantically again and again until I had no strength left. My heart sank as I slumped down on the rear seat by the motor. Had I jeopardized my whole trip, just to save a few dollars? I had planned for so long and been so careful with every detail, yet I had not started and run the motor at home or had it professionally tuned up. I felt like an absolute failure and a fool.

In my disappointment I cried out to the Lord trying to understand why this happened. Was the enemy trying to stop me from making this trip? Was this God's way of forcing me to take a day off to sit around and relax, so I would be well rested for this trip? Was there severe weather ahead or other danger that I would miss by being held up here for a day? Was there something I had overlooked on the boat, or something else the Lord needed me to do here before he would allow me to get started? I reluctantly accepted the fact that I was in his hands and that this was his trip. He had gotten me here safely and his will and his timing were perfect. I would start my voyage when he wanted me to, and I knew that worrying about it or trying to out guess him was more foolish than not starting the motor at home.

Just then two well-dressed couples came down the stairs to the docks and stopped to admire my boat. One of the men said it was beautiful and complimented me on the name. Thanking him, I shared my trip plan with them. When they heard what I was planning, they smiled with admiration and one man said that he envied me, because he had wanted to take the same trip for years. I told them about my motor problem, and asked if they knew anything about outboards. Without hesitation, one of them climbed aboard to help me, even though he was dressed for a cruise and not for mechanical work. The man tried several different settings and adjustments and gave the motor numerous pulls but was unable to get it to start. He mentioned several things that he thought could be wrong and apologized for not being more of a help. Before they moved on, he told me that the marina next door had an excellent service department and said that the guys there were experts on any type of marine engine. I was thrilled to hear that, thanked them sincerely and added a loud "God bless you" as they walked off down the dock toward their boat.

Not wasting any time, I walked quickly across the boat yard and took a shortcut between the buildings to the marina next door. A good looking young man with dark hair had the radio blaring and was up to his armpits in the engine compartment of a large boat. He greeted me politely, but I sensed that I was just another intrusion in his already busy day. Wiping his hands, he turned down the loud rock music and sipped a beer as he listened to my problem. "You mean you took the motor off and put it away for the winter without running it out of fuel or winterizing it?" He asked, with a surprised tone that made me feel pretty dumb. "Your carburetor's full of varnish and gunk, it needs to be dismantled and cleaned. Can you take the carb off and bring it to me?" He asked matter of factly. I felt that I would have had a better chance of performing heart surgery, than to remove the carburetor from my motor over twelve feet of muddy canal water. "Look, I'm really busy today," he began with an impatient tone, but then paused and softened as he saw the disappointment in my face. "Ok, I'm here until five; I'll be over in a while to check it out and we'll see if we can get you going." I eagerly thanked him, shaking his hand almost off with gratitude. "Thank you Lord," I praised silently, as I headed back to the boat with my feet barely touching the ground. My spirit soared as I crossed the parking lot and spotted my Christian flag floating proudly at the top of the mast, now visible from anywhere in the boat yard.

Since I had time to kill, I organized and checked out my equipment. I put things in the most convenient locations so that once I got underway, everything would be easily accessible. I loaded both cameras with film and put them on the counter near the plates, napkins and utensils. I didn't know how I would prepare food and steer the boat at the same time but I would find a way to do it. I plugged in the stereo headphones and untangled the cord from my spotlight in case I had to run at night. A little green heron landed on a nearby boat, its iridescent feathers glistening in the afternoon sun. Grabbing one of the cameras and my longest lens I carefully snuck up on him. When I got close enough for some great shots my camera froze up on the third click of the shutter. I grabbed my second camera body out of the boat and attaching the long lens went after the bird again, only to have that camera freeze at the first snap of a picture. Both of my cameras had dead batteries and were now useless until I replaced them. If my motor had started right up, I would have sped away from the dock long ago, starting the trip of a lifetime with thirty rolls of film and no working camera aboard.

Three thirty became four o'clock, still with no sign of the young mechanic. The afternoon shadows lengthened and my patience shortened as I watched four o'clock slowly turn into four thirty. "Please Lord, let him show up, please let him make it." Any moment now I would hear footsteps and see his head appear as he descended the steps to the docks with tools in hand, just like the cavalry coming to save the day in a western movie. At four forty-five my patience and hope changed to sadness and dread as I realized that he wasn't coming. "Maybe he's going to come over when he's finished for the day," I thought hopefully, as I walked back over to his marina to see what had happened. When he saw me come in, his body language told me that he felt really bad. "I'm sorry man," he blurted out before I could speak; "I got busy and forgot all about yuh." Trying not to look as disappointed as I felt, I thought about what to do next as I wondered if I would ever get going. "Listen,

I'm gonna be here early tomorrow," he said. "I'll come right over first thing and check it out before I do anything else. I'll have your motor purring like a kitten in no time."

As I thanked him and headed back, I thought about the advantages of starting out early and having the whole day to find safe harbor, rather than rushing off tonight with just a few hours of daylight left. "Lord, I believe that it's your will and your timing that has me still here for whatever reason. Please work it out that I won't have to pay the marina another fee for spending the night here, since I already paid them too much for launching the boat," I prayed. Since the boat was ready, and I had the rest of the night free, I took the van and trailer to Wal-Mart to buy camera batteries and other important items I had forgotten. After selecting the right batteries, I picked up a hooded raincoat with elastic pants and a mechanics tool kit, in case I needed to work on the motor again during the course of the trip.

When I got back to the marina, I parked the van and trailer in the high grass at the back of the property where they would be out of the way until Dan came to get them. I put the cash that I promised Dan in the glove compartment, and then locked the van before walking back to the boat. As I paused on the platform before going down the steps, I was surprised to see the tall, slender body of a white heron standing on top of a dock piling right next to the boat. There seemed to be an angelic quality about the bird, as though God had placed one of his angels on guard to watch over the boat while I was away. I admired its graceful beauty and the ethereal glow of the white feathers in the fading light. "Lord, why did you make them white in Florida and gray in New York?" I asked, even though I thought I knew the answer. "Does being so white help them endure the harsh sun in southern climates, or did you make more varieties and colors for us to enjoy, just so we would be more in awe of you?"

Although it wasn't dark yet, the full moon had risen above the marsh on the other side of the canal. Being so low in the sky it looked like a huge silver wafer and was the perfect backdrop for the harbor scene below. There was something about boats at twilight that made me wish I was an artist. The peaceful stillness and beauty of that night overwhelmed me as I descended the steps to the dock. I felt overjoyed to be there (even though I was behind schedule) and I fondly remembered why I loved being on the water and traveling by boat so much. Once inside the boat I turned on the radio. A Christian station was playing an old hymn, which resonated loudly inside the cabin and floated out over the still water. It was one I hadn't heard before, but the very first words that boomed out at me were: "He will sail with me. . . . My boat will be in his hands across the river." I then looked at the painting of the young sailor with Jesus. A narrow beam of light was coming through the window, highlighting the face of Jesus and the face of the boy as it fell on the picture. "Thank you Lord, for the ways that you encourage me and remind me of your presence," I sighed, as my view of the picture became blurred by tears. Knowing that God had his reasons why the boat was still there, I was anxious to know what they were and see how this delay would become a blessing.

A black crowned night heron landed silently on the dock piling next to me. My pulse quickened as I looked at the large bird that stared back at me from just a few feet away. How stately and noble it was sitting there in the moonlight. I marveled at the perfect design of the long legs with their big feet for wading, and the thick heavy beak for catching fish. Every feather was the right size and shape and the few contrasting highlights of color on the white body seemed like they had been hand painted by a master artist.

The most striking feature was a crown of black feathers on the top of the head that reminded me of the crown of thorns our savior wore on the cross. I wondered if the Lord had sent this kingly bird (with a crown) as a symbol of himself, to remind me that he was watching over me as closely as his feathered creation seemed to be at that moment.

I was awakened the next morning by the brilliant Florida sun as it streamed into the cabin. I was thrilled that I had fallen sleep in the oppressive heat and that no flies or mosquitoes had bothered me, even though the hatch and cabin door were open all night. When I launched the boat, the manager had invited me to use the boater's locker room to take a shower. Since the marina next door didn't open for an hour, I used the time to shower and shave for the first time in three days. Although it was hard to feel "dry" after a shower with that much humidity, I did feel fresh, alert and ready to face the day as I left the locker room. When I passed the marina office, a pang of guilt stabbed my heart as I thought about spending the night at their dock without permission or additional payment. I knew that it was critical that a Christian be honest and above reproach in the smallest things. With the lettering on my boat and my Christian flag, it certainly wouldn't look good to others if I tried to bend the rules or get out of paying for a service. Reluctantly, I tried the door only to find it locked. No one seemed to be around so I promised myself I would try again later. Maybe if they knew I had engine trouble they would give me a break, since I had already paid so much to launch there. Not wanting to take any chances, I went right over to check on the mechanic. I wanted to make sure that he was still coming over first thing that morning as he promised. Maybe I was starting to grow on him, because he seemed friendlier as he assured me that he would be right over as soon as he opened up the shop. I also learned that his name was Ken.

As I walked back to the boat, I felt the Lord speaking to my heart that Ken was one of the reasons that I was still on Amelia Island. In fact, Ken may have been the main reason that the Lord brought me to that marina and kept me there. I felt him telling me to come on strong with a Christian witness and salvation message for Ken. I could see the Lord using this handsome young man to touch the hearts and lives of young people in that area for many years to come. I prepared an "ambush" for him by tuning the boats radio to an upbeat, contemporary Christian station and turning the volume up loud so he would be listening to it as he worked on the motor. Sorting through my pile of tracts, I tried to find a couple that would appeal to a down-to-earth, hard-working young man in his mid twenties. I then untied the boat and retied it so the motor was as close to the dock as possible for easy access. While I waited I rinsed down the boats hull and topsides with the fresh water hose on the dock. I praised the Lord for allowing me to have such a beautiful boat, as I watched the water bead up on the newly waxed surfaces with great satisfaction. It was after nine, so I tried the marina office again to see if anyone was there yet. To my surprise and delight it was still locked and dark within. I concluded that they didn't have Saturday hours at all during the slow midsummer season. I accepted that as God's way of working things out so I didn't have to pay for a dock spot for the night, and I praised him for yet another blessing.

When Ken came down to work on the motor, I did everything I could to help make the job easier for him. As he worked, I told him that there must have been a reason the Lord kept me there overnight. He opened up to me, saying that he wasn't very religious but he believed in God and he did pray. He said that he just got word that a friend was in a motorcycle accident last night and was now in intensive care with internal bleeding. "Wow Lord," I thought, "your timing is perfect! You really do put me in the right place at the right time!" Now I knew why he wasn't supposed to fix the motor yesterday. That morning, after hearing about his friend's accident, he would be more open and receptive to what God wanted me to share with him. I began by sharing how real and how good God had been in my life. I talked about how he had used me, blessed me, guided me and allowed me to experience things that had to be "miracles". When I found out that he was an avid hunter, the rest was easy. I told him about my videos and my ministry, and how the Lord had allowed me to share his message with hunters everywhere. When I spoke about hunting with my son, he told me that his fondest memories were from deer hunting with his dad, and he shared a story with me about their favorite tree stand.

When he finished working, the motor not only started with one pull, but purred smoothly and quietly at the lowest speed indefinitely. As I shook his hand to thank him I reinforced again how real God was, and how much he loved him. I then laid a hand on his shoulder, and still clasping his hand prayed earnestly and passionately for his injured friend and also for him. I prayed that God would show himself to him in a very real way and that Ken would invite Jesus to live in his heart and direct his life. He shook my hand firmly as he thanked me. Before he left, he reviewed the maps and charts of the Intra Coastal Waterway with me, to make sure I got headed in the right direction. That was another blessing, because I learned that I was supposed to turn right at the end of the canal to go north, and not left as I was told before. The blonde marina employee had misunderstood my question, telling me to turn left at the end of the bay outside the canal, and I had asked only which way to turn at the end of the narrow canal. I sent him on his way with a hearty thank you, a brochure describing my videos, and a couple of hunting tracts that outlined the testimony of two famous hunters who were also outdoor writers.

Finally, at long last, with the motor purring softly, I untied the boat and gave the bow a gentle shove away from the dock and into the current. Pushing the tiller hard over, I made a sharp U-turn and headed slowly down the canal toward the Intra Coastal Waterway. With tears of joy welling up in my eyes and my heart filled with love for God and his timing, I praised him as I reviewed his reasons for making me spend the night on Amelia Island.

» He had used me to touch a life that in turn might touch many other lives.

» Now I knew which way to turn to head north, so I did not start my trip by going the wrong way.

» I was rested, refreshed, clean and feeling positive after the ordeals of driving, launching and rigging.

» Both cameras had brand new batteries installed and were loaded and ready for use.

» I now had rain gear aboard, stowed conveniently for quick access.

» I had a complete set of mechanics tools aboard, in case I needed to make any repairs.

» All of my equipment, food, sails, hardware and accessories were organized and easily accessible.

As I reached the end of the canal and turned to point my bow northward, I noticed a beautiful rainbow in the sky ahead. The giant arch seemed to beckon me like a gateway to the beginning of my voyage. "Thank you Lord for the blessings of Amelia Island and that I am finally underway," I prayed. "Please continue to be with me now as I travel and prepare me for whatever lies ahead."

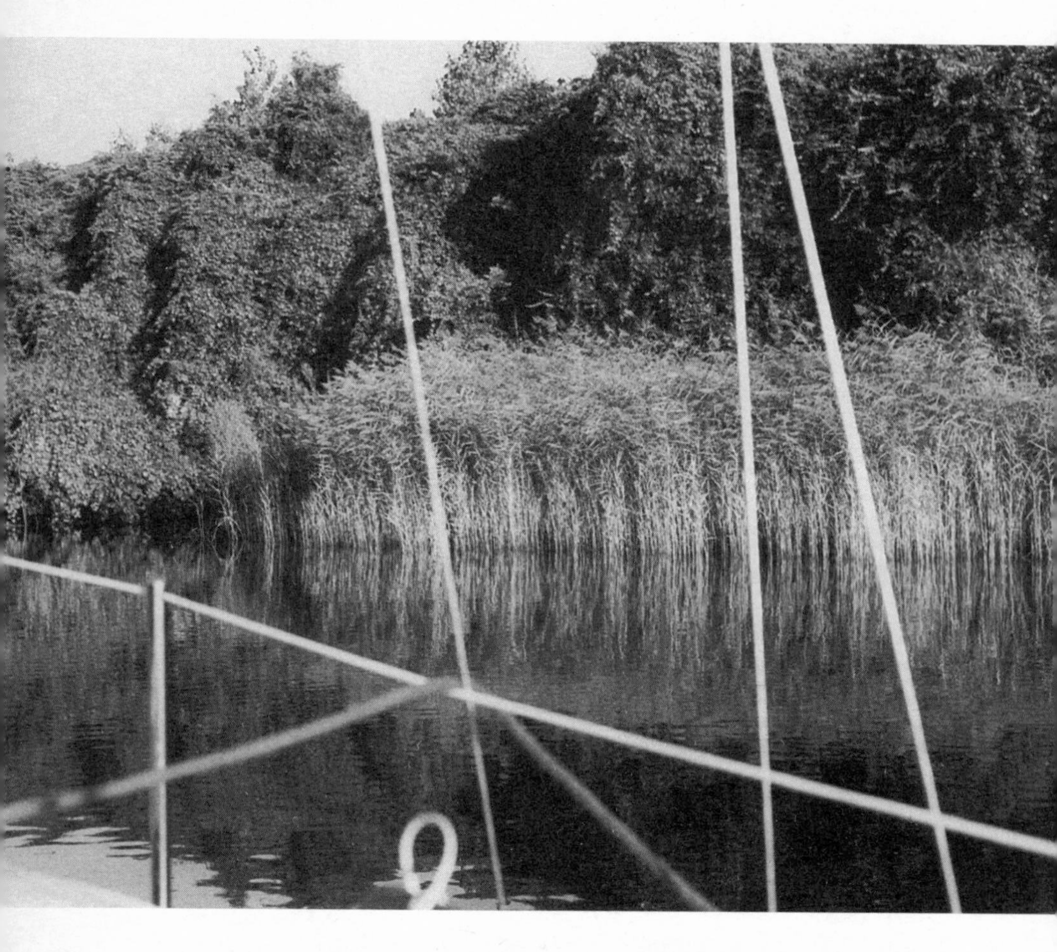

Chapter 6

Up a Canal without a Motor

As I headed out into the large sound beyond the canal, I realized that not all of the Intra Coastal Waterway was a narrow grass lined river. I was now in a large expanse of water that stretched ahead of me for at least seven miles and was three to four miles wide. The sound was shaped like a fat Y with the right fork leading out into the open Atlantic. In that direction I could see large pleasure boats and fishing vessels, heading out and coming in and could actually make out ocean swells and large breaking waves even from that distance. The left fork was the Intra Coastal Waterway (ICW) stretching northward toward home. This was the left turn the blonde man had referred to when he gave me directions. Praise God that Ken had straightened me out, or I would now be heading happily for Miami instead of Savannah.

Fully exposed on that stretch of open water, I felt a brisk northwest wind blowing across my bow. That was the first time I felt any breeze since I had been in Florida. As I moved farther out, a rolling chop came diagonally at me from the northwest. The heavy bow and keel of my well-designed vessel sliced effortlessly into the small rollers and I began to enjoy the gentle up and down motion of the boat as it stepped over each small wave. I had gone about three miles when without any warning the motor started to run rough and then died. Almost in shock I pulled the start rope, as I tried to figure out what could possibly be wrong. It started right up again and seemed to run fine, so I continued on, hoping that the stall was just a one-time fluke. After a few more minutes it died again, and this time, to my great frustration, it would not restart no matter how many times I pulled it. I was dead in the water, adrift and at the mercy of the wind and the waves so I had to think fast! The wind was getting stronger and the sky was getting darker as my boat, with no sails up, was "sailing" sideways across the sound toward shallow water!

My first thought was to throw an anchor and call for a tow on my ship to shore radio. I didn't want to think about how much I would have to pay someone to come out and tow me in for repairs. Then I felt foolish, as I remembered that I was sitting in a fully rigged sailboat on a windy day. "I can sail back in easily with this northwest wind," I thought, as I tore at the sail covers to get the sails up quickly. A boat that big was really fun to sail, once your sails were up and you had her under control, but trying to get the sails up alone was not a job for the faint of heart, especially in a strong wind. Sails and ropes flapped wildly, stinging my face and hands as a light rain began to fall. I scampered back and forth on the wet decks trying not to slip and fall overboard as I rigged for sail power. When I finally grabbed the tiller and pointed her in the right direction, the sails filled and she leaned left as the bow plowed forward, slicing aggressively through the water. I had forgotten how exhilarating it was to feel a boat move powerfully through the water under sail, and I hoped I could use sail power often on that trip. I was thrilled that the wind direction allowed me to point my bow at the mouth of the canal and sail right at it. At that speed it didn't take long before I approached it, but then a troubling thought occurred to me. Even though I had covered the three miles back to the canal quickly, the wind might not let me turn left and sail the two hundred yards up the canal to the marina dock. Even if the wind direction was right, I feared that in the sheltered confines of the canal, there would not be enough wind to move me.

My worst fears were realized. As I reached the canal and turned left to go up the narrow, boat-lined channel, my sails went limp and I began to drift helplessly toward the swamp grass on the right. As I ran frantically toward the bow to get out an anchor, two men in a rowboat with an old motor came out of the canal. I asked if they could tow me the short distance up the canal to the marina, which was now visible on the right side. Quickly looping two dock lines together to make a tow rope, I tied it to my bow cleat and threw them the other end. I had my doubts about the little skiff with its small outboard towing something that big. But the distance was so short; I thought they could somehow get me there, even if it took a while. The heavy set man in the back looped the rope through a ring on the starboard side (which I knew was a mistake) and revved the engine. The small rowboat turned sideways as the forty eight hundred pounds of sailboat behind it moved only slightly. Just then a well-dressed man in a powerboat came out of the canal and slowed to ask if I needed help. I sensed from his tone that he wanted to appear helpful, but really didn't want to be bothered. He said that he had to check on something out in the sound, and would be coming right back. If I still needed help when he returned, he would stop to tow me in.

I told the men in the rowboat to tie the rope to the center of their transom, as close to the motor as possible and go slow. I prayed under my breath that this would work, because I sensed that they were about ready to give up. This time, as they started slowly forward, their boat turned sideways a little but began to move up the canal and I moved with them. I steered hard away from the marsh grass, trying to compensate for the fact that their tiny boat didn't really want to tow me straight. The nice thing about a sailboat was that once you got one moving, it would keep gliding for quite a distance and you could steer it because the steering didn't depend on the thrust of a motor. The bad thing about a sailboat (when coming into a dock) was that once it was gliding forward it would keep moving, long after the motor was turned off. Without a motor to kick into reverse to slow my approach, I would be coming in hard and fast. When I was only a hundred yards from the dock, a strong gust of wind pushed me sideways and all that weight turned the small aluminum boat like a toy. Afraid of running into me, the man in the back untied the rope and dropped it into the water so he could straighten out and avoid me. Panic stricken, with no time to grab a rope or drop an anchor, I drifted helplessly into the expensive boats tied up along the right side of the canal. "No!" I shouted as I dropped to the gunwale with my feet dangling over the side awaiting disaster. I planned to sacrifice my body and do whatever It took, to cushion the impact and prevent damage to my boat and the boat I was floating into, that I was sure cost six figures. Reaching out with my feet, I hoped to stop two tons of sailboat by flexing my leg muscles and pushing off as hard as I could. Miraculously, that brought me to a stop just a few inches from the other boat. The wind and current continued to push me into it and I stood up pushing off with both hands and a foot to keep the two vessels separated. One of the stainless steel cables that held up my mast was actually rubbing against the other boat, but thankfully not in a place where it could scratch it. Since the entire weight of my boat was now on my body and the cable, I feared that the taught cable would snap, forcing me to make time consuming repairs or abandon the trip. Just then, the power boater returned and reluctantly agreed to tow me, making it very clear that he couldn't stay long or help me get tied up. As he grabbed the tow rope and started forward, I pushed off with all my might and praised the Lord as I pulled away from the yacht without scratching it. I had to gauge my speed and steering carefully as I approached the dock, knowing that I would have only one chance with this man's help to get it right. If I waited too long to have him drop the rope, I would come in too fast and plow into the dock. If he dropped it too soon, the wind and current would stop me from reaching the dock and I would be right back where I was, drifting into other people's boats just short of my destination. If the latter happened, I would have no way to make it the last few yards to the dock since my reluctant helper would be gone. Carefully steering a "can't miss" course toward the dock, the instincts I had developed from years of sailing took over as I waited for just the right moment and then yelled "drop the rope" as loud as I could. I glided diagonally into the dock still moving pretty fast. I was glad that the dock had built in bumpers since I didn't have time to put out my fenders. As I jumped to the dock and grabbed the boat, it took all of my strength to bring it to a stop and hold it gently against the dock in the current. I praised the Lord for getting me in without damage and without having to pay for a tow.

As soon as I was tied up, I walked next door to let Ken know that my engine was still not right. His partner told me that he was out on a boat with a customer and would be back soon, so I went down to the dock at Ken's marina to wait for him to come in. While I waited, two good natured older men came down to look at a boat and I exchanged greetings with them. When I found out that one of them was Ken's father, I took the opportunity to brighten someone's day and give a compliment. I told him that his son was a hard worker and a very nice young man, and that he had been a great help getting my motor started. I spoke about my ministry to hunters and told him that his son had said that his favorite memories were from deer hunting with his dad. As he heard those words, his eyes softened and his aging well tanned face broke into a smile from ear to ear as he nodded fondly in agreement.

When Ken came back, he was surprised and disappointed to hear that my engine had quit, but being a man who took pride in his work, he was willing to come over and figure out what had happened. A quick inspection told him that a small gasket on the fuel hose connector was leaking. Since he didn't have one in stock he attached the fuel line from the tanks directly to the fuel intake valve inside the motor so there would be no chance of a leak. Before he allowed me to get underway again, he insisted on running the motor (in gear) for at least an hour at the dock. After a full hour the motor still hummed smoothly, pushing waves of water down the canal as the boat strained at her ropes. After that test, Ken pronounced the motor to be one hundred percent dependable and ready for the long trip. I thanked him sincerely and promised to pray for his friend as he helped me untie and pushed me away from the dock. Heading down the canal toward the ICW, I wondered what God's reason was for allowing yet another delay. As I thought about the frustration of breaking down, wasting time and being towed, something occurred to me. What if I had been out in the swamp somewhere in the middle of Georgia, thirty miles from the nearest marina when my motor quit? Suddenly, losing a few more hours, coming back to the dock and even my struggles in the canal with no motor didn't seem so bad. I praised the Lord again for his wisdom and his timing which I still believed to be perfect.

As I headed down the canal, three massive black tails rose from the water ahead of me. To my delight three rare Florida manatees were swimming up the canal toward me. I enjoyed the sight of those slow moving gentle giants as they passed close to my starboard side. The enormous adults and their tiny calf were graceful in their obesity as their flabby, walrus-like bodies glided past me. The huge rounded tails rose from the muddy water and slowly fell again as they swam. As they moved away, they almost seemed to be waving goodbye with their tails, wishing me "God Speed" on my journey and giving me permission to finally leave Amelia Island. The rain had stopped and I felt confident and secure in the knowledge that the motor had been serviced and thoroughly tested by an expert. The peace that passes all understanding came over me as I listened to the smooth drone of the outboard and with my hand on the tiller steered once again out into the open water of the sound.

There was a stiff rolling chop quartering towards me and a strong wind in my face out on Cumberland Sound. Buoys and navigational markers seemed to be everywhere which confused me at first. Some were numbered and color coded to guide vessels out to the ocean, while others marked dangerous reefs and shallow water. The ones that I needed to recognize and follow were the official numbered markers of the Intra Coastal Waterway. Those were large red triangles and green squares mounted on poles, towers and buoys. They were sequentially numbered, and lined the ICW all the way from the Florida Keys to New England. All ICW markers had a small yellow square or a small yellow triangle printed on them regardless of their overall shape or color. This differentiated them from the signs used to mark all other shipping lanes, rivers and canals that joined or passed through the Intra Coastal Waterway. I had learned from my research that when traveling north on the ICW, I had to keep any marker with a yellow triangle to my left, or port side. I also had to keep any marker with a yellow square to my right, or starboard side. I would find out as I went along that most of the time the yellow triangles were printed on the big red triangular shaped markers and the yellow squares were printed on the big green square ones. After a few days and a little experience I would learn to keep the red triangles to my left and the green squares to my right, but the first few hours were challenging and frustrating as I tried to find those markers and make sure I was headed in the right direction.

There in the large expanse of Cumberland Sound with green squares and red triangles marking rivers, canals and channels to the ocean, it was difficult at first to find the markers for the ICW. Everything around me looked wrong and somehow different than it did on the chart. I was used to reading maps as I zipped along at sixty-five miles per hour, but now I had to adjust to how long it took to cover even short distances at a speed of seven miles per hour! At one point I ventured close to shore to check out a red marker and found myself in dangerously shallow water. My depth alarm beeped loudly, showing me that I was only in four feet of water and would run aground if I went any farther in that direction. With one eye on the depth finder, I carefully came about and steered cautiously away from the shallows. Confused and unsure, I moved across the sound in the right general direction until I came upon a numbered ICW marker. My frustration gave way to relief and confidence, as I looked at the chart and realized that I knew exactly where I was. I began to understand that the chart was right on. I needed to adjust my impatient mind to moving slowly, and to remember that at that speed it took quite a while to travel between two points that looked close together on the chart. Once I had a reference point, I could see an endless line of red and green markers stretching northward ahead of me. Like a line of thin, unmoving, widely spaced soldiers, they stretched toward the horizon, outlining my path toward home. A path that I hoped would be as easy to follow as the yellow brick road.

25

CHAPTER 7

I Didn't Know God Made White Pelicans

As I passed each ICW marker I was thrilled that the numbers descended in order, and that each marker agreed with the color, number and location that was shown for it on my chart. Just as I was beginning to think it was easy and kind of fun, the wind came up, the sky darkened and it began to rain hard, really hard. Quickly putting the maps and charts inside, I closed the cabin door and donned the rain gear I had purchased the night before. As the wind and my forward progress drove the rain into my face, I praised the Lord for keeping me on Amelia Island an extra night and giving me the wisdom to purchase foul weather gear. This is not fun, I thought as the cold rain drove into my eyes with such force that I could hardly see. I should have gotten swim goggles to protect my eyes, but I never thought it could get that bad. There were a couple of other options besides standing out in the downpour. I could stop, anchor and wait it out, but trying to move around on the rain washed decks getting out anchors and ropes in the driving rain seemed even less enjoyable. I could rig a tent over the boom with my tarp and bungees to protect myself, but I would also have to anchor to do that, and trying to rig a tarp alone in that much wind would make a great scene for "Americas

Funniest Home Videos". At that point the best alternative was to tough it out and keep going. *It can't rain this hard for long,* I thought, as I prayed that the wind and the rain would let up soon, and that I could see well enough to keep going until it did.

A short time later the rain slowed to a drizzle and then stopped. The sky brightened and the sun appeared through an opening in the clouds. "That's more like it, thank you Lord," I praised, as I untied my hood and eagerly unsnapped the ill-fitting plastic suit. Shaking the water out of it I folded and stowed it in the cockpit compartment to my left for easy access. Since I was manning the boat alone, I had developed a way to steer by holding the wooden tiller between my legs as I stood facing the bow. That way my hands were free to read the charts, take off rain gear and perform other tasks, while staying on course and maintaining my forward progress. I would be flying solo for the first leg of the trip to Charleston. I had made arrangements to meet my family and tie up at a marina there for three days. My son Tom had been accepted into the Army Reserve Band as a percussionist. He would be finishing his basic training at Fort Jackson, South Carolina in a few days. The plan was to leave the boat in Charleston harbor and attend his graduation ceremony with my wife and two of my daughters. After the ceremony, we would spend a couple of days with Tom until he had to leave for the next phase of his Army training. My wife Mary would then join me for a week as I continued my trip up to Norfolk, while the girls returned home. When we arrived in Norfolk, Mary would fly home and my sailing buddy Marty Douglas would join me and stay aboard until I reached New York City. Marty had been with me before, on a week long trip on Lake Ontario. He loved sailing trips, and planned one of his vacation weeks this year so he could join me. Being an adventurer, he wanted to be part of the "big water" phase of my trip, on Chesapeake Bay and out into the Atlantic to New

York Harbor. Although I looked forward to having a "crew" aboard; there was something special about the sense of accomplishment and solitude of manning a boat alone. As I took in the sights and smells of open water, I could feel the presence of the Holy Spirit guiding me as I cruised steadily from one marker to the next. The air was heavy and sweet after the recent rain, and I felt at peace there with the Lord as my only companion.

As I made my way across the wide waters of Cumberland sound, weather conditions changed several times. I had to don and take off my rain gear more than once, as bands of heavy rain passed through, followed each time by clearing skies. I came through areas where strong winds slowed my progress and short stiff waves slapped at my bow. At one point a large power yacht came roaring by from behind and passed me at high speed. He was hurrying to get out of the rain and into a safe harbor, something I was not able to do traveling at my slow steady speed. I was impressed that something that heavy could skim so lightly over the water, but I was not prepared for what happened next. Before I could react or brace myself, the four-foot "tsunami" produced by something that big, pushing water out of the way that fast, slammed into my port side rolling my boat over onto it's side and causing me to lose my balance and fall to the deck. Things crashed to the floor inside the cabin and the mast swung wildly from side to side as the boat righted itself. That was not good, or very smart, I thought, as I questioned whether a twenty-five foot sailboat was too small to make this trip. Even in the protected confines of that inland waterway, I had been tossed like a toy and almost capsized on the first afternoon. I promised myself to be more alert for large boats that might pass me from either direction. I knew that I had to react quickly if a wake that size came at me again. I would need to point my bow right into it and plow through it, rather than letting it hit me broadside causing a knock down or a roll over.

As I continued on, the sky cleared and the wind died down. There was now more blue in the sky than there were clouds, and the warm sun felt good on the back of my neck. "I must be in Georgia by now," I thought, so I began to sing the old song "Georgia on my mind" as I cruised effortlessly on the glassy water. "Thank You, Lord, this is really nice," I thought, as I glided along a narrow winding river in the sunshine. As I wound my way along the banks of that peaceful river under a blue sky I rejoiced inside. At least for the moment things were exactly the way I imagined they would be. A few ducks and shore birds stood on the beach or swam in the shallows near shore. I told myself that the Lord had placed them there, just to add life to the scene and to entertain me. I smiled inwardly as I imagined him telling them where to sit, so I would have something to look at and enjoy as I went by.

As I rounded a bend in the river, a new scene appeared, and I noticed a flock of large white birds standing on a sand bar ahead. Having produced several wildlife videos, I thought I could identify most American birds. But I was surprised and puzzled by the odd shaped bodies of these creatures. They were too big to be seagulls and they were too short and dumpy to be any kind of heron, egret, or crane. They were standing in a group like geese or swans, but even at that distance I could tell by their short necks and awkward bodies that they couldn't be waterfowl. I had never seen or heard of any white bird that size and shape, and could not imagine what they were. As I got closer, I saw the long wedge shape beaks, tucked down against thick curving necks that rose from heavy awkward bodies and I knew they had to be pelicans. A smile came to my face as I passed them at close range. "Lord, I knew you made white herons for the southern states, but I never knew that you made white pelicans," I said, shaking my head in disbelief. "Thanks, Lord, for letting me see them, I learned something new today." They stared at me blankly with comical faces that only a mother could love. Their clumsy bodies seemed to be assembled from the spare parts of other bird species, yet they were somehow elegant in their snow white plumage. I wondered if God had designed pelicans as a prank, on a day when he was in the mood for a good laugh. Maybe he created them just to make us smile, as the comic relief of the bird world.

I was beginning to feel good about the trip and my confidence soared. Now that I was starting to relax and enjoy myself, a rumble in my stomach reminded me that I hadn't eaten anything since early that morning at the dock. Most of the food I brought with me was left over from our annual Fourth of July picnic at the lake. Planning ahead, and trying to be a good steward, I had frozen several packages of hot dogs, hamburgers, and rolls that were left from that gathering. I also salvaged squeeze bottles of mustard and ketchup, along with plastic cups, plates, napkins and utensils. Trying to keep all that meat fresh for as long as possible in summer heat, I cooked half of the hamburger patties on the grill at home and then froze them again. I then kept the cooked meat, the raw meat and the rolls frozen solid until the day I left, placing them in the boats icebox under frozen containers of blue ice. I hoped to use that meat up as soon as possible, eating things in the order they thawed out, and buying fresh ice for the icebox daily. Since I was cruising well, I didn't want to stop and anchor to prepare a meal, so I rigged a crude "auto pilot" to steer the boat while I got out some food. By stretching a couple of bungee cords across the cockpit and around the tiller handle, I created a way for the boat to steer itself for short periods of time. By adjusting the bungees until the boat was maintaining a straight course I could actually leave the tiller for a minute or two. Then I could jump down into the cabin and quickly get out a few things, or make a sandwich, as I kept a watchful eye on the direction the boat was heading. If she started going the wrong way, I would scramble back to the tiller and readjust my course and the bungees, until I felt that it was safe to let go of it again. By repeating this process several times, I could accomplish a lot, and still maintain my forward progress at full speed ahead.

Rather than try to cook while cruising alone, I got out a couple of cooked hamburgers, rolls, ketchup, an ice cold Diet Pepsi and my king size bag of M&Ms. The burgers and rolls had thawed out but were ice cold, so I placed them on a paper plate in the sun to warm them up. After about twenty minutes I coated them liberally with ketchup to create the world's greatest burger sandwiches. Even though the meat was cold, and the rolls were damp, I felt like I was eating manna from heaven. The hot sun had softened the M&Ms, making them messy to eat and proving to me once and for all that they do melt in your hands. Even though they were a chocolate mess they tasted great, and the ice cold Diet Pepsi was colder and sweeter than mountain nectar on that hot day. I guess when you're starving and doing something you love, anything can taste like a meal fit for a king.

As I enjoyed my feast and steered with the tiller between my legs, I absorbed my surroundings and relished that moment as much as any other one I can remember. Watching the sun reflect off the still water, I took in the beauty and the solitude of the marsh. The words from an old TV commercial came to mind; "It doesn't get any better than this," the ad claimed. As I praised the Lord for giving me that special moment, I knew that it did get better than this, far better than this, when we are in heaven with him for eternity.

Chapter 8

The Anchor Holds

After an hour or so I found myself back in big water on the Cumberland River. The Cumberland appeared to be over a mile wide and stretched out ahead of me as far as I could see. Since I was out in the open, I could feel a brisk wind in my face again and it seemed to be getting stronger. As I moved up the river, watching my depth finder and steering my way from one marker to the next, I noticed some ominous looking black clouds coming my way. Things were still clear overhead, but in front of me a dark curtain of menacing clouds had been drawn across the sky and was moving toward me at an alarming rate. The streaks I saw under the gloomy clouds told me that it was already raining hard a mile or two up river in the direction I was heading. I felt a sudden chill in the air and the wind picked up as the choppy water began to look as dark as the sky. Looking straight up, I became more concerned, as the friendly patch of blue above me got smaller. The wind was pushing the clouds my way and I was motoring toward them, so the storm approached me that much faster. I had to make a quick decision: Put on the rain gear, batten down the hatches and keep going, or anchor now, before the downpour, and hunker down inside the cabin to ride it out. It wasn't a pleasant experience steering through the wind driven rain earlier and now it looked like things could get even worse. At that moment

I saw something else that helped me decide. Two miles ahead, now visible in sharp contrast to the dark water and sky, were the large whitecaps of huge breaking waves in a line across the river. "Those are either ocean surf breakers crashing on a beach, or waves of more than five feet, in a large, open body of water," I thought, swallowing hard as a flood of questions raced through my mind: "Is that the ocean? I don't have to go that way, do I? There must be a turn into a protected creek or canal before I get there . . . the Intra Coastal Waterway can't have waves that big, can it?" I decided that it would be foolhardy to go any farther in that direction until I knew what lie ahead, especially with wind and rain imminent.

Weighing all the factors, I decided to get as close to the right shore as possible, throw both anchors off the bow and ride it out. It was important not to get into water that was too shallow, in case the high winds pushed the boat for a distance toward shore before the anchors dug in. About seventy yards from shore I found ten feet of water and cut the motor. As I scrambled forward to get out the anchors the sky opened up and the rain started. The anchor ropes which had been so neatly coiled before the trip were now tangled from highway travel and wave action. As the strong wind pushed the pilot less craft rapidly down the river and towards shore, I tore frantically at the tangled ropes as big cold drops of rain pelted my head and neck. In my panic and the urgency of the moment I made the ropes more tangled by pulling on them too hard as the boat drifted toward the shallows. With God's help, I finally got one anchor and all of its rope free, and dropped it into the water. With one rope out of the way the job was easier, and after another minute of kneeling on the slippery deck in the downpour, my wet hands uncoiled the second rope and got that anchor over the side. With the ends of both ropes tied to the bow I threw all of the rope into the water. Since an anchor holds a boat by digging into the bottom and not by its weight, the more rope you had in the water the more shallow the angle of the rope would be. The boat's weight would then drag the anchor across the bottom and it would be much more likely to dig in and hold securely. With two anchors out, I had twice as much chance that one of them would hold me. The brush on shore looked very close now, and I feared that I had taken too long to get the anchors down. Being careful not to slip on the wet decks and fall overboard, I ran back to the cockpit to check the water depth and close up the cabin. Looking at the shoreline, I could tell that the boat was still moving sideways with the wind as the slack in the ropes was taken up. As the anchors began to drag, the digital read out on the depth finder said I was in seven feet of water and then quickly changed to six. At three feet my keel would dig into the bottom and I would become hopelessly stuck and possibly sustain damage to my vessel. With one eye on the depth finder and one eye on the brush, I prayed earnestly in the driving rain as the shore loomed closer and the water depth dropped to five feet. "Lord, please let the anchors dig in before I drift much farther," I whispered, staring anxiously at the depth finder in my rain soaked clothes. If the anchors didn't grab, my only chance to avoid running aground was to restart the engine and try to motor away from shore, dragging the anchors with me. As I moved toward the outboard to start it, I felt the boat lurch and then turn sharply to point up river as if a giant underwater hand had grabbed the anchor ropes and given them a gentle pull. "Thank you Lord!" I shouted, as one look at shore told me that I had stopped moving. A glance at the depth finder told me that I was in five feet of water, and with the boat now pointing at its anchors and into the wind, I knew I could ride out almost anything. Although my rain soaked clothes clung to my skin and made me feel cold and uncomfortable, I began to loudly sing the song: "The Anchor Holds" as I opened the cabin doors to go inside.

Once inside the warmth and protection of the cabin, I got out of my wet clothes, dried myself with a towel and slipped into a dry sweatshirt and jeans. The rain beat furiously on the cabin top and poured across the windows as the strong wind rocked the boat up and down, but I felt safe and secure. Looking out the window toward shore I could tell that I hadn't moved and I noticed a gnarled old tree growing up out of the brush that looked almost dead. It was the only tree in sight, and it reminded me of a photo I had seen of a famous ancient tree that grew out west called the Joshua tree. I dubbed it the "Joshua Tree" and used it as a point of reference to make sure I didn't move, and that my anchors were still holding fast.

Wearing warm dry clothes and in the safety of the cabin, I now felt physically refreshed and mentally positive. There was something about overcoming adversity and dangerous, stressful situations that invigorated the body and mind. Looking at my charts of the Intra Coastal Waterway, I learned why I had seen big breaking waves off in the distance. A few miles ahead, the Cumberland River entered St. Andrews Sound. A sound is a corner of the Ocean that makes a dent or pocket in the coastline that is too big and not protected enough to be called a bay. Depending on the direction of the wind on any given day, a sound can be as calm as a pond or as rough as the open Atlantic. The chart showed me that in order to continue north on the ICW, I had to go several miles out into St. Andrews Sound until I came to red marker number thirty-two. I would then turn left and follow the markers toward land, until I was in the safety of the river that ran behind Jekyll Island. The chart also showed me that there was a wide area of breakers ahead that occurred when the large swells of the sound crashed and broke against the currents and shallow water of the river. This powerful wave action piled up a long sand bar that stretched across the mouth of the river. Apparently there was only one spot that was deep enough to get through the treacherous shallows with their massive breaking waves and out into the open water of the sound. The ICW markers would lead me to it, and I prayed that I could navigate it successfully.

When the drumming of the rain on the cabin top slowed to a pitter patter and then stopped, I came out to look around. The sky was beginning to brighten, and the wind was dying down, so I made the decision to pull the anchors and try to get across St. Andrews Sound right then. If I could just make it to Jekyll Island and get behind it, I could anchor safely for the night in a protected spot, far from the wind and crashing waves of the Atlantic. The closer I got to the breakers the bigger they looked, but the markers led me to an area where the ocean swells marched steadily up the river unchanged as they passed over deep water. As I headed for the deep channel and out into St. Andrews Sound, I was frustrated that there were no more ICW markers ahead in any direction. I was now in five foot ocean swells with an occasional wave being even bigger than that. I was able to quarter diagonally into the waves, rising to climb the watery hills as they lifted me up, then slammed me down into the valleys, with spray coming across the bow and blowing back in my face. St. Andrews Sound was an unprotected corner of the Atlantic, so being on it meant being out on the ocean. To my right was open water all the way to Africa and endless waves coming at me from as far as the eye could see.

The only thing worse than being out in waves that big, was being out there without knowing which way to go. Apparently marker thirty-two was either missing, or so far out in the sound that I could not see it yet because of the waves. Without it, I had no way of knowing which direction to head, or how far out to go before I could turn left and head for Jekyll Island. I could see the island off to my left and it didn't seem very far away. My heart and my instincts told me not to venture out into the deep swells of the sound, but to turn left now and head straight for the safety of the island. But to my left, a sea of large breakers boiled and crashed, indicating shallow water all the way to the island in that direction. If I went that way, not only would I run aground, but being stuck and immovable the boat would then be pounded by the massive breaking waves into a pile of fiberglass debris. As I continued farther out into the sound, I began to pray passionately: "Heavenly Father, please show me the course that I need to follow, and help me to make it through this area of open water. Please help me to steer carefully in these huge waves, avoid the shallows and get back into calm protected water as soon as possible."

A few minutes after my prayer, a large motor yacht came along, heading in the same direction that I was. It was far enough away so its wake did not affect me, and it headed right out into the sound as if the captain knew exactly where he was going. "Thank You Lord," I praised, watching it carefully and memorizing exactly where the large boat went. About three miles ahead, the boat made a sharp left turn and headed right for the island. Although I was disappointed that I had to go so far out, my prayers had once again been answered as God showed me the route I needed to follow. I was deeply moved as I glanced at the picture of the young sailor with Jesus, and realized that he had pointed my course through the waves, just as he was doing in the picture. He used a boat, instead of literally pointing with his finger, but at that moment I could feel his presence more than ever, and knew that his hand was on my shoulder as firmly as it was on the shoulder of the young boy.

For the next hour and a half the boat was tossed like a piece of driftwood, as it rocked and wallowed its way through the powerful ocean swells. Unlike a larger vessel, "God Speed" was not big enough or heavy enough to set a course and plow right through the waves in a straight line. I had to feel my way through the hills and valleys of water, steering a zigzag course. I gripped the tiller tightly, following the trenches between the waves whenever possible, then turning sharply to meet the next wave head on with the point of my bow. After an hour of battling the waves that way, I turned left and steered toward the side of Jekyll Island where I had seen the large yacht disappear. On that heading the waves hit me from the right and the rear, causing me to rock forward and roll sideways as they carried me forward toward my destination. Throughout that ordeal I glanced at the picture often, to remind myself that God was with me, knowing that if I had his hand on my shoulder, I had nothing to fear. I still shuddered when I saw the huge breakers crashing in the shallows nearby, and I continued to call out to him for protection until the boat glided into the calm water of the river behind Jekyll Island. I felt like I had just stepped off of one of the world's worst amusement park rides and was now standing on solid ground. As I breathed a sigh of relief and praised the Lord, I felt like he answered by sending a dolphin to escort me up the river, its dorsal fin gently breaking the rippled surface as it swam beside me for a short distance. If dolphins could talk, I imagined this one saying: "You made it; welcome to Jekyll Island. The Lord was with you all the way, and he got you safely across the big water."

As I rounded the corner of the island, I passed a beach with people sunning and swimming. Men had waded out with bathing suits and fishing rods to cast, and they waved as I passed by. It was a beautiful summer evening after a day of rain, and as I looked in the sky I saw a rainbow that began in the water and ended somewhere on the island. "Thank you, Lord, for leading me safely through the waves, and for the rainbow that is a reminder of your presence and your promise to us," I prayed. "I praise you for the blessings and protection that you give me, and I ask that you continue to be with me." As I finished praying, a smile came to my face. I thought about how quickly things had changed and how different they were from just thirty minutes ago.

Voyage of the Heart

CHEYENNE
CHEYENNE
MSJ 11

Chapter 9

Meaner than a Boat Yard Dog

After leaving the sunbathers and fishermen behind, I passed under two massive highway bridges with numerous cars and trucks whizzing by overhead. I wondered if anyone in a vehicle above was looking down and admiring the small sailboat below, wondering where I was going and wishing they could be cruising with me instead of rushing home from work. Farther up river, I passed a large yacht club with stately old brick buildings. My guide book for marinas and facilities told me that it was the Jekyll Island Club, an exclusive upscale yacht club that had a lot of tradition and history. After winding my way down a smooth grass-lined river for an hour, I came into a wide area that was the central hub of several intersecting bodies of water. The narrow channel that I was in formed the letter "T" where it entered a much wider river and came to an end. This mile wide river ran left and right in front of me and appeared to open up even wider to my right and branch off in two directions. Looking straight across the big river, I saw a very high, very long highway bridge ahead of me on the other side. Under that bridge, another river flowed away from me as it left the main river directly across from my entry channel. It looked like there was a good sized city on that river just beyond the bridge on the left side.

Looking at my chart I got frustrated, because nothing I saw

matched anything on the printed page. I was supposed to go under a big highway bridge, but on the chart it was not at an intersection where one large river left another at right angles. I was supposed to be in the Brunswick River, but was that the wide river flowing to my right or the one straight ahead going under the bridge? The chart showed the city of Brunswick Georgia on a river, but not near the intersection of two major rivers and nowhere near a highway bridge. To make matters worse, there were colored, numbered navigational markers everywhere, but I could not find any more ICW markers. Confused and perplexed, I headed toward the bridge in the fading daylight, hoping that I would spot an Intra Coastal marker or something else that would tell me where I was. As I approached the bridge, I still wasn't sure if I had to go under it or not and it was getting dark fast.

To my right was a large rocky island covered by tall trees. A long wooden dock stuck out from it and two power boats were suspended from boat hoists at the end of the dock, telling me that someone lived on the island. The island was accessible only by boat but was not completely surrounded by water. It was on the corner of the swamp at the intersection of the two rivers, bordered on one side by marsh and on the other sides by water. The water on the "dock" side of the island was sheltered from the wind by the high rocky shoreline and tall trees and it was as smooth as glass. Noticing that a security light at the end of the dock was just beginning to glow, I decided that the calm, well lit area would be a great spot to anchor safely for my first night at "sea". Motoring slowly in toward the calmest water, my plan was to get as close to the island and the light at the end of the dock as possible. As I watched the depth finder, my instincts told me that the water would be deep close to the steep rocky shoreline, and I was right. Taking her in to about eight feet of water, I left the motor purring softly in neutral as I sat on the bow sorting out the wet anchor ropes. In my eagerness to get going again at the "Joshua Tree", I had not taken the time to coil them up and stow them properly. As I worked with the ropes, I noticed white herons, white egrets, and other white birds flying in to land in the trees on the island. They made quite a racket calling to each other, as they came from every direction, a few at a time and landed there until the trees were full of them. It seemed like I had discovered the night time roosting area for every white bird in Georgia, so I named the place "White Bird Island". Everything seemed too good to be true; I was close to shore, close to the lighted dock, yet still in good deep water. I felt safe sleeping with the birds in that peaceful, secluded spot, and was pleased that the Lord had led me there, but I couldn't believe what happened next.

As soon as the first anchor splashed the water, the island erupted with noise and confusion as two large, ferocious rottweilers charged out onto the dock and began barking at me wildly. I was glad that they were sixty feet away, as they paced frantically up and down the dock barking and trying to find a way to get at me. Apparently the owner of the dock didn't want any uninvited guests on the island. As the incessant barking continued, I feared that the owner would come out to see what the commotion was about, and ask me to anchor elsewhere. That would mean even more work, and it would be difficult and dangerous to move and find another "safe" spot now that it was dark. Fortunately, the owner did not come out, but I knew that it would be hard to get any sleep unless the dogs accepted me and settled down.

Calling my wife to let her know my progress, I learned that she wouldn't be able to join me in Charleston and cruise with me up to Norfolk. I also found out that Tom's Army orders had been changed, and he was now free and willing to take my wife's place for that leg of the trip. I was disappointed that my wife couldn't share this experience and these memories with me. But the way things had gone so far, I knew that she would not enjoy this and I did not want a negative experience to sour her on sailing forever. Having not seen my son during his nine weeks of basic training, it would be great to spend time with him and have my hunting and fishing buddy along on such a memorable adventure.

I started out at one o'clock that first day and went about forty miles before I anchored there. The more I looked at the charts the more confusing everything seemed. The river going under the bridge should have been the McKay River, and I was supposed to go that way to continue north, but there was not one ICW marker anywhere to verify that I was in the right spot. The position of the bridge was all wrong. The highway bridge over the McKay River was nowhere near the intersection of two major rivers as this one was. Rather than get more frustrated, I decided to trust God and believe that He would give me the guidance and direction I needed in the morning.

The constant loud barking drove me crazy and made it impossible to sleep, but after a couple of hours the dogs gave up and quieted down. At about one thirty, I was startled awake by the loud clunk of the keel making contact with the bottom. *I couldn't have bumped bottom,* I thought, *I'm anchored in eight feet of water!* I bounded quickly up the stairs to check my depth finder and see what was happening. When I anchored, both ropes were stretching toward shore with the boat pointing at the island and pulling away from it. During the night the wind changed and the boat had swung toward shore. Since a sailboat anchored from the bow will always point into the wind, the anchor ropes now led off toward open water and the back of the boat was very close to the island. I was now twice the length of my anchor rope closer to shore than I had been when I anchored, and the tide had gone out, putting me in three to four feet of water. Without panicking, I sat on the bow with my feet dangling over the side and pulled on the thickest anchor rope, coiling it on the deck as the boat moved out and I gained line. My plan was to pull the boat out to deeper water where the anchors were dug in. When I was directly over the anchors, my depth was still just four to five feet, and I knew I would be in trouble if the tide continued to go out. My only choice was to pull the anchors, go out deeper and anchor again. Completely exhausted, I groaned at the thought of having to face that grueling, time consuming task again at two o'clock in the morning.

The sounds of the anchors being placed on the deck and the motor starting up roused the dogs and they rushed back out on the dock barking crazily. "Oh no, not those two again," I muttered, "I'll never get any sleep tonight." When I got out to eight feet of water, I dropped both anchors and hoped that the dogs would quiet down again so I could finally get some sleep. Just then, I cringed as the owner of the dogs came out on the dock to see what they were barking at. It was a tall middle aged woman who couldn't have been too happy about being awakened at that hour. At that point I was just relieved that it wasn't a grumpy old man with a shotgun, and I began to yell apologies and explanations to her in a voice loud enough to be heard over the dogs. "I'm sorry, I meant no harm," I began. "I'm trying to get to my sons graduation from boot camp, but I seem to be lost," I shouted (hoping that might trigger some sympathy and she wouldn't ask me to move). "I just needed a safe place to anchor for the night," I continued. "I didn't know you had guard dogs that would create such a disturbance, I'm very sorry."

The woman was surprisingly pleasant and understanding, considering the hour and the circumstances. She apologized for the dogs and said that she did not mind me anchoring there because it was a good safe spot. Seizing the opportunity, I asked for some directions and found out that the river going under the bridge was not the McKay River or any part of the Intra Coastal Waterway. To get back to the ICW heading north, I needed to return to the wide river I had come from (which was St. Simons Sound) and go out and around the back side of her island to the left. I thanked her sincerely and said good night as she took the now quiet dogs with her back into the trees and disappeared. "Thank you Lord!" I praised, as I realized that even this night filled with problems seemed to have a purpose. I had gotten directions in the middle of the night in an area where there was no place to stop for directions. If the dogs didn't wake their owner, I would have gone under that bridge in the morning and many miles in the wrong direction, only to retrace my route when I discovered my mistake. At sailboat speed, a mistake that big could have cost most of a day, throwing me far enough behind schedule to miss my son's graduation ceremony. I had also learned how much the tides could change the water depth in just a few hours, and how important it was to use a bow and a stern anchor to stay in one spot, rather than two bow anchors.

In the morning, I rose and dressed in the predawn darkness feeling like I hadn't slept all night. My fifty-two year old body felt like it was dead and I was running on empty. I dreaded the thought of trying to get the anchors up, knowing that they might be deeply dug into the bottom. My back and shoulder muscles ached from moving the boat and pulling up anchors and my hands and fingers were sore and swollen. Wetting a wash cloth in the melt water from the ice box, I washed my face with it hoping that it would perk me up. The small anchor came free with a mighty pull, but it was quite a job dipping it up and down in the water to wash off all the mud before I could bring it aboard. The heavy main anchor would not budge on the first try when I pulled with all my might, so I moved the boat around it, pulling hard from different directions until it finally came up surrounded by a cake of mud twice its size. After washing the big anchor and coiling and stowing both anchors, I sat on the front deck physically exhausted trying to figure out what to do next. One fuel tank was empty and most of the ice was now water, so I planned to get gas and ice at the first marina I found. I also decided to try hailing another vessel on the radio for some directions, as soon as I got underway.

Making my way slowly back to the motor I summoned enough energy to give it one good pull and it began to purr softly. As I wearily sank down on the rear seat, I noticed how beautiful the full moon looked, hanging low in the sky over the bridge. As I stared at the moon, the peace that passes all understanding filled my heart in spite of my weariness, and I began to pray: "Lord give me the strength and the energy I will need to continue on and to do what you have called me to do. I ask that you come against the enemy and his attempts to frustrate me and wear me down. Please soothe my aching muscles and swollen hands and help me to cover a great distance today. Show me the direction that I need to go, as clearly as you are pointing the way for the boy in the picture, and help me find a place to get fuel and ice. Please live in my heart and travel with me today, in Jesus name I pray, Amen."

As if my prayer was their cue, the white birds on the island began flying out of the trees and over the top of my mast. At first there were just a few, then more and more in ever increasing numbers until the sky overhead was filled with them. The graceful wings were even more starkly white against the deep slate blue of the dawn sky. I sat in awe of that spectacle as the wide, endless stream of white bodies moved overhead and stretched toward the sunrise like a legion of angels flying on ahead of me. Tears welled up in my eyes as I praised the Lord for allowing me to be part of that scene and for again reminding me of his presence. Gently nudging the motor into gear, I moved smoothly away from the island, heading for the open water of St. Simons Sound as the red sun rose from the water ahead.

Voyage of the Heart

195

Chapter 10

Bold Adventurer or Aging Fool?

"This is the sailboat God Speed, hailing all vessels and marinas; can anyone help me with some directions?" I spoke loudly into the microphone of my ship to shore radio with a sense of urgency in my voice. "This is the sailboat God Speed, hailing all vessels, can anyone read me?" "Yes captain, I read you loud and clear," a deep voice boomed back at me through the tiny speaker. "You've got the captain of an ocean going "Sea - Tow" tug, how can I help you?" asked the friendly voice. "I seem to be lost," I began. "I spent the night near a big highway bridge, anchored on the lee side of an island that has a dock with a couple of small boats on it. It was the night time roosting spot for hundreds of white herons and egrets. I need to go under the Lanier Island Highway Bridge, and continue north on the ICW up the Mackay River, but nothing I see looks anything like my maps and charts.

The captain of the tug explained: "It sounds like you were anchored on the west side of Marsh Island. You're confused, because the big bridge you saw is brand new and is not on your charts. The bridge you are looking for is still quite a distance up the line. Come back out from Marsh Island and away from the bridge into the open water of the sound. Turn left and follow the buoys down the middle of the sound until you come to red buoy number twenty. If you turn left after you pass that buoy, you will see the red and green markers for the ICW north. They will lead you to the Lanier Island Bridge and right up the McKay River."

"I can't thank you enough," I replied. "Where can I get some fuel and ice?" He told me that just before I went under that bridge, there would be a marina to my right a short distance up the Frederica River. He advised me to hail them when I rounded buoy number twenty for directions to their dock. "God bless ya captain," I responded, "You just made my day and saved my trip!" "Happy to help," he said cheerfully, as he signed off. "Thanks again Lord," I said aloud, as I headed for the buoys in the center of the sound.

When I passed buoy number twenty and made a left turn I could see the line of red and green markers stretching ahead of me and a major highway bridge off in the distance. When I realized I was back on track, my confidence swelled as I reached for the radio again. "This is the sailboat God Speed looking for a marina near the mouth of the McKay River. This is the God Speed, I am heading north on the Intra Coastal Waterway and need fuel and ice, can anyone read me?"

"This is the Lanier Island Marina" answered a confident female voice, "we can supply both of those needs and we would be happy to accommodate you. I'll stay on the radio with you captain and talk you right in to our docks. "This is cool when you're not lost," I thought with a smile. "I could really get used to this lifestyle and being called captain." The woman was pleasant, courteous, and very helpful as she directed me through the mine field of buoys and markers toward her marina. I was hard to help, because I didn't know the area and found myself questioning everything she said. The marina was located near the highway bridge, so I wanted to steer for the bridge and didn't understand why she kept sending me to the right. I found out later, that what looked like open water ahead, was really a shallow, grassy mud flat. If I headed right at the bridge, I would have buried my keel in the bottom and been stuck there indefinitely.

That was yet another lesson to let go and trust God's guidance. He had provided a willing guide and a place to get supplies, yet I still had trouble following his lead, even after everything thing he had done for me. Feeling pretty sheepish, I vowed that I would follow the woman's directions. I also thanked her for having patience with a grumpy, worn out old sailor that was operating on no sleep. Her voice remained pleasant and her words were encouraging as she stayed with me, patiently giving me shortcuts to get there quickly and avoid shallow water.

The marina where I was headed was just a mile up the Frederica River. I would have to take a short detour up that river, and then come back out into the sound to go under the bridge and up the McKay. The Frederica was blocked off just beyond the marina by the low approach span to the Lanier Island Bridge. The woman said they were located just before the impassable bridge on the left side of the river.

When she got her first look at my boat, she expressed surprise that it was so small, because she was expecting a larger vessel. As I approached the marina, she told me to stay out in the middle of the river and go almost to the bridge. Then make a sharp U-turn to my left and come into the gas dock with my starboard side to the dock. She warned me that being so small, the strong current would make it difficult for me to come into her dock. The trick was to come in slow enough to touch the dock gently, yet fast enough to make it there and grab something, before the current pushed me away from the dock and down the river. I knew only too well that a sailboat was not well suited for coming into a dock. The slower the motor ran, the less control you had over steering and forward progress. Once you kicked the motor out of gear you became a lame duck, completely at the mercy of the wind and the current.

While still in the middle of the river, I tied off the steering tiller with bungees to hold a straight course, while I got out my boat fenders and cushions. I had two large rubber boat fenders with me and some low budget home made fenders I created using fat yellow pool "noodles" and some rope. I then scrambled all over the deck hanging the fenders to protect my starboard side from what could be a hard impact with the dock. I also hung an old boating safety cushion and my throwable horseshoe life ring over the side, to further protect the shiny white surface I had so lovingly scrubbed and polished.

As I made my U-turn, I could feel the strong current pushing me toward the dock and I hoped that I could slow down enough to come in safely. As I reduced speed I felt the current begin to turn me sideways and push me away from shore and back out into the river. "This is gonna be tricky," I said to myself out loud. The only way to get there with that much current was to speed toward the dock, and then pop the motor into reverse and rev it like crazy to slow down just before I slammed into it. I'm really glad I've got a person waiting on the dock here to grab me and cushion the blow. Just then a sickening thought occurred to me. When I anchored for the night, I took the dock rope off the front bow cleat and stowed it away so it didn't tangle with the anchor ropes. In my eagerness to get going that morning, I hadn't taken the time to get it out and reattach it. Now I was coming in bow first with no front rope for the woman on the dock to grab and hold. With no one else aboard it was now too late to do anything about it, as I closed on the dock hard and fast. At a distance of about ten feet I cut my speed, popped the motor into reverse and revved the motor to full throttle backwards. The boat slowed quickly and the woman grabbed my safety rail as she cushioned the impact by pushing and holding me off with her foot. "Give me a bow line quick," she yelled. "I won't be able to hold her long in this current." My heart sank as I had to reply that I did not have a bow line attached. Panic stricken I jumped to the bow, hoping to quickly attach and throw a rope, only to find that the strong current was already turning the bow out into the river and the outboard toward the dock. The woman held on tenaciously, trying with all her might to turn the boat and bring it in sideways against the dock, but without a bow and stern rope to pull me in she was fighting a losing battle. Although she made a valiant effort, the boat turned out of control in the current until the outboard (which was still running) almost banged into the dock. As I scrambled back to the motor to protect it from damage, we both decided that she should let go and push me away, before the boat and the current pulled her off the dock.

Wow, that did not go well at all, I thought, as I made a wide circle in the river to position myself for another run at the dock. Slowing the motor I left the tiller for a moment to attach and secure a bow line. I placed the coiled end on the starboard rail and did the same with my stern line so both could be easily grabbed by someone on the dock. After my first failed attempt, I felt that I now had a better feel for approaching the dock in this current. "Lord, please help this to work this time," I muttered softly as I again closed on the dock. "You grab the bow line and I'll jump off with the stern line," I shouted loudly, making sure she heard me over the sound of the motor. As the front fender made contact with the dock the woman grabbed the coiled rope and pulled my bow in sideways. Kicking the motor out of gear I waited for the gap between boat and dock to close and then with one jump joined her on the dock holding the stern rope.

We both breathed a sigh of relief as we gently brought "God

Speed" against the dock and tied her securely, putting equal tension on both the front and the back ropes. Then I shook hands with the woman and thanked her for her help and her patience. In a sincere, respectful tone she replied that she was happy to help, and added with a smile that it was her job. She then said that I was not the first sailboat to have trouble coming into that dock. The pleasant, deeply tanned young woman wore a baseball cap with a ponytail coming through the hole in the back of it. She smiled easily, seemed eager to please, and had a way with people and with boats. I told her about the trip I was taking and that it was something I had dreamed about doing for many years. She nodded with approval as she said that it sounded like a great adventure and also told me that her name was Melissa. She told me to catch my breath and then come into the office when I was ready to purchase fuel and supplies. As I went below to begin the unpleasant task of digging out the fuel tanks, Melissa went back into the office to take an incoming call on her ship to shore radio.

With my body twisted like a pretzel in the cramped confines below the deck I unhooked the fuel tanks and somehow muscled them through the hatch and out into the cockpit. As I stood on deck to lift them over to the dock a loud clear voice came through the radio to break the silence. "How about you Mel; what're you up to this morning?" began a young man's voice.

"I just had a terrible ordeal with an old timer in a small sailboat," Melissa answered. "The guy just about wrecked his boat and motor trying to come into our dock, and almost pulled me into the river in the process," she chuckled. I had forgotten that my radio was still on and tuned to the marina-hailing channel, and apparently Melissa hadn't thought of that possibility either. "This guy's using swimming pool noodles for boat fenders, and he's trying to go all the way to New York in a 25 foot sailboat," she continued, "I hope he makes it." "I guess everything is relative," I sighed, thinking about how I saw "God Speed" as a large impressive sailing "yacht." "He sounds like an eccentric old nut," the young man continued. He then went on to say that the national weather service was tracking two hurricanes that were supposed to hit the coast right where I was going, and he wondered if I knew about them. "I'll make sure he does," Melissa answered. She then went on to ask the man: "Didn't you tell me that you've always wanted to take a trip like that? Don't be too critical; that might be you some day."

The young man answered that he did admire my courage and sense of adventure as he signed off. Melissa closed the conversation with a friendly tone, saying that she had to see what I needed, and give me some directions and precautions

After overhearing that conversation, I sat in the cockpit staring down the river with a bruised ego. Feeling depressed, I compared the way I saw myself with their perception of me. I thought I was an experienced captain and adventurer, yet in their eyes, I was just an eccentric old timer. It was hard for me to hear and accept the idea that maybe I really was just that. "Maybe I am just a dreamer," I thought, a sea faring "Don Quixote", off on a great adventure in my own mind, and yet to those I encountered just an aging fool. It was certainly too late to turn back and I knew that how God saw me was the only image that really mattered. I vowed to keep going and enjoy the trip, regardless of how people might see me.

Just then Melissa came down the dock with a smile, and my spirits brightened as I helped her fill my tanks. After putting them aboard, I went inside to purchase ice and she insisted on going over the maps and charts of the area with me. Apparently, many of the buoys and markers in that area had been changed and renumbered since my chart was printed in 1994. That was why I was confused and had trouble finding the McKay River. Melissa crossed out the non existent buoys and drew in the new ones on my chart. She also made sure that every buoy and marker had the correct number on it as far up the ICW as she had gone. Then she gave me directions to get safely back out into the sound, up the McKay River and under the Lanier Island Bridge. Before I left, she warned me that two hurricanes were developing, and that one of them was scheduled to make landfall right where I was headed. She advised me to keep one ear on the weather radio at all times and to be careful. Whatever her opinion of me was, it was obvious that she wanted to help in every possible way, and that she was sincerely concerned for my safety. I knew that the Lord had brought me to that marina for a reason, and that her help was heaven sent. As I thanked her and said goodbye I told her that I hoped to write a book about my voyage someday and that maybe she would be in it. I also left a Christian tract with her, and made her promise to read it during a slow time, because it might change her life. With her help I was able to get away from the dock much easier than I had come in, and with a hearty God Bless you and thanks for everything, I headed for the sound, promising myself that I would follow her directions exactly.

Voyage of the Heart

Chapter 11

The Coast Guard Searches for "God Speed"

As I passed under the Lanier Island Highway Bridge and headed north on the Intra Coastal Waterway, I again found myself in narrow, winding grass lined rivers. Even though I was in the back country marshes, I saw the occasional fin or tail of a dolphin break the surface as a group of them cornered a school of bait fish in the shallows. At one point the McKay River touched the Fredericka River and my Chart showed that I could choose either one to continue northward since they separated there and then came together again nine miles up the line. I chose the Fredericka because it was narrower, a slightly shorter route and seemed to be "the road less traveled."

When the two rivers came back together, I entered a wide area known as Buttermilk Sound.

A brisk southwest breeze was coming over my left shoulder, so I put up the jib and added a couple of knots to my speed by using sail power with my motor. It was exciting to finally have a sail up and the wind behind me. I marveled at how the boat lifted and drove forward as it responded to the pull of the sail and the power of the wind. The joy of sailing was short lived however; since it wasn't long before I had to take my jib down to enter another series of narrow rivers.

As I wound my way up the Little Mud River and then the North River, I passed a couple fishing from an old discolored skiff with an antique motor. The heavy set woman in the front waved with a smile, proudly holding up a small fish she had caught. The old timer sitting in the back looked about as old and worn out as their boat, and I wasn't really sure if he was her husband or her father. I waved and gave them a thumbs up sign for their fish. "Nice going, don't catch em all," I yelled across with a smile. The woman laughed and the man nodded with a smirk. "God bless ya, have a good day," I called out over my shoulder as I moved away from them. I hoped they had noticed the emblem and name on my boat and that somehow I had reminded them about God and brightened their day a little. At that point, cruising down the narrow protected rivers was effortless, so I tuned in to the weather channel to get a forecast.

. . . "Yesterday Hurricane Alex was stalled and gathering strength one hundred and fifteen miles south east of Savannah," said the robotic radio voice. "This category one hurricane is now moving slowly northwest toward the Carolinas with sustained winds of sixty-five knots per hour. Alex is expected to become a category two hurricane, with winds of eighty-five knots as it passes Cape Fear. This storm will make landfall near Cape Hatteras, on the outer banks of North Carolina." "Oh Lord what am I doing out here?" I said softly, swallowing hard as I thought about the forecast. I'm moving north toward Savannah and the Carolinas and so is the hurricane. The only bright spot, was that the storm was still out over the Atlantic, far from shore, moving diagonally north and in toward the outer banks, while I was moving slowly up the coast inland. With a two day stop in Charleston for Tom's graduation, there was a chance that the hurricane would hit North Carolina and be gone before I got there. "The National Hurricane Center is tracking two other storms at this time," the mechanical electronic voice droned on. "Tropical Storm Bonnie has just been upgraded to a category one hurricane. It will pass over the Dry Tortugas today as it continues to track northward toward the Florida panhandle. It is expected to make land fall near Apalachicola, Florida in five days and continue north through the coastal states toward New England." *Great!* I thought, *that one is supposed to hit Florida and then move right up the coast. I am a sitting duck right in its path.* If all that wasn't enough, my heart sank further as the monotonous voice continued. "Tropical Storm Charlie is now approaching Cuba. This severe storm is rapidly gaining strength and may soon achieve hurricane status. If it continues on its present course, it will pass to the west of Cuba and move north east toward Florida and the coastal states. The current wind and atmospheric conditions are ideal for this storm to dramatically gather force. The National Hurricane Center states that given the weather factors that now exist, Charley could become the worst hurricane to hit the east coast in twelve years. It may achieve category four status with maximum sustained winds of one hundred and thirty-five knots before making landfall in Florida."

Wow! I groaned as my heart sank, one hurricane will make landfall ahead of me, while another comes right up the coast behind me. If there's anything left of me after that, it sounds like the granddaddy of all hurricanes will be coming through a few days later to finish me off. I promised myself that I would listen to the weather channel intently each day. I had to be flexible enough to change my float plan according to the weather forecast. I might need to stay holed up for a day or two, or push myself hard, cruising both day and night to stay ahead of the storms and make up time. I knew that even if I avoided the hurricanes, I would be very likely to encounter high winds, heavy rain, hail or lightning.

After winding my way up Old Teakettle Creek, Creighton Narrows and the Front River, I was able to put up both sails on a long stretch of open water on Sapelo Sound. By putting a bungee around the tiller to hold a straight course, I was able to scramble to the front to hoist sails, only to run back and grab the tiller each time the boat began to drift off course. After two or three tries, I had the sails up and was back at the tiller steering. It felt good to be under full sail with the wind at my back. But I realized how much work it was to do all that on my own. "That really took a lot out of me," I thought, sweating and breathing heavily from the exertion. My chart showed that five miles ahead I had to turn and enter a narrow river. At that point, I would need to go forward again to bring the sails down and depend on my motor. After putting so much effort into getting them up for that short distance, I decided it really wasn't worth it to use sails without help, unless I was going to be in open water with good wind for several hours.

After leaving the sound, I found myself motoring smoothly down narrow rivers. I had somehow been able to bring down and cover the sails without stopping, and I was starting to enjoy myself in spite of the weather forecast. A light wind rippled the surface as it rustled through the sea of marsh grass on both sides of the river. The endless waves of green nodded and bowed as they were shaped by the ebb and flow of the wind. Light colored valleys seemed to race away from me as a strong gust pushed its way through the grass. The sound of insects, birds and frogs rose from the summer marsh with such a loud shrill chorus, it seemed like every living creature was praising the Lord.

I found an excellent Christian station on the radio, so I plugged my headphones into the extension cord I had rigged up near the motor. The phones blocked out the drone of the motor and allowed me to enjoy the music loud and clear as I steered for hours on end. The sun was brutally hot as I knew it would be and its reflection off the water hurt my eyes. I donned sunglasses and a wide brimmed straw hat that I bought for eight ninety five at a convenience store. It was the kind of hat that made you think of Huckleberry Finn sitting on the river bank fishing with a bamboo pole. I found that by sitting on a cushion on the gunwale of the boat with my back against the safety cable I had a commanding view of the water ahead. Before the trip, I installed a pivoting tiller extension handle that allowed me to steer effortlessly from there, or anywhere else in the cockpit. By draping a life vest over the safety cable for a back rest and sprawling my legs on the seat, I found a position where I was comfortable enough to steer all day.

I must have been quite a sight sitting there with my back against a yellow life vest. Definitely not your classic yachtsman, I was nodding to the music in my big headphones, while wearing my country straw hat and a pair of horn rimmed sun glasses I had found. Anyone seeing me would have thought I was a cross between a hillbilly and James Dean. Being practical and having limited funds, I chose to be functional rather than fashionable. To feel better about my appearance, I convinced myself that there were few people along that stretch of the river, and that the gators and frogs really didn't care how I looked.

As the long, hot day wore on I was pleased at how well things were going. The motor was purring like a kitten, the numbers on the ICW markers were right on and I seemed to be cruising through several pages on the charts rather quickly for a small sailboat. By mid afternoon conditions changed as I felt the first evidence that somewhere ahead of me a hurricane was moving toward the coast. The sky was still clear but the wind picked up until it was so strong that it was almost unbearable. It was a biting wind that blew steadily in my face with no sign of letting up. The relentless wind changed the smooth river to a rugged washboard of moving ridges as it whipped across the surface. The parade of short stiff waves marched aggressively toward my bow, slapping sharply against it as I rose and fell to step over them. "Wow! Its blowing like stink out here," I said out loud. "I don't think I've ever felt wind this strong, under a bright blue sky." The fierce wind made the cables holding up the mast begin to hum and whine and I could feel the boat vibrating beneath me as the wind and chop slowed my forward progress. The wind was so strong that when I turned a corner and it hit me broadside, the boat leaned over the way it does when you're sailing, even though I had no sails up.

This is no fun, I thought. *I hope these conditions don't last long; I can't stand out in this kind of wind all day.* Then I praised the Lord that I was in a small protected river and that the sky was blue overhead. I shuddered to think what it would have been like in a large body of water with that much wind, especially if rain was being driven into my face by that gale.

The relentless wind stayed with me for several hours and then began to lessen as I approached the open waters of St. Catherine's Sound. That large body of water had a two mile wide opening to the Atlantic on the eastern end. I had to cross diagonally north east through the middle of the sound to get behind Ossabaw Island and into the Bear River. Once I was in the Bear River I would be in protected waters again. But the mouth of the river was located near the opening of the sound, just one mile from the fury of the open Atlantic. As I crossed the sound I would be exposed to ocean winds and waves for about three miles or thirty minutes. Once I was in the middle of the sound there would be no turning back and little margin for error. I would have the Atlantic Ocean to my right and four miles of open sound to my left. Although this wasn't the largest body of water I would have to cross on this trip, a nervous fear gripped me, as I thought about the wind conditions that day. Even though the wind had lessened, any big body of water had to be pretty wild right then. I thought about waiting for things to calm down, and then I thought about my son's graduation from basic training. If I waited until morning I might not get there in time to see it. I weighed the option of being tossed around for just thirty or forty minutes and then being back in a narrow river again. If I could just make it across, I might be able to cruise safely for days without having to cross an open area again.

"Lord I'm gonna go for it; keep me safe," I cried out, as I pointed my bow toward the tiny ICW marker two miles away in the middle of the sound. Before long I was quartering into five footers as I picked my way carefully through the valleys and over the crests of each big wave. "This is just as I feared," I said to myself with a white knuckle grip on the tiller. I rocked and wallowed my way through the waves trying to dodge them and roll with the punches as much as possible. I could see the open Atlantic off to my right and the white crests of huge ocean waves as they swept into the sound and toward me from as far away as the eye could see. My hope was that when they hit the shallow water and outgoing currents of the sound they lost some of their force and size. As they marched toward me like a never ending army, I encouraged myself by thinking that I wasn't getting the same waves as a boat ten miles out to sea. I saw a large fishing trawler coming into the sound from the ocean, and I wondered if he was coming in because it was too rough out there, or just coming in at his normal time.

Looking out over the ocean and slightly to the north I noticed a very dark patch of sky. As I stared at the ominous black clouds I saw several bolts of lightning come from them to strike the water below. *Whoa, that storm is a bad one,* I thought. *I'm glad its way out there and not right over me.* I swallowed hard as I realized that the large area of black clouds could very well be Hurricane Alex. From what I had heard on the radio it was in the right general area. I estimated that it was even with Savannah, yet still quite far off shore, and it seemed to be moving north and west toward the Carolinas.

"Oh Lord, please get me safely across as soon as possible," I prayed loudly. "Please keep your hands on the motor and keep it running until I get back into protected waters," I continued, with a deep sense of urgency. The motor had been running flawlessly for two days but I knew that if it quit out there I could be in serious trouble. It was way too rough to get any sails up alone and letting go of the tiller even for a second to anchor or get to the radio could be disastrous in waves that big. As fears of the motor quitting passed through my mind, my heart sank as I realized that I had made a terrible mistake. Looking at my watch, I saw that I had been running on one fuel tank for over six hours. I had learned that each tank was good for about six hours of steady cruising before it was empty. It was a tricky operation to disconnect the gas line from one tank and reconnect it to the other one. I had to leave the steering tiller and squirm around below decks in order to do it, but there was no way I could let go of the tiller now. Even with a bungee on it, the boat would never hold a course in those waves. There was no "course" out there anyway; a live person had to be at the helm to dodge and weave through the huge waves, avoiding as much punishment as possible. "What a dummy, what was I thinking," I shouted, scolding myself for being so absent-minded. "I should have switched over to the second tank before starting across the sound. If I run out of gas out here, I'm gonna have a horrible experience and I might find myself in a life or death situation."

I began to pray earnestly, as I zigzagged my way across the

sound trying to avoid the biggest waves. "Heavenly Father, please help me make it across and into calm water before I run out of gas in the first tank. Please put your angels around the boat to pull me swiftly through these waves to safety. I pray, Lord, with all my heart that you will not let me run out of gas out here in the middle of the sound." As I ended my prayer, I bent down a little so I could see the picture on the wall inside the cabin. As I looked at the face of Jesus, I felt my fear subside. The gentle strength of his hand on the boy's shoulder and the love on his face reassured me as confidence again swelled within me.

The farther out in the sound I went, the bigger the waves got and the harder the wind seemed to blow. Whenever a wave crashed over the bow or I slammed down into a valley, spray was blown back in my face by the strong wind. The wind driven salt spray stung my cheeks and eyes, blurred my vision and soaked my clothes, but all I could do at that point was keep going and trust God. "C'mon, Lord, get me through this," I asked repeatedly. "Keep the motor running, please don't let me run out of gas now," I pleaded passionately. I closed the cabin top with my free hand so things inside were not soaked by the salty water, but I could not put the cabin doors in place while steering, so the maps and charts did get wet.

After being tossed like a toy for almost an hour, I reached a position just off the mouth of the Bear River and the motor was still running. "C'mon Lord I'm almost there," I breathed anxiously, "Please keep me going just a little while longer." As I left the sound and moved up the river behind Ossabaw Island, the wind was still fierce, but the big waves gave way to a three inch chop. When I realized that I had made it, I raised my free hand toward heaven and began to shout praises to the Lord with my salty lips. As I headed up the river and into the marshes again, I saw that the whole sky was now dark and a severe storm looked imminent. It was at that moment, as I thought about what to do next, the engine sputtered to a stop. "Thank you, Lord, for letting her run so long," I praised, as I squeezed into the storage space to disconnect the empty tank and reconnect the full one.

When I got moving again, the sky looked even more threatening. I needed to anchor and close things up, or find a marina fast. My guide book for marinas and yacht clubs showed a small marina just two miles ahead down a side channel. I decided to make a run for it and hoped I could make it there before the storm hit.

AUTHOR'S NOTE:

Many months after my voyage, my wife admitted to me that when she heard about the hurricanes approaching Florida and the Carolinas she called the Coast Guard to have them check up on me. They called her back to say that their search and rescue helicopter had spotted me, moving slowly up the Bear River in Georgia behind Ossabaw Island. They also told her that I had a hurricane ahead of me and one behind me. I never knew that the Coast Guard had searched for me and spotted me that day until six months later, long after I returned home from this memorable trip.

TREASURE D

Chapter 12

Any Port in a Storm

A couple of miles ahead, a side channel came into the main river from the left. Although it looked like a man made channel it was labeled Killdeer Creek on my charts. According to the guidebook, Hidden Harbor Marina was located about a mile up the creek. The book said that it only had limited facilities, but I just needed a place to tie up before the sky unleashed another downpour on my wet and weary body. Right on the corner where the creek turned left, a faded, antique Sunoco gas sign hung on a couple of old posts sticking up out of the marsh. Below it, there was a hand painted white sign that had the word marina and an arrow pointing up the creek. My instincts told me that this small marina in the back country swamps of Georgia would not be fancy, but at that moment it was an oasis in the desert.

I smiled inwardly and pretended to be an old time sailing captain shouting orders to his crew:. . . . ."Do you really think it's wise to take a sailing vessel into the swamp cap'n?". . . . ."Look at that sky, mate, its blacker than the inside of a barrel. We're in for a blow I tell ya, and there are hurricanes about. We've got to get her in somewhere and right quick at that me lads. You know what they say boys, any port in a storm, that's right me hearties any port in a storm. Step lively now mates and watch our depth, the chart shows the center of the channel to be shallow and we don't want to leave her high and dry."…..

The chart showed a sandbar and shallow water in the center of the creeks mouth, so I stayed to the right as I turned the corner and started upstream. A short distance up the creek, a side channel went to the left while the main creek continued straight. I thought the marina would be straight ahead, but another white sign with the word marina and an arrow seemed to point down the smaller channel to the left. As I turned left I had an uneasy feeling that something was wrong. I was now in a tiny creek, and there didn't seem to be anything ahead but marsh as far as I could see. Just then my shallow water alarm began to beep, telling me that I was only in five feet of water and then it quickly dropped to four. My boat had a shallow water keel, but still needed at least three feet of water to float. If I went any farther I risked getting stuck and it didn't look like there was a marina ahead, so I turned around and headed back toward the main creek.

Back at the "T" where I turned left into the smaller creek, I was greeted by a sight that has left me puzzled to this day. The white marina sign with the arrow now seemed to point to the left as I approached it. It was pointing down Killdeer creek in the direction I was heading before I turned left into that side channel. That meant that the marina was just where I thought it was, and I was headed right for it when the sign pointed me the wrong way up the small creek. The sign was pointing to the left a moment ago and now it was pointing straight down the creek. Were my eyes playing tricks on me, or was it loose on the pole and moved with the wind? A closer look told me that it was mounted haphazardly on the pole. It was not pointing straight down the creek and not really pointing to the left either. It could actually look like it was pointing in either direction, depending on the angle you saw it from. Did my eyes deceive me, or had the enemy played a trick on me to get me stuck, or make it take longer to find the marina so I would get caught in the rain? As if in answer to that question, the rain started, and quickly changed from a light shower to a downpour. As I covered the last half mile to the marina without rain gear, water flooded my face, and ran down my neck and back as it soaked through my clothes.

The wind was blowing fiercely again as I rounded a bend and saw the marina. It was located on the left side, in an area where the creek widened into a tiny "bay". There was a section of dock along the shore that looked like it was the visitors dock. Farther down, several dock fingers jutted straight out from the shoreline for boaters who had rented a slip for the season. As I approached the docks I noticed several things about the place: There were no sailboats and no really big boats. The docks were lined with small fishing boats, skiffs, runabouts, and a couple of small commercial crabbing vessels. Most of the boats were well worn old timers that had long ago lost their luster. The buildings appeared to be shabby and run down and the docks looked rickety and in need of repair. I was touched by the quaintness and antiquity of the place, and didn't know that places like that still existed in the year 2004. I felt like I had driven the boat through a time warp and into "The Twilight Zone." Out in the main river, beyond the narrow entry channel, time and modern day America went by, but back here in the "Hidden Harbor" it looked like the land that time forgot.

As I approached, a sad looking unfriendly man with a sweat-stained baseball cap came out on the dock to help me come in. Everything about his face, demeanor and body language told me that he didn't like me, or just didn't like people in general. He reluctantly grabbed the lines I threw to him and with a halfhearted effort tied a couple of quick knots and began to walk away. As I tried to thank him, he nodded with a grunt and a scowl as he plodded resentfully back down the dock. "Wow!" I thought, did I do something to make that guy dislike me, or does he dislike everyone?" "Maybe it was the Christian name and emblem on the boat and he didn't like Christians?" Remembering that I was in Georgia, I looked at the New York registration on the boat thinking that maybe he hated all "Yankees". Then I thought about my ethnic background. I was an Italian with a dark complexion and a dark beard, and my skin was even darker now after several days in the sun. In my naivety and love for people, had I overlooked the fact that there were still some people in America that resented minorities? Although I was Italian, I could have easily passed for a Mexican, a Puerto Rican or an Arab to someone who didn't know me. The thought occurred to me that it might embitter a person to have someone from a race they hated show up in a boat they couldn't afford and then have to serve them. It would also add insult to injury if that person was out traveling in a boat while they had to work.

It bothered me deeply that the man disliked me, and I vowed that during my short stay there I would do whatever I could to show him the love of Christ and try to change his opinion of me. Before I could do anything else, I needed to get out of my soaking wet clothes and slip into some dry ones. I never realized how good a warm dry sweat shirt and comfortable pair of dry jeans could feel until I slipped them on over my damp chilled body. In my quest to make it to Charleston on time, I would have kept pushing north until dark and then anchored somewhere out in the swamp, but I guess the Lord had other plans for me that night. Now I could dry my clothes, get fuel, eat a good meal and rest. If time allowed, maybe I could find a way to reach out to that man even if it was only with my actions, my attitude and a smile. I remembered young Ken, the mechanic from Amelia Island and wondered if the bitter old man was the reason the Lord brought me to this marina. Some fishermen looked at me oddly as they came into port and I got the feeling they didn't see many sailboats in there. "God Speed" was a rare craft, because it was a good sized vessel with a shallow water keel. Most cruising sailboats would never make it up the shallow creek, with their four and five foot fixed keels.

I noticed that the grumpy older man kept looking down at my boat as he worked near the marina office and I wondered why I bothered him so much. As I stood on the dock now warm and dry to plan my "evening in port", I realized how much my boat stood out there. Although certainly not one of the biggest sail boats, in my eyes she was one of the prettiest. The heavily waxed surfaces of the shiny white hull were a stark contrast to the decay and neglect of the muddy, discolored, algae covered docks. I really enjoyed seeing her there with her lettering and Christian emblem silently proclaiming my beliefs. I knew that God had gotten me this far and even brought me in here tonight for a reason, so I was honored to have my boat be a floating billboard for him. She shone like a bright light in a dark place next to the grubby fishing boats, rotting docks, run down buildings, and rusty live bait tanks.

I made a mental list of everything I could get done while I had the time and the facilities. Having no idea when I might have gas pumps, a shower or a dryer again, I decided to make my time there really count. "Let's see now," I thought, "job number one: pay for my slip, get gas and be nice to that man. Job number two: take a shower and shave. (Which I hadn't done in two days) Job number three: dry all my clothes if there's a dryer. Job number four: eat a good meal and listen to the weather radio to check on the hurricanes. Job number five: call home. Job number six: go to bed early so I can wake up before the sun and get going at first light."

As I carried my empty fuel tank down the dock, crabs scuttled away from the sound of my footsteps on the mud below. I was embarrassed when the gruff man turned on the pump for me to fill my tank and I couldn't get the cap off. I wasn't eager to ask for his help, but I didn't have much choice. He grudgingly reached down shaking his head and with one twist of a big weathered hand had the cap off. After I paid for the gas and my slip, he asked if I wanted to take a shower and I replied that I did. "C'mon," he said, "I'll show ya the showers." As we walked to unlock the shower building, I told him that I was heading for Charleston to see my son graduate from basic training. He said that his name was Jim and that his son had also been in the army a few years back. I was thrilled, because that was the first time he spoke to me in a normal voice with no animosity and I sensed that he was starting to soften a little. The rusty door to the shower room was stuck at first, but after a hard jerk it opened and a crab scurried out of the shower stall and ran right between the two of us. The floor of the shower was covered with sand and the coin operated washer and dryer in the next room looked like they had been there since the fifties. But I didn't care, I just saw a hot shower and warm dry clothes. As we walked back, I asked questions about the fishing boats, what kind of bait he sold and how the fishing was, trying to show an interest in his work and his home area. He answered each question with few words, but each time he spoke, his tone seemed friendlier. As he turned to go into the office, I thanked him for his help and said that I probably wouldn't see him in the morning because I hoped to leave at first light. I extended my hand for a handshake and felt a surge of joy as he hesitated and then awkwardly reached out to take my hand. As I shook his hand firmly, I looked him square in the eyes and said with all the sincerity and love I could muster: "God bless ya brother, thanks for everything!" He looked into my eyes and nodded thoughtfully, then without saying a word slowly turned and went into the office. "I wish I could have said more," I thought sadly, "I should have said so much more." What I really wanted to say, and tried to say with those few words, my handshake and my eyes was: God loves you, Jim! You are a special, precious child of his, and he wants to bless your life. He wants to live in your heart and he wants you to feel his love. Invite Jesus into your heart and he will wash away the hurt and the disappointment that has made you bitter and angry. No millionaire cruising on the finest yacht is more special or more important to him than you are."

"Well Lord, I didn't say what I wanted to, but maybe my boat lettering and friendliness planted a seed in his heart that you can water later on. I hope I brightened his day a little and changed his opinion of Christians, "Yankees," minorities, sailboat owners, or whoever it was that he disliked when I arrived.

Back at the boat, I grabbed my toiletries and my wet clothes and headed back to the laundry and shower building. After showering and shaving for the first time in two days, I felt like a new man. As I walked back to the boat nuzzling my face in the arm load of warm dry clothes, I thought about how good they felt and how good I felt. I praised the Lord that he brought me in here and that my damp, weary body and my spirits were dry, refreshed and renewed. Back on board I feasted on cold precooked hamburger pieces dipped in ketchup for appetizers and then ate a whole hamburger patty in a roll smothered with taco sauce for the main course. Dessert was a handful of M&Ms that had been melted into a lump by the heat, with a tall glass of ice cold milk. I laughed inwardly as I thought that my wife would have never taken a shower in that building after seeing the crab. I was thrilled that roughing it could be so enjoyable and that surviving dangerous situations and the adventure of "camping" on the water made the crudest food a sumptuous repast and the most rustic accommodations seem like the Trump Towers.

As I ate, I listened intently to the weather station on my ship to shore radio. "Hurricane Alex is still located over the Atlantic just ninety miles south east of Charleston and about fifty miles from shore." the monotone voice began. "It is expected to gather strength as it moves northwest toward the coast during the next twenty-four hours," concluded the announcer. "Not so good, I thought. That's right where I'm going. Lets see now, I'm about a hundred and fifty miles south of Charleston, and I'm hoping to cover seventy-five miles each day and be there in two days. That would put me in the area where the hurricane is right now tomorrow night. Of course the hurricane is forty or fifty miles out over the ocean and I will be inland. The key fact that gave me hope was that the hurricane was there now and I would be there tomorrow. If Alex kept moving north on its present course it could be eighty miles farther up the coast by tomorrow night. I seemed to be about twenty-four hours behind it. "Wow," I thought, "it's a good thing I didn't start this trip one day sooner." As that thought crossed my mind, I remembered that I would have started cruising twenty-four hours earlier, if I had not been held up by motor problems on Amelia Island. My emotions got the best of me again, as I praised the Lord for his timing, and promised myself that I would stay on his schedule for the rest of the trip and not mine.

The hurricane was ahead, and the forecast called for lots of showers and thunderstorms, but the charts showed that I would be in narrow protected waters most of the way to Charleston. With that in mind I decided to trust God and leave at first light, keeping my eyes on the sky and my ears glued to the weather radio, in case Alex decided to change course and head my way.

As I lay on my berth staring at the ceiling, I thought of a way that I could take one more shot at Jim's heart before I left. "The guy lives in the back country swamps of Georgia and he probably grew up around here. He's got to be a hunter or a fisherman," I thought. "Maybe he does both, or at least used to when he was younger." I had several tracts aboard from my outdoor ministry. Each one featured a famous hunter or fisherman that had a TV show or wrote for a magazine. They contained a salvation message and a personal testimony telling how each man found God and how he changed their life. They were written by down to earth outdoorsmen in terms that Jim would understand and be able to relate to. I would leave a stack of my video brochures, and a stack of tracts with a note, asking if they could be placed on the counter in the marina office. Maybe Jim would see me in a different light if he knew that I produced hunting videos. Hopefully, he would also read one or more of the tracts and be touched by the story of a famous outdoorsman that he respected. If he was willing to let them sit on the counter for a while, there was always the chance that other men would pick them up and read them. If one life was changed because they were there it was well worth leaving them.

"Lord, keep me safe as I move toward the hurricane and thunderstorms tomorrow. Allow me to get to Charleston in time to pick up my wife and daughters at the airport and make it to Tom's graduation. Help me to sleep well and wake up before the sun. Please touch Jim's life and help him to come to know you and love you. Use the tracts I leave behind to touch hearts, and show me if a life was changed because of this trip, Amen." My heart was full with the peace that passes all understanding, and it was a joy to hear the soft lapping of water against the hull and feel the boat gently rocking me to sleep, as my head settled deeply into the softness of my pillow.

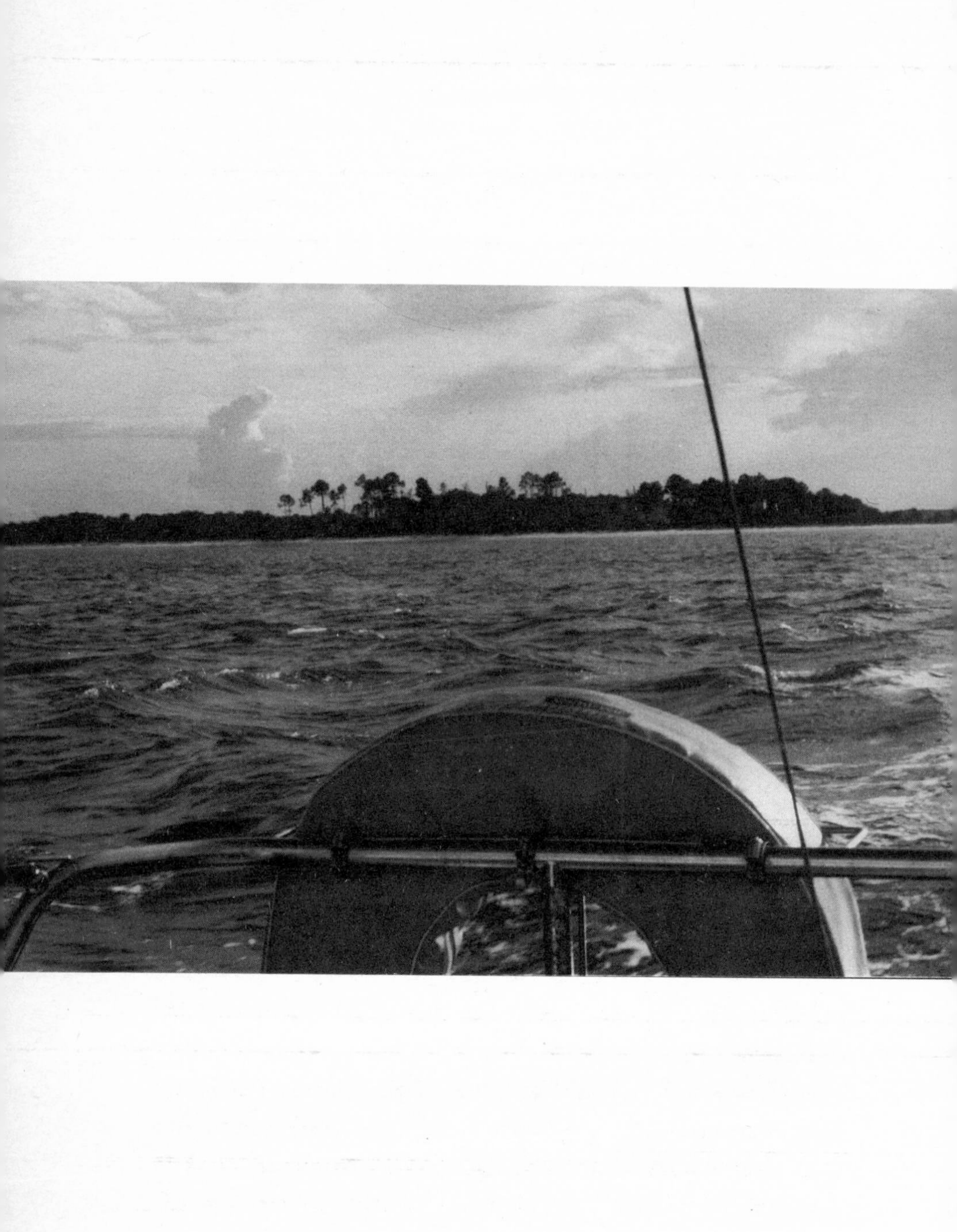

Chapter 13

Hurricane Ahead of Me–Hurricanes Behind Me

My eyes opened suddenly in the semi darkness of the boat's interior. The security light on the dock was shining right into them through the cabin window. When I saw it, I remembered where I was and reached for my watch, only to find that it was three thirty in the morning. I had hoped to be up before the sun, but another hour or two of sleep would have been nice with such a long day ahead of me. My personality usually didn't allow me to fall back to sleep once I was awake and that was the case that morning. My active mind jumped quickly from hurricanes, to Army graduations, to how many miles I could make today if I started now, and then back to hurricanes. Since I was too excited to fall asleep, I said my morning prayers and then began to figure out what to do with the extra time until it was light enough to get going. I dressed warmly for the cool dampness of morning, but in layers so I could strip down while steering as the day warmed up.

Standing on the dock in the predawn blackness, I could see the red and green flashing lights of each ICW marker out in the main river. I watched each one flash and die in succession like a giant strand of widely spaced Christmas lights showing the safe channel to the north as far as my eyes could see them. I could almost run at night, I thought, in an area like this where most of the markers have a flashing light on them. I could slowly steer my way from flasher to flasher in the dark using my powerful spotlight to scan the water ahead for obstacles and find markers that didn't have a light on them. The green markers had a green light on them and the red ones had a red, and the chart tells you which numbered markers are lighted and which ones are not.

I had to go seventy-five miles each day to reach Charleston on time. With a hurricane ahead of me and two behind me, there was a chance of being held up by bad weather. With that in mind, I decided to get out my spotlight and get started before the sun came up. I used the marina bathroom one last time and then hung a plastic bag on the office door filled with brochures, tracts and a note. "Dear Jim," it read. "Thanks for your help and hospitality. These brochures tell about the videos that I produce and sell. Also enclosed are some pamphlets with some great tips and advice for deer hunters and fishermen. I wondered if you would be willing to leave them on the counter and point them out to guys you know who hunt and fish. Thanks for everything and God bless you. Dave Tripiciano - "My Father's World" Video Productions." I made it sound like I was trying to advertise my videos to guys who came in, but my main reason for leaving them was to get him to read a salvation message as told by a famous outdoorsman. At the very worst, I hoped that Jim would take a minute to read one before discarding them.

The motor started with one pull and I praised the Lord for how well it had been running as I eagerly untied the bow and stern ropes. With my trusty spotlight slicing through the foggy blackness of the swamp, I slowly moved away from the dock lights and into total darkness as I started down the channel. The powerful "antique" light had been given to me many years ago. The rusty old spotlight had a sealed beam like a car headlight and threw as much light as one. Now, in the cave-like darkness and fog that surrounded me, it was worth its weight in gold as it illuminated the tall marsh grass and reflected off the black water ahead. After a few minutes, my eyes adjusted to the darkness and I was able to make out the shadowy outline of the marsh grass against the night sky and the shimmering watery blackness of the creek. Staying centered between the dark walls of grass on both sides I moved slowly and cautiously down the channel, using the spotlight to scan the water ahead for floating debris, or large swimming reptiles.

As I approached the corner where the creek "teed" into the main river, it was almost five o' clock. It was now light enough that I could just make out the silhouette of the old Sunoco gas sign that pointed up the creek to the marina. My pulse quickened as feelings of joy about my early start mingled with fear and dread as I thought about the hurricane and severe thunderstorms ahead.

Just then my thoughts were interrupted by the loud beeping of the depth alarm. It was shockingly loud in the dawn stillness and I was instantly gripped by fear as I realized what had happened. I had stayed in the center of the creek, far from the marsh grass on either side to safely navigate the channel in the dark. But had completely forgotten about the sand bar that blocked the mouth of the creek where it entered the main river. The chart showed me yesterday that there was just two feet of water in the middle of the creek at the entrance and I had steered right into it. The depth alarm beeped frantically as the numbers dropped from five to four to three and a half feet in a few seconds. "Oh no," I whispered panic stricken. "Am I really that absent-minded? How could I let this happen?" The numbers dropped so quickly that before I could react I was over the sand bar with no time to turn, back up or slow down.

I felt bitter disappointment and frustration overtake me, as the joy of my pre dawn start gave way to thoughts of spending the day stuck in the mud, or aborting the trip because of damage to the boat or motor.

"Lord Jesus, get me through this," I cried, desperately raising my free hand toward heaven. "Please Lord; don't let me get stuck, not here, not now when I have a chance to get so far today." I continued to shout: "Please Lord, get me through," as I watched the depth drop to 3.2 feet and then 3.1. Then I felt a drag on the boat as if a giant underwater hand was slowing me down and realized that my keel was sliding through sand and muck. Shining the light in the water, I could see that I was still moving forward as the boat and motor churned up the bottom leaving a wide muddy wake behind me. "I might plow through this and break free into deep water, if I can just maintain my forward progress," I thought. "C'mon Lord, keep me moving forward," I pleaded, revving the motor for more thrust and hoping there wasn't a sunken tree or boulder on the bottom.

My heart leapt when I felt the boat pull free from the bottom and begin to speed up. The depth finder numbers went from three to six feet, as quickly as they had gone the other way and the depth alarm stopped beeping. Apparently the tide was coming in and the water was just deep enough for my three foot keel to slide over the bar and into deep water. I breathed a sigh of relief, thankful that the water was not a few inches shallower.

As I turned left into the main river, I could see the colored lights of the ICW markers interrupting the darkness as they flashed in succession ahead of me. I praised the Lord loudly and repeatedly for getting me through the shallow area and allowing me to overcome a mistake that could have meant disaster. Then I prayed that he would keep me alert and vowed that I would be very watchful of water depths, so an incident like that didn't happen again. It was now light enough to see the marsh grass, but still dark enough that the flashing lights really stood out. There was great comfort in seeing them there like a line of faithful friends showing me the safe route north. They appeared and then disappeared in the darkness, each one having less than a second of glory before another one had its turn. As I pointed my bow toward the first one I hoped that the route would be as easy to follow throughout the day and in the coming days as it was at that moment.

Chapter 14

Lost

I cruised easily that morning, winding my way through narrow rivers and wider rivers as the sky and the marsh grass gradually brightened around me. I didn't notice when the lights on the markers stopped flashing, but it suddenly occurred to me as it got light that they had stopped. I could tell that the sun was above the horizon now without looking at it from the steady warmth on my right arm and shoulder. The low sun of early morning illuminated the damp grassy wall on the left side of the river, making it sparkle with the deepest most brilliant shades of green. What a striking contrast, I thought, to the dark, somber greens of the same grass on the opposite side that was still in deep shade at that early hour. The color of the marsh grass was a great object lesson, showing me the difference between the life of a person who knew the Lord and one who did not. A life that reflected the light of the world shone vibrantly with all the color and brilliance of the grass on the left. While a life that did not reflect his light was dark, somber and muted without any true "color" or joy.

My early start made the morning seem like an eternity as I motored for hours through marshy bays and creeks that seemed like they went on forever. I tried to distract myself from the sameness of the never ending sea of grass, by studying the charts and listening to Christian radio with my headphones. As the sun got higher and temperatures rose, I was able to strip off one layer of clothes at a time while steering, until I wore just a tee shirt and shorts with my funny straw hat and "old school" sunglasses.

The route was clearly marked and easy to follow as I made my way from one colored marker to the next. After I passed through a narrow land cut called "Hells Gate", the Intra Coastal Waterway made a left turn at red marker number eighty-six in the middle of the Vernon River. Since it was so easy to follow the markers all morning, I had been lulled into a false sense of confidence and wasn't really watching the chart closely. When the route turned sharply left at marker eighty-six there were several more markers just beyond it that continued straight ahead in the direction I was heading. Those led me across the Vernon River into a windy bay and then out into the open waters of a sound. The markers I followed were not ICW markers, but local navigational markers that guided boats out into the sound. Since they formed a straight line after marker eighty-six, I followed them and didn't notice that their numbers were wrong and that they didn't have the symbols found on ICW markers.

As I bounced around in the wind blown chop with no land to my right, I wondered if I was going the right way. The chart didn't show any big bodies of water, especially not that big and there were no more markers visible. The last ICW markers I had seen had numbers in the eighties, but now I couldn't find one anywhere. Lost and confused, I was desperate to get back on course before I wasted even more precious time.

I noticed a yacht club with tall masts and large powerboats on a side channel before I entered the sound. I turned and headed there at full speed, hoping to get the directions I needed to get back on track. There was a wide variety of power and sailing yachts there, and I noticed several well dressed people on the docks and in their boats. My plan was to get close to the docks and try to hail someone for directions. That would be much easier and take far less time than coming in to tie up. One large power cruiser with two deeply tanned older couples aboard was just backing out of its slip as I approached. Coming along side of them I throttled down to a soft idle so I could hear their responses.

Before I could open my mouth to ask directions, the man at the wheel yelled out exactly what I needed to hear, as if he had read my mind: "If you're looking for the ICW northbound, you have to go around that island with the trees on it," he said pointing. "Once you get to the back side of the island, turn right keeping the island on your right and you will begin to see the ICW markers again. "There's a sharp left turn at marker eighty-six in the middle of the river that you missed. Don't feel bad, it's easy to miss it if you don't know the area. You've got to watch your charts and the markers close there, or you will over shoot it and follow the wrong markers," he concluded. I thanked him and wished them a great cruise, then I sped away toward the island he had pointed out. I was amazed that he knew just what I was going to ask before I opened my mouth. Apparently I wasn't the first one to miss the turn at marker eighty-six and pull in there for directions. It must have been a daily routine for members of that club to answer the same question for first time ICW travelers who missed that turn.

I smiled, as the thought occurred to me that maybe I had made the wrong turn for the right reason. By pulling in close to those docks only God knew how many people had seen my Christian flag and emblem. If I stayed on course, I would have passed many miles from that upscale yacht club and the one person that needed a reminder that day wouldn't have had one. Again I praised the Lord for his timing, and reminded myself that I was on his schedule and not mine.

As I rounded marker number eighty-six, I could see the next ICW marker farther up the river and everything looked right again. Now in a wide area where the Vernon and the Ogeechee River joined to form one river, I steered into a brisk wind, plowing my way through wind driven whitecaps. As I pounded my way through the stiff chop and salt spray it began to bother me that I was bouncing around in rough water again. It also disappointed me that all I ever saw was marsh grass in every direction. Even though I was having memorable experiences and could feel the Lord blessing and using me, I wished the scenery would change, so that steering all day would be more enjoyable.

As I fought my way through the waves and past two more ICW markers, I could feel that my fifty-two year old body (awake since three thirty) wanted to give up. I was physically exhausted, mentally drained and tired of swamps, wind and waves. I wanted to lie down and sleep for a couple of days, but it wasn't even noon yet. I knew that if I stopped to rest I would never make it to my son's graduation, or home before school started in September. Steering with my legs, I fumbled with the flapping pages of the chart in the wind, trying to see what lay ahead of me that day. After a few more miles, that wide river ended at the base of a hill. Then I would turn right into a narrow river and be in sheltered, calm waters for the rest of the day.

I realized that I had been awake, steering and fighting waves for eight hours, and hadn't eaten anything yet, so I tried to motivate myself to keep going with a pep talk: "C'mon keep going you can do it . . . Just a little farther and you'll be in calm water . . . Right up there at the bend is a narrow protected area, you can cruise effortlessly and have some food to pass the time . . . if you can just make it that far, the rest of the day will be cake . . . get into calm water and get some food in you and you'll feel better . . . keep pushing all day, you can do it, and then you'll sleep great tonight . . . You can't miss Tom's graduation . . . you're almost there, keep going."

"Lord, your Word says that your strength is perfect when our strength is gone. Please give me the strength and the energy to keep going," I prayed, hoping that conditions would be better ahead, and that I would feel energized after eating something. After what seemed like an eternity, I reached the end of that wide, rough stretch and turned right into the Burnside River. When I rounded the bend a shout of "thank you, Lord!" sprang from my lips, as I saw what lie ahead.

A series of hills to the west sheltered that river from the wind, making the watery surface as smooth as glass. Instead of endless marsh grass as far as the eye could see there were upscale homes with well groomed yards, flower beds and palm trees on both sides of the river. Most of the properties had well maintained docks, with large boats and many of the yards had swimming pools. At that moment, I understood what the ancient Israelites must have felt like when they got their first glimpse of the "Promised Land" after spending forty years in the wilderness. "Wow, this is more like it," I thought. When I planned the trip, I pictured myself cruising through cities and towns, enjoying the sights and scenery of each state. One of the highlights of traveling on the New York State Barge Canal was cruising right through villages and people's yards, admiring their boats and their property. The time would slip by quickly and cruising would be much more enjoyable now that I was passing through "civilization".

This is the life I thought, as I poured ice cold milk into a bowl of Honey Nut Cheerios and began to enjoy them while steering with the tiller between my legs. I had to hail the operators of two lift bridges on the radio, asking them to open for my mast as I approached. Both of them were very accommodating, respectfully calling me "Captain" in their heavy southern accents. I got a big kick out of being called "Captain" and I thanked them both with a hearty "God bless you," as I passed beneath them waving. Later, a large power cruiser named "Gator Roy" came slowly from behind to pass me. An older man sat on the bridge steering with a beer in his hand and a sad expression on his face; he appeared to be alone on the boat. I waved with a smile yet felt sorry for him, because he was cruising on such a beautiful day in his big impressive boat, and yet he seemed so empty and alone. I could tell that something was missing in his life and I knew what it was. I tried to hail him on the radio but got no response, so I continued on my way, hoping that he had noticed the name and emblem on my boat.

As I continued to enjoy the day, a dolphin surfaced and swam along next to me for several minutes, playing with my boat as if it was another dolphin. I was blessed by its playfulness and exuberance as it splashed and played in my bow wake, crossing back and forth under the boat with effortless speed as it greeted me with clicking and squealing sounds. "I'm motoring at seven miles per hour and it's swimming circles around me just for fun," I thought, as I admired its power and perfect design. Only a loving Creator could have designed something that big that could move so fast with a flick of its tail, and given it a love for man and a playful, fun loving personality.

AGGIE GRAY

Chapter 15

Hunkered Down in a Blow

Hours later I came to the end of a canal and found myself looking straight out into the open Atlantic, even though the chart said I should be winding my way through narrow waterways. I had done it again. I hadn't been watching the chart closely and had missed another turn. Going back to the last spot where rivers forked, I saw why I had missed it. An ICW marker at a corner where a small river turned off the main river was partially hidden by the marsh grass and I hadn't seen it at all. Turning down the smaller river, I saw to my disappointment that there were no ICW markers in that direction either. Frustrated and upset with myself for wasting more time, I called on the radio for directions. A very nice tug captain answered, but said that he didn't know the Intra Coastal Waterway very well. Being confused and preoccupied on the radio, I didn't notice that the sky was getting real dark, real fast. As I continued to talk to the skipper of the tug a downpour began with no warning.

Because I was on the radio when it hit, I couldn't close the cabin doors quickly, so the maps and charts got wet and the rain soaked everything in the cabin before I could batten down the hatches. Right about then I spotted the shape of the next marker, sticking out of the water about a mile down the river. As I motored toward it shaking my head with disappointment, I knew that the enemy had taken another shot at me and succeeded in stealing my joy for a moment. I promised myself that I would not let him get me down or cause me to lose heart. I knew that if he was taking shots at me, I was doing something very worthwhile, and that strengthened my resolve to press on. I promised myself that I would be absolutely paranoid about checking the chart when I came to any fork in the river no matter how "main" one of the forks looked. I had learned once and for all that the "obvious" way wasn't always the right way.

The route continued to be interesting, as I passed marinas and mooring areas where large groups of boats were anchored. There were restaurants, boat dealers and commercial fishing vessels that were scarred by rust from many years of hard work in a salt water environment. The word Savannah appeared on several boats, so I thought I was somewhere near that city although I never saw it. I did see large developments of new waterfront condos being built, and an incredibly large sailing yacht that had to belong to a multi millionaire.

An hour later on a wider, more deserted stretch of the river, I spotted a marina ahead on the right that seemed to have an easily approachable gas dock. Since I would need fuel soon, I decided to pull in there to fill the tanks and take a badly needed break. Having learned from experience, I made sure all fenders and ropes were in place before I came in. As I approached, a friendly older man with glasses came out on the dock to help me. He warned me that there was a lot of current there, and as I slowed to dock speed I saw that he was right. Not wanting another experience like I had with the young woman, I decided to circle and come around again. On the second pass, now fully aware of the current, I came in strong and hard waiting for the last possible second to kick the motor into reverse. As she nestled gently against the dock, I threw him the front rope and confidently jumped off with the back rope, feeling like Kurt Russell in the movie "Captain Ron".

The small thin man introduced himself as Larry. He was very helpful and eagerly answered my questions about the local area. As he filled my tanks, I told him about the trip I was on and that I had dreamed about taking it for many years. His eyes filled with admiration and his tone was supportive as he helped me put the tanks aboard and brought me a bag of ice. I learned that he was from Westfield, New York, a small village in Chautauqua County, close to where I attended college and my first teaching job. He had a sweet spirit and a servant's heart which made me think he was a believer. To see his response, I told him how the good Lord had sailed with me, blessed me and protected me so far. He nodded politely, but his expression and body language told me he didn't have the same beliefs that I did.

As we talked, I learned that I wasn't at a marina. I was standing on the gas dock of an exclusive waterfront resort and country club with three golf courses. Each day, several boats loaded with tourists left from those docks to cruise to Hilton Head Island for shopping and sightseeing. I had arrived just as a tour boat was preparing to board for the trip, so there were many well dressed couples and families waiting on the docks and crowding into the small snack store to buy drinks. I smiled and nodded as I thought about God's perfect timing. He had brought me into that fuel dock right when a boat load of tourists was just standing around.

After using the men's room, I went into the store where I grabbed some soda, and then I paid Larry for everything. Without being asked, he followed me down the steps to the boat to help me cast off. Before stepping aboard, I shook his hand earnestly as I thanked him for his help. I told him that he was one of the few people I had met that truly had a servant's heart and that the Lord had put him in the perfect place to bless people with that gift. "Keep serving people and the Lord will bless your life," I said, as I handed him some tracts to read. He smiled and thanked me as he untied my ropes and shoved me into the current. I shouted "God bless you" over my shoulder as I raised my hand to wave to the small, unassuming man, who stood waving from the dock as if he was saying goodbye to a friend. I was touched and a little ashamed as I reflected on the fact that many Christians (including myself), did not have the servant's heart of a Larry. "Lord," I prayed, "help me to be more like Larry. Help me to be a humble, unselfish man, eagerly helping and serving others. Help me witness to other people more with my actions and my behavior than with words or tracts, Amen"

After pulling away from the gas dock, I motored right by the countless tourists waiting on the docks to board their tour boat and those already on the boat. Waving politely to them as I passed, I continued down the river toward Hilton Head Island. Thirty minutes ahead, the river ended as it opened into Calibogue Sound. That large body of water stretched north to my left and south to my right and Hilton Head Island lay ahead of me on the opposite side of the sound. That long narrow island also stretched north and south with its west side on the sound and its east side on the ocean. As I moved out into the sound, the boat load of tourists from the resort caught up to me and passed well to my right, heading for the island. Even from the middle of the sound I could make out the classic barber pole stripe of the Hilton Head Lighthouse. My guide book pictured it, and described it as a famous historic landmark of the area.

As I turned left and headed up the middle of the sound, an ominous blanket of black clouds swept toward me from the north. I knew I was going to get wet, but my first instinct was to keep going and try to make it to the river at the north end of the sound. I could dry out wet clothes and warm my body, but I would not have another chance to see my son graduate from basic training, so I closed things up, donned the rain gear and pushed ahead at full speed into the approaching storm. " . . . Darn the rain, full speed ahead . . ." I said, trying to paraphrase the words of a famous naval commander in an attempt to be funny and relieve some of the fear I felt as I looked at the sky ahead. I swallowed hard as I remembered that hurricane Alex was moving up the coast north of Savannah and that I was now well north of Savannah. Although the storm was supposed to be a day ahead of me, I guessed that I was seeing the bad weather that followed on the outer fringes of a hurricane.

The blackness of the sky closed in completely, shutting out even the smallest trace of blue and then the wind picked up. I felt the cool breeze in my face change from gentle to vicious in about two minutes and then it began to rain. Big drops, no huge drops of cold rain struck my face and exploded on the cabin top like miniature bombs. Within seconds I was in a torrential downpour so heavy that I had to hold my arm above my eyes to protect my face from the pounding it was taking from the oversized rain drops. "I can do this," I said, "only three more miles and I will be in narrow, protected waters again and it can't rain this hard for long." My mind and my spirit were determined to keep going, and I might have made it, if the enemy hadn't thrown two more obstacles at me that I wasn't expecting.

Fog! Seemingly out of nowhere, fog began to envelop the sound and obscure the shoreline. Because of the rain, the visibility was terrible, but the fog made it almost zero. I took a compass reading while I could still see, so I could navigate with instruments if I lost all sight of land. I noted the compass heading for my course northward, and the heading for the Hilton Head lighthouse just in case. As I pounded my way through the salty chop, enduring the fierce wind and pelting rain, the white curtain closed around me, completely obliterating the view ahead. I was plowing blindly into the fog at seven miles an hour with my rain gear flapping in the wind like the clothes on a scarecrow. At that point I was only able to see thirty feet ahead, so motoring at full speed into the whiteness made me nervous. My compass would show me my course in the fog as surely as Jesus pointing the way in the picture. But the compass wouldn't show me a large steel buoy or ICW marker sticking out of the water, or worse yet a boat load of tourists hurrying across the sound to get out of the rain. Since my situation had changed from uncomfortable to life threatening, I slowed to half speed and began to weigh my options. Should I keep steering slowly into the fog using my compass, and give a loud blast on my whistle every few seconds, or turn and run toward Hilton Head Island? I could see nothing through the fog ahead, but behind me and to my right the shoreline of the island and the lighthouse were still faintly visible.

Just then, as if to answer my question a bolt of lightning split the sky, followed by a thunderous boom that startled me even though I knew it was coming. Without wasting a second, I pushed the tiller hard over, pointed my bow at the lighthouse and raced toward the island at full speed. *That settles that,* I thought. I had no desire to be standing under a thirty-two foot aluminum lightning rod, especially when it was the tallest object for miles around in the middle of open water. "I might be reckless, but I'm not crazy," I thought, trying to be funny, in an attempt to make light of a desperate situation. The strong wind was now behind me, so I made good time and the lighthouse grew rapidly larger as I closed the distance between myself and the island. Coming in to about eight feet of water, I killed the motor and scrambled forward on the slippery decks. With rain stinging my face I somehow got both anchors off the bow and let out all of the anchor rope.

Once inside the warm, dry interior of the cabin with the doors in place, I felt more secure. Ripping off the wet rain suit, I knelt on the floor and sprawled my chest, head and arms on the nearest bed cushion in a position of complete surrender and relaxation. I marveled at how soft and comforting the cushion felt against my cheek and how good it was to be completely relaxed if only for a moment. I could feel the boat drifting as the wind and waves pulled the slack out of the ropes. Then I felt it slow down as the anchors began to drag. In a few seconds there was a solid jerk as an anchor dug in and the boat turned sharply to point into the wind. I knew that I would be fine as long as lightning didn't strike the mast. I had no reason to move so I just knelt there, listening to the sound of the thunder and feeling myself rise and fall with the gentle up and down motion of the boat.

I noticed that my rain pants were torn from catching on a bolt and my clothes were wet, but none of that seemed to matter now that I was safely hunkered down. Not wanting to lift my head from the comfortable warmth of the cushion, I watched the lightning flashes through the rain washed window. I was almost lulled to sleep by the drumming of the giant rain drops and the movement of the boat, but I caught myself drowsing and forced myself to stay awake, so I could push on as soon as conditions changed.

Chapter 16

Learning to Trust My Compass

The force of the wind and rain gradually began to diminish, and soon I realized that I hadn't heard any thunder in several minutes. Reluctantly raising my head from the cushion, I stood and stripped off my wet clothes, knowing how important it would be to get going again as soon as I could. Drying off with a towel, I slipped eagerly into the warmth of a comfortable sweatshirt and dry jeans. The moment the sound of rain drops on the cabin stopped, I opened things up and went forward to pull the anchors. The air was fresh and sweet, the fog had lifted, and the sky was beginning to brighten.

The north end of the sound was clearly visible as I motored smoothly in that direction with renewed confidence. I praised the Lord for getting me through the storm, for giving me a time of rest, for the comfort of dry clothes and for the brightening sky ahead. The ICW markers led me into a series of slender rivers where I enjoyed winding my way past the beautiful waterfront properties of Hilton Head Island. I was impressed by how sturdy and elaborate the docks were, each one extending several hundred feet out from the shore. Every dock was built on closely spaced round pilings and was at least fifteen feet above the water at low tide. Each one had the facilities for lifting a large boat out of the water and up to dock level. I assumed they were so high and extended so far out because of the tides, and I could see from the algae and barnacles on the pilings that the water rose to just a few feet below dock level at high tide. They had been designed for beauty as well as function and many of them had gazebos, sitting decks or attractive boat houses on them that matched the main house.

Farther ahead in a narrow area bordered by trees my stomach reminded me that I hadn't eaten anything since my bowl of Honey Nut Cheerios that morning. I treated myself to two cold pre cooked burgers on rolls with ketchup and some M&M's with milk. Inhaling them eagerly while steering, I was again pleased by how delicious the most rustic food tasted when you were starving. I changed my mind an hour later, when my stomach got queasy, and I began to wonder if the burgers or the ketchup had gone bad, having been on ice since I left New York.

As I turned a corner, the narrow creek opened into a very large body of water. My chart showed that I had entered Port Royal Sound. I saw that I would have to steer through the widest part of it to get across to the Beaufort River. Although I would cross larger sounds farther north, this would be the longest distance across open water so far this trip. There were no ICW markers in the middle of the sound, so I would be steering across open water, with nothing to aim at. The chart simply gave me a compass heading. After passing the last visible marker, I would have to trust my compass and hold a course of eighty-nine degrees for seven miles across the sound, until I could see red marker number twenty-six. After turning left between twenty-six and twenty-seven, I would again see the familiar red and green markers leading me up the Beaufort River.

As I pointed my bow into open water I praised the Lord for two things:

1. It was a beautiful summer evening with blue skies and little wind, so the open water of the sound had only gentle rollers

instead of the wind driven ocean waves I faced when crossing the other sounds. That was a big blessing, since this was quite a distance across open water, and I had already weathered a storm that day.

2. I was given a brand new lighted compass for Father's Day to replace the broken one that came with the boat. If not for that gift, I probably wouldn't have purchased one on my shoestring budget. I didn't think a compass would be necessary on this type of trip, since I thought I would be winding my way through scenic rivers, creeks and canals all the way.

I moved across the sound with one eye on the compass and one eye on the gently rising and falling water ahead, holding a strict course of eighty nine degrees. I saw that the Lord was giving me another object lesson, and this time using the compass. In order to cross the sound I had to completely trust the compass to guide me. I could not see which way to steer on my own, so I had to believe that the compass was pointing me in the right direction. That is the kind of faith God wants us to have in him. He wants us to know that even when we can't see the course ahead or the final outcome, he will guide and direct our life exactly where it needs to go, if we believe and trust him as our "compass".

The vast expanse of moving water around me was not as intimidating with a blue sky overhead and no wind, so I began to relax and enjoy the rocking and nodding of the boat as it bobbed and lifted in the gentle rollers. Far to my right, I could see where the sound opened into the ocean and to my left was Parris Island, the home of a United States Marine Corps base.

My faith in the compass turned out to be well founded. After forty-five minutes of keeping the pointer at eighty-nine degrees, I approached the other side and saw the next Intra Coastal Waterway marker dead ahead. Turning left between number twenty-six and number twenty-seven I headed north up the Beaufort River and around Parris Island. The word MARINES was printed on a water tower and visible from a great distance. That reassured me and gave me even more confidence in the compass and my ability to follow the chart. It occurred to me that I was in South Carolina now and had been for some time. *I guess they don't have colorful signs on the Intra Coastal that welcome you to each state, like they do on the highway,* I thought with a smile.

Seeing some uniformed men moving near a building, I thought about my son, just finishing basic training at Fort Jackson and I wondered how he was doing. I was very proud that he made it into the Army Reserve Band, and blinked back a tear as I realized how much I missed him. If I arrived on time, I planned to leave the boat at a marina in Charleston and somehow get to the Charleston airport to rent a car. Then I would drive to Fort Jackson, picking up my wife and daughters at the Columbia airport on the way to the base. The day before graduation was family day and Tom was allowed to leave the base. We hoped to spend time sightseeing with him, treat him to dinner and stay to see the ceremony the next day. After the ceremony, Tom and I would drop the girls off at the Columbia airport and drive back to the marina. After we unloaded Tom's things, someone from the marina would have to follow us back to the Charleston airport to return the rental car and bring us back to the boat. It would feel strange to be on land again, driving a car, eating in a restaurant and sleeping in a bed, but right about then it sure sounded good.

It was almost dark and I was still eighty miles from Charleston. I had to be there tomorrow night for everything to work out as planned. Knowing that I went sixty miles yesterday and about seventy today, I knew that I would have to start early, push hard and have an almost perfect day to make it there before sundown. It wouldn't be any fun poking around in Charleston Harbor in the dark. Especially if I was trying to find a marina that I hadn't been to before.

As I followed the river around Parris Island, I began to look for a side channel on the opposite shore for a safe place to anchor that night. When I reached the back side of the island the river forked in two directions, but there were no more ICW markers. Because of the wrong turns I had already made and my tight time schedule, I desperately needed reassurance to know that I was going the right way before I went any further.

Up ahead, I spotted a well tanned couple sitting in a kayak, so I moved toward them to ask directions. They were watching a group of dolphins on their right side, so I passed to their left and slowed to a stop as I spoke. "Is this the Intra Coastal Waterway north to Charleston?" I shouted, pointing straight ahead. "Yes sir, you're going the right way," the young man answered as they both smiled up at me. The woman's bikini top fit loosely and left little to the imagination as she leaned forward, so I quickly diverted my eyes to look at the dolphins. "Do you know if there's a marina or safe place to anchor for the night up ahead," I asked. "As soon as you go under that highway bridge, you'll see a marina on your left," the man said, pointing up river. He then went on to say that the town of Beaufort was only a couple of miles beyond the bridge and he believed there was a marina there also. "Thanks a lot; you guys just made my night," I said with a smile. "God bless ya, have a nice night," I called out, as I kicked the motor back into gear. I moved slowly away from them, trying not to toss them with my wake or scare the dolphins. It looked like they were having a great time. *If more couples went out dolphin watching together, marriages might last a whole lot longer than they do nowadays,* I thought.

As I neared the bridge, I could see that there was a small marina on the left just beyond it. It appeared to be closed for the night, so I decided to tie up to the fuel dock and pay for my stay in the morning. The dock ran parallel to shore to make it easy for boats to come in and out. As I approached it and slowed down, the strongest current I have ever felt swept me quickly along the dock and pushed me out into the river. It was so strong that I quickly decided that it would not be wise to try to come into that dock in a sailboat alone. Just past the last marina dock, there was a small grassy cove where a small sailboat was anchored. Knowing that it would soon be too dark to see anything, I pulled in and anchored about fifty yards beyond the other boat and about the same distance from shore.

I got into my berth quickly, knowing how critical it was to get an early start the next day, but it wasn't until I lay there and began to relax that I realized how mentally, physically and emotionally exhausted I really was. I started to thank God for getting me that far, protecting me in the storm and giving me a safe place to anchor, but I must have fallen asleep in the middle of a sentence, because I don't remember ever finishing that prayer.

Voyage of the Heart

Chapter 17

Aground at Four AM

Although I fell asleep quickly, I slept restlessly, and only for a short time. As I lay there staring at the stars through the open hatch, moonlight streamed through the cabin window. The moon was so bright, it looked like dawn was coming, but I knew it was still the middle of the night. I was afraid to look at my watch, because then I would know how little sleep I got and how long I still had to wait for morning. I finally gave in and checked it, only to find out that it was one o'clock in the morning. Too excited to sleep, I popped my head through the hatch, amazed at how light it was and how beautiful the moon looked. The calm black water reflected a silver pathway that led toward the full moon, and I was surprised at how far down the river I could see. Every light on shore was clearly visible, and so were the lights of Beaufort, which lay on a bend in the river ahead. The closely spaced ICW marker lights led off down the middle of the river toward the small town, flashing at me as if they were beckoning me to follow them.

If I pulled anchors now and went very slow, I knew I could navigate by using my spotlight and following the flashing lights. I had fished and cruised many times in the dark and felt very comfortable doing it, especially in the moonlight. I still had eighty miles to go and absolutely had to be there tomorrow night. If I waited for daylight and had a perfect day with no stops or delays (which hadn't happened yet), the best I could hope for would be to arrive just before dark. At that hour the Marina would be closed, so I couldn't take them up on their offer to keep my food in their freezer or take me to the airport. If I started now, even at two or three miles per hour, I could cut ten to fifteen miles off of the eighty before it got light. That would leave me a distance to cover that I could easily do in one day. I would arrive early, and have plenty of time to get the boat secured, shower, and pack whatever I needed for the two days I would be at the Army base. If I arrived while the marina was open, I could put my food in their freezer and get a ride to the airport. I might even be able to drive to Columbia that night and treat myself to a cheap motel room. I would be dead tired, but I could collapse into a real bed in an air conditioned room. Being close to the airport, I could sleep late and maybe even feast on a continental breakfast in the morning. Then I would be waiting for them as they stepped off the plane, just like the "Old Spice" man that returned from the sea.

It sounded so good, that I decided to give it a try, believing that the Lord had roused me early, just so I could make it there comfortably the next day. To my delight both anchors came up easily and were not covered with black gook. Motoring slowly toward the line of flashers, I scanned the water ahead with my spotlight and "bam" a triangular ICW marker jumped out of the darkness at me the instant the light hit it. Apparently the numbers, symbols and borders on the markers were made from the same reflective paint that made highway signs so visible at night. Carefully picking my way from one marker to the next, I was able to go two miles down the river to the downtown area of Beaufort. There the main street of the town crossed low over the river and my progress was blocked by a swing bridge.

My first thought was that they didn't have a bridge operator on duty at two AM, so it looked like I had reached the end of the line for my early start and good idea. Just to see if someone was there, I approached closely, hailing the bridge operator on the radio and honking my hand held air horn three times. I had done that at all of the other bridges and they had opened, but here I got no response. That's strange, I thought, checking my guide book. It says that this bridge opens at any time of the day or night on demand. Disappointed, I headed for a well lit "board walk" area along the main street, built for boaters who wished to visit the town. As I approached, planning to spend the night there, I spotted a couple taking a walk along the river so I hailed them. "Do you know what time the bridge opens," I called loudly. "They open all night, go over there and blow your horn and wake em up," answered a deep, pleasant, African American voice. I smiled, because his accent was so heavy, it took me a second to figure out what he said. "Thank you," I called out, as I headed back toward the bridge. Now that I knew someone was up there, I was determined to get their attention and get them to open so I could continue on my way. I tried hailing the operator again on the radio, knowing that all the bridge operators had been monitoring channels thirteen and sixteen. Then I honked my air horn again and again as loud as I could, but got no reaction, so I gave several loud blasts on my band director's whistle, and still got no response from the bridge.

An idea came to mind: I could tie up and walk over to the bridge office. If someone was there but asleep a polite knock on the door should rouse them, and I could then ask them to open the bridge. It would be well worth the walk if I could keep going and gain any amount of mileage toward Charleston before daybreak. As I motored back toward the main street, I noticed a marina near the board walk with a well lit fuel dock. I decided that it would be smarter to tie up there, in case I couldn't get the bridge to open. It would be a safer, quieter place to sleep, and I could top off my tanks in the morning before leaving, eliminating the need for a fuel stop on a day when every mile and every minute really counted.

After securing the boat, I started the long walk to the lift bridge, but stopped short after only a few steps. Right on the window of the fuel dock office was a poster with bridge information that read: "Attention Boaters—The Lady Island Highway Swing Bridge Opens On Demand For Boats Twenty-Four Hours A Day. All Bridge Operators In The State Of South Carolina Monitor VHF Radio Channel Number Nine. Quickly jumping back into the boat and switching the radio to channel nine I tried the bridge operator again with the boat still tied to the dock. To my delight an older southern voice answered immediately. He explained that regulations did not allow him to open for a horn or a whistle, but now that I had identified myself on the radio, he would be happy to open for me as I approached. "Thank you Lord Jesus," I praised audibly, as my fingers snatched eagerly at the knots, trying to get them untied quickly. I was just pushing away from the dock, when I heard the clanging bells and saw the flashing lights as the gates came down to stop traffic on the highway above. "Praise the Lord, he's stopping cars already. I better get over there so he doesn't have to hold up traffic too long," I thought. By the time I hit the bridge he was wide open and I sailed through without even having to slow down. "Lady Island Bridge operator, thanks a lot for opening so quickly, you're the man," I chimed happily, as I passed below him waving. "God bless ya and have a great night," I concluded. "Y'all do the same Cap'n," was his reply.

On the other side of the bridge, things were a little different. I was in a much wider river now with fewer dwellings or lights on shore. As I moved away from Beaufort, the street lights and other lights of the village that brightened the sky earlier were no longer with me. The moon was lower in the sky and had gone behind some clouds, so things were much darker than they had been an hour ago. The good news was that I had a flashing green marker dead ahead to reassure me so I headed right at it in the darkness. There were just enough scattered lights on both shores so I could tell where land was and where the middle of the river was. As I slowly passed the green marker I was happy to see two more red flashers ahead lining up to make a bee line down the middle of the river. The first one was about a mile away and the second a short distance beyond that. This is too easy, I thought, the markers line up like ducks in a row. The channel goes straight down the middle of the river, right where it should be. I felt so confident, that I didn't even look at the chart or scan the water ahead with the spotlight. *I can't believe I'm cruising down a river in South Carolina in the moonlight, thank you Lord, for giving me such a rich full life.* I began to sing to myself as I slowly gained mileage toward Charleston in the dark: " . . . Gonna run all night, gonna run all day . . ." I sang happily, not realizing that I had made a terrible mistake that could have cost me the trip and my boat.

I was in the middle of the river, heading straight at the distant flasher that was also in the middle, not aware that several unlighted markers curved sharply to the right as the deep channel turned right and hugged the shoreline for a while, coming back out into the middle right about where the next flasher was. The deep channel was on the right side, because a big sand bar ran right down the middle of the river for almost half a mile between me and the next flashing marker. The water over the bar was so shallow (I learned later), that at low tide the chart showed it as dry land. Because I wasn't looking at the chart or using my spotlight, I had missed the unlit markers and the sharp turn of the channel to the right and I was motoring happily right at the center of the sand bar in the dark!

Unfortunately, there was one more factor that sealed my fate, and left me wide open for disaster: I needed at least three feet of water to float, and my depth finder had a shallow water alarm that would beep loudly whenever I came into five feet of water or less. Another feature on the device was a deep water alarm. I had no use for a deep water alarm, but the previous owner had set it to beep whenever I was in fifty feet of water or deeper. It panicked me several times during the trip, beeping as I passed over deep water in a sound or was in the middle of a river. I promised myself that I would reset it, or disable that feature, but I hadn't taken the time to do it. Until I could change it, I had learned to live with it, ignoring the beeping when the numbers told me I was in deep water.

As I approached the sand bar, it began to beep loudly to warn me of the disaster ahead, but it said that I was in deep water, not shallow water. Looking at the digital readout in the dark without my glasses the numbers 50 told me that I was in fifty feet of water. That didn't surprise me, since I was in the middle of a wide river. I ignored the beeping and calmly continued to steer a course straight ahead through the darkness toward the flashing light.

With no warning, the boat hit something so hard that it rose up from the water as though Moby Dick was coming to the surface right under it, and I stopped moving forward. The tiller moved and jumped in my hand and then became rigidly locked in place as the rudder buried itself in the bottom. The motor made strange sounds as it churned in the mud trying to push a boat that would not move, so I kicked it out of gear. "What happened?" I cried out with my heart pounding wildly. "What could I have run into, way out here in fifty feet of water?" I asked myself, still in shock and disbelief. I moved in to take a closer look at the beeping depth finder which was now showing a depth of twenty feet, and then I groaned loudly, dropping to the seat and shaking my head as I realized what had happened. The depth finder wasn't showing 20 feet, it was showing 2.0 feet. That meant when I read 50 feet, I was really only in 5.0 feet of water. In the dark and without my glasses, my aging eyes had missed the decimal point and now I was aground in the middle of a wide river at four AM. I tried to break free from the sandy bottom by gunning the motor to rock the boat back and forth, but gave up after a few minutes when I saw that I wasn't getting anywhere. Bitterly disappointed, I knew that if I couldn't get going soon, I would have no chance of making it to Charleston that day.

As I sat there, upset with myself and devastated by the whole situation, many thoughts passed through my mind. It was dark, so no one could see how foolish I looked stuck out there in the middle of the river and it was a good bet that no one would run into me in the dark, because all the other boats would be in the well marked channel (where I should have been) far from this sandbar. If I damaged my hull causing a leak, or bent my rudder so I couldn't steer, my great "voyage" was now over, and I had to figure out a way to get what was left of my boat back home. There were professional tow boats on the ICW that made a living towing boats that were out of gas, had motor problems or run aground. I knew that if I called for one on the radio, the fee would wipe out most of my gas money, so I prayed for the tide to lift me off and hoped that it wouldn't take too long. Adding insult to injury, my tide chart said that low tide would not even occur for another hour! That meant the water level would keep going down for an hour, before the tide started to come in and the water got gradually deeper again. Since the water was only two feet deep, I was afraid to imagine what the sand bar and the boat would look like in an hour with the tide going out.

Anyone who has seen the part of a sailboat that is underwater knows that the hull tapers down to a point at the bottom. This narrow "fin" or keel stabilizes the boat and counter balances the force of the wind on the sails when sailing. If you set a flat bottomed boat on land on its bottom it will sit there upright. But if you set a sailboat on land; resting on the point of its keel, it will roll right over onto its side. I didn't know how much more the water would go down in the next hour, but I hoped that "God Speed" would not be left lying on her side on dry land in the middle of the river like a beached whale.

Since there was nothing else to do, I sat inside the cabin waiting, praying and writing down all the details of the trip, including my current predicament. I thought it would be good to have a "Captains Log" of my voyage in case I ever sat down to write a book about my adventure. I felt the boat gradually lean toward its starboard side as the water around it receded. Very slowly, it tipped more and more, until it was heeling as much as any sailboat would when sailing broadside in a strong wind. As it continued to tip even more, there was no place to sit comfortably, so I had to sit on the floor with my feet braced against the opposite berth as things began to fall off the shelves and land on the floor around me. At first, I pictured the boat tipping over so far that the entire river would come pouring in the cabin door, trapping me inside and drowning me. But then I realized that was impossible. A fixed keel sailboat could tip only so far even with no water, because the heavy keel would always stay down holding the mast up. The water was going down and away from all decks and doors as it receded, and it was impossible for twelve inches of water to pour into a cabin door that was five feet above the river bottom.

At four forty-five, still fifteen minutes away from low tide, the boat was laying on its side so badly that I hoped it had reached the point where it couldn't tip any more. I looked at my watch constantly, hoping and praying that five o'clock would come quickly, so the water would start getting deeper again. At four fifty-five the outer edge of the starboard deck was under water and there was no longer any way to get into a comfortable position aboard. Finally five o'clock came and went, but the boat stayed in that position. Six o'clock also came and went and still the boat laid there in the mud without moving an inch. Being a fresh water sailor, I didn't know much about tides, but I thought that when they reached their lowest point they started to go the other way. Apparently that wasn't the case. I learned that once the water reached low tide, it stayed shallow for quite a while before it started to get deeper again.

In spite of how bad things seemed, the Lord gave me a feeling of peace and security through that ordeal, but I began to question why he allowed it to happen, especially on a day when my time schedule was so tight. I tried to ask him as I prayed: "Lord, I praise you that I am safe, but why did you allow this to happen today?" "Did this happen because I rushed off in the middle of the night without asking for your protection and blessing?" "Did you want me to have the time to write things down so I can write a book about this someday?" "Is there a tow boat captain or Coast Guard crewman that will come to know you because they came to my rescue today?" "Is this your way of forcing me to stop and rest, because I planned to push myself all night and all day today, or did you allow the enemy to take a shot at me just to test my faith?" "Are you testing me, the way you tested Job and Paul in the bible, to see if I will still trust you and praise you through catastrophe and disappointment?" "Well I will, Lord, I will!" "I trust you even now as I sit here aground on this sandbar with my boat looking like a shipwreck!" "I praise you and love you with all my heart, and if this is the end of the trip and my boat, then I praise you for the experiences and memories you have given me this week." Please help me to get home one way or the other, and continue to use me and this boat to do your work. In Jesus' mighty name I pray, Amen.

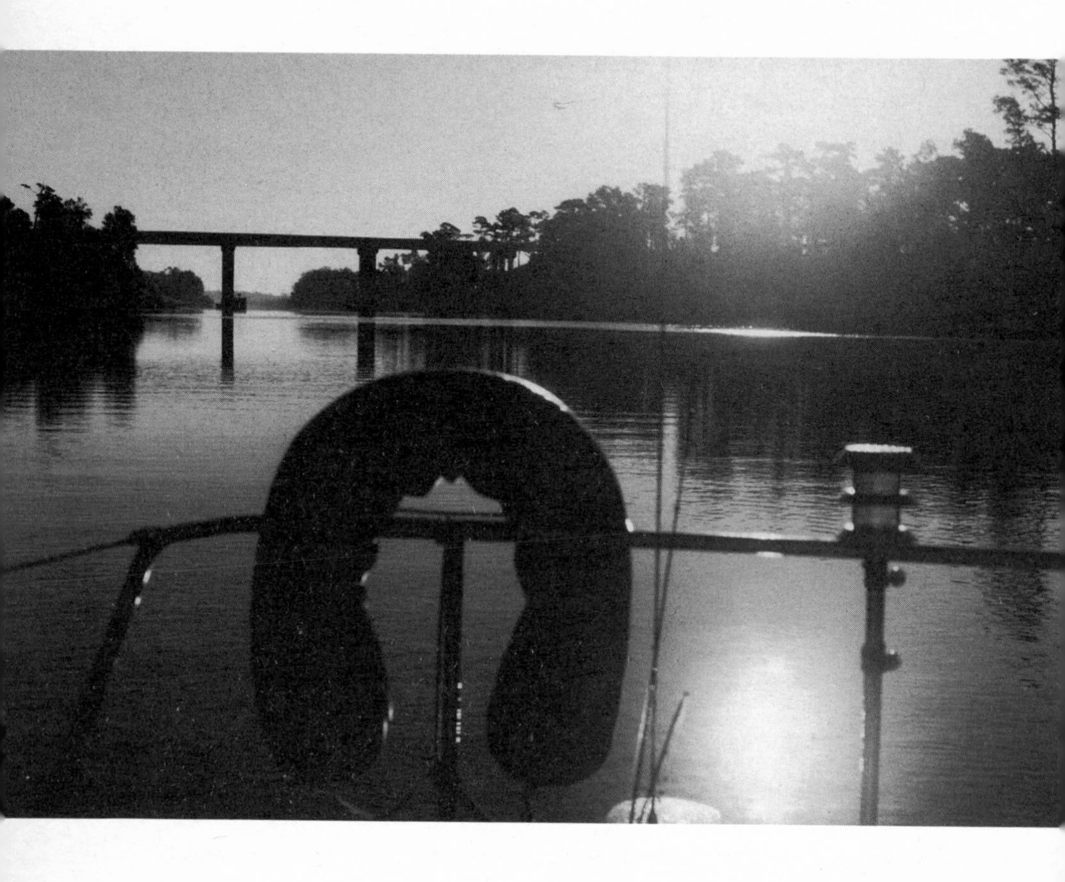

Chapter 18

Singing to the Dolphins, Feeding the Gulls

At seven o'clock, I noticed an almost imperceptible correction of the boat as it started to come back the other way. The boat had gone from an upright position to lying on its side in twenty minutes so I hoped it would come back up just as quickly. It had been daylight for an hour now and I realized that if I had just waited until morning to pull anchors and get underway, I would have been safely past this spot by now, heading for Charleston. Since I no longer needed running lights, I turned off all the electronics to save my battery in case I needed to use the radio to call for help.

By seven twenty, the boat had gained a couple more degrees of correction, but it seemed to be a painfully slow process, taking much longer to right itself, than it had to lie down. Having been up since one o'clock, I felt my body shutting down, so I wedged myself against a berth on the badly slanted floor and fell asleep for about thirty minutes. When I woke up, I could tell that the cabin door was not as crooked as it had been before, but it was still far from being level. Going outside, I stood on the highest point of the deck on the port side. With my toes overboard I held the mast cable, leaned out and jumped up and down with all my weight. To my surprise the other side bobbed up and the boat came level! Trying to move the tiller, I could tell that it was still stuck, but now that she was upright it seemed like I might really get out of there.

I did some quick math, and found that if I could get going again within the hour, I might still make it to the marina in Charleston that night. I could tell by how little the boat moved when I walked around, that it was still in the sand, but the water was rising rapidly. While I waited, I put more minutes on my cell phone, straightened up the cabin, and organized the things that had fallen off the shelves.

At about eight twenty, the boat seemed to rock and move normally when I walked around, and I could move the tiller handle a little so I eagerly tried the motor. When I revved to full throttle, a cloud of mud and silt billowed back in the prop wash as I pushed the tiller handle back and forth. I could feel the rudder moving in sand, making it hard to turn and I hoped it didn't break. The bow moved back and forth as I steered hard from side to side hoping to rock the boat free. At first I wasn't sure if I felt it, or imagined it, but it seemed like the boat was moving! Sure enough, with the motor roaring and churning the muddy water, I felt it slowly, lethargically, plowing through the sand. Then my spirit soared as I felt it break free from the bottom and surge ahead normally. Praising the Lord with all my heart, I pointed the bow toward deep water.

As I made my way toward the ICW markers near shore, I was so happy, I pretended to be Captain James T. Kirk of the starship "Enterprise": "Scotty, damage report," I barked, as I took a mental inventory of any damage I had sustained. Then I switched to a high pitched Scottish brogue and replied: "Well Captain, she seems to be steering normally, so I don't think we've damaged the rudder. We're still afloat, and the cabins not filling with water, so there's no sign of a leak yet. Looking up at the mast and rigging, everything seems to be ship shape aloft. Who knows what kind of problems might crop up in a day or two, after putting that kind of stress and strain on a vessel? I'll tell you, she can't take much more of that captain, she can't take much more!"

I laughed loudly at my own foolishness, but was thrilled to be underway again. Now in the safety of the well marked channel I praised the Lord as I headed full speed for Charleston, hoping that the wind and current would be behind me all the way. My positive outlook grew as I realized that the weather was great that day. The puffy white clouds had animal shapes, and the sky seemed bluer than ever as I thought about coming through such a traumatic ordeal unscathed. Running wide open, I did not want to waste precious time missing a turn, so I followed the chart carefully and verified each marker number. Keeping one eye on the depth finder, I steered the straightest course possible, cutting corners and hugging the inside of curves to cut off a few yards of distance and a few seconds of time where I could.

By mid morning, beads of sweat were running down my forehead, as I felt the South Carolina sun bake the top of my straw hat. Large power cruisers blew by me like I was standing still, causing massive waves in the confines of the narrow rivers. It was interesting to note the heart attitude of the people on each boat that passed me. Many zoomed by at full speed, not even looking back to see my plight as I was tossed helplessly and almost swamped by the waves they left behind. Others reduced their speed dramatically as they approached a small sailboat. Then they cruised slowly past, smiling and waving and did not resume full speed again until they were well beyond me. My boat seemed tiny and insignificant next to the huge yachts, each one worth more than my house, but I remained enthusiastic because I knew that the message I was carrying, was worth far more than any boat I would encounter.

I couldn't help but wonder what they thought or said about me as they passed. I wished I could have been a fly on board with them to hear their comments. What did they say about the funny little man in the straw hat, steering the small sailboat with the large name and Christian flag? Did they even know what kind of flag it was? Some of them probably thought I was a nut, but I hoped that at least a few had been somehow touched or reminded of God as they passed me.

Later on I passed a young family with children in a ski boat, and watched as each child took a turn being pulled along on an inner tube. I smiled wistfully when the happy screams and laughter reached me. My heart warmed as I recalled and fondly missed the days when my own children were little. I remembered pulling them along behind a motoring sailboat as they laughed and cheered each other on. Those "low budget" rides were a big deal to them, and they always seemed to have a ball, even though we were moving at a snails pace by comparison.

Three shiny wet fins sliced the surface as a group of dolphins appeared and began to race and play in the wake of my boat. I wondered if the happy clicking and squealing sounds they made were their way of shouting and laughing at each other, just like the children in the ski boat I had passed. Feeling silly, I took on the deep, inner city tough guy voice of "Rocky Balboa" as I said: "Hey guys, how ya doin?" Their happiness and exuberance was contagious, and I felt an inner joy well up in me as I watched their playful antics. I began to sing to them loudly in a heavy, old fashioned Italian accent. Using the tune to the classic Italian tarantella, I made up the words as I went along: "Hey - a - Joe - a - wha - da - you - know - a - whats - a - matta - for - you? You - swim - and - play - in - the - sun - all - day - I - say - whats - a - matta - for - you! Hey!" I laughed out loud at how silly I was being, yet inwardly praised the Lord for giving me so much joy on that beautiful day.

Later I noticed a few gulls circling over the water ahead. Occasionally one would dive to catch a minnow or pick up an edible piece of floating debris from the surface. I thought about how the precooked hamburgers had made my stomach queasy the last time I ate one. They had been fully thawed for several days now and even though I tried to keep them on ice, I found that ice didn't last very long in the Carolinas in August. I decided to give the gulls a treat, and see if these wild birds would respond to being fed, as well as the ones that begged for scraps of food at public beaches and outdoor restaurants. As soon as I broke off the first piece of hamburger and threw it in the air, they were on me like fleas on a dog, circling and diving at the boat in hopes that I would throw more. As I broke off pieces and threw each one as high as possible, they were sometimes able to catch them in mid air and if not, quickly dove to scoop them out of the water. When one bird grabbed a tasty prize, several more would attack it, in an effort to pull the meaty morsel from its beak. I smiled at their antics as I enjoyed the aerial "circus" above me. I don't know where they came from, or how the word spread so quickly that a crazy old timer was throwing hamburger into the air, but within minutes, the half dozen birds turned into thirty or forty. My boat must have looked like a garbage scow as the cloud of gulls circling and wheeling overhead dove and flapped at me squealing and shrieking. I laughed, as I thought of the old horror film "The Birds" by Alfred Hitchcock, thinking how this could have been a scene from that movie.

As the day wore on, I called the marina in Charleston to let them know my progress. They were courteous and helpful, saying that I could put all my perishable food in their refrigerator while I was away from the boat for a couple of days. They also offered to give me a ride to the airport so I could pick up the rental car to drive to Columbia. Everything seemed to be working out well, but in order for those things to happen, I had to arrive at the marina before they closed for the day at seven. My calculations told me that I should be there by six thirty, but the marina owner said that I would have to come through a lift bridge just before Charleston. The bridge, located on a busy highway, did not open for any boats between six and seven o'clock due to rush hour traffic. I would have to make it to that bridge before six or I would be held up for a full hour and lose any chance of making it to the marina by seven. Needless to say I was thrilled when I rounded a bend in the river and saw the bridge dead ahead at five thirty.

"This is the captain of the northbound sailboat "God Speed". I am requesting that the Charleston lift bridge open as I approach," I spoke into the radio, calmly and respectfully. "Absolutely not!" a stern woman's voice shouted back at me with a harsh unfriendly tone. "State highway regulations prevent me from opening this bridge for any boat traffic between the hours of five and six thirty PM," she snapped. Her loud voice and hard nosed attitude made me wonder if she had been a drill sergeant in the military before she operated a bridge. "What is the name of your vessel and your home port?" she barked sharply, making me feel like I was being questioned by the Gestapo. "God Speed, from Youngstown, New York, ma'am," I replied sheepishly. "Anchor right there until six thirty captain, but under no circumstances are you to block the approach to the bridge for other vessels, do you understand?" she growled. "Yes ma'am, understood," I replied. I was crushed and sick with disappointment as I hung up the microphone asking myself what I had done to get this female bridge operator so upset with me.

"How could this happen?" I thought. My emotions went from the top of Mt. Everest to the bottom of Death Valley, as I realized that my chance of making it was now gone. The marina owner didn't know the correct bridge time schedule and his mistake had given me false hope. Shaking my head sadly, I tried to understand why the Lord would bring me that far, only to have me miss making it by just thirty minutes. Devastated, I slumped to the seat in the hot cabin, trying to accept the fact that I would now have to wait a full hour for the bridge to open.

I called the bridge operator again, trying to smooth things over with her and make sure there were no exceptions to the rule. "Charleston bridge operator," I began politely. "I meant no disrespect. I am not from this area and was not aware of your time schedule. A marina owner told me that you were closed between the hours of six and seven. I am traveling from Florida and need to be at a marina in Charleston tonight before seven, to make connections to see my son graduate from basic training at Fort Jackson." Hearing that, her tone softened a little as she replied: "I'm sorry, Captain, even if you had the governor aboard; my orders are that this bridge will not open during that time." She stated that fact with the same resolve and determination as if she was guarding a bridge in Iraq. "I will open for you promptly at six thirty," she finished curtly. I thanked her as I signed off and then began to think about what to do next. First I called the marina and explained my predicament to them. They confirmed that once I got through the bridge, I would still be eight miles away, and traveling at sailboat speed I would not make it there before they closed. The man offered to put two large coolers containing ice outside the office door for me. If I put all my perishable food in them, he said they would put it in their refrigerator as soon as they arrived the next morning. I thanked him sincerely as I signed off, still worried about a ride to the airport. As I sat in the stifling heat of the cabin, I thought about the other unplanned stops and delays that had turned into blessings or ways to meet and touch others. I felt foolish and a little guilty that I still had to be reminded that I was on his schedule and not mine. After thinking it through, I accepted that delay as his will, but I was anxious to have him show me the reason for it.

Voyage of the Heart

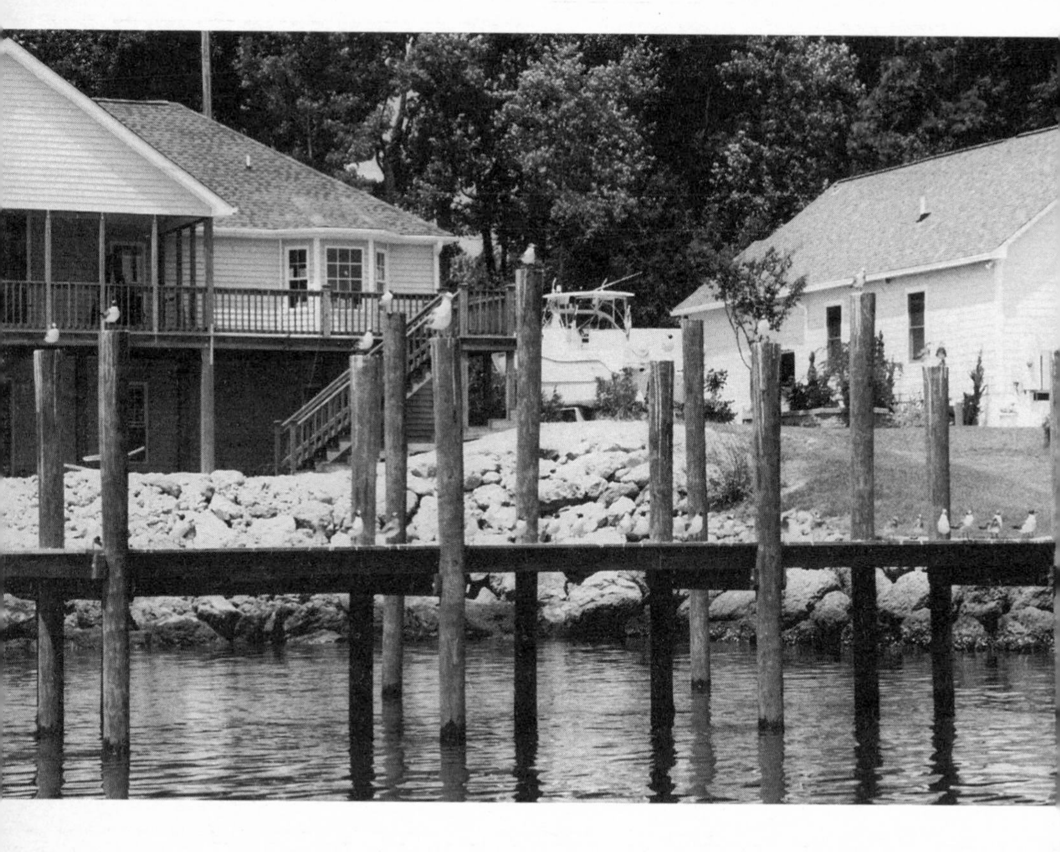

Chapter 19

Help from an Unlikely Source

While I waited for the bridge to open, I packed everything I would need to stay in a motel for a couple of nights near the Army base. I also prayed that the Lord would provide a ride to the Charleston Airport, so I could rent a car to get there. I organized the cabin, bagged the garbage and put all perishable foods in two large plastic bags so I could lock up and leave the boat quickly once I arrived at the marina. The cabin was like an oven and my clothes were soaked with sweat as I bustled about, taking a mental inventory of everything I had to do, to leave the boat for two days. I was drained from pushing myself all night and all day and my ordeal on the sand bar, but somehow the Lord gave me the strength to keep going in spite of the heat. I worked fast, then I sat outside in the fresh air to cool off. Six thirty finally approached and I pulled my anchor and restarted the motor so I could pass through the bridge as soon as it opened.

At exactly six thirty, I heard the clang of the warning bells and saw the red lights flash as the stop gates came down stopping traffic on the highway above. "Sailboat God Speed, you may now approach the bridge to continue north, please stay to your right as you come through, because I have two other vessels waiting on the north side that are southbound," the woman's voice came through the radio now with a more friendly tone. "Charleston bridge operator this is the sailboat God Speed," I replied. "Thank you for opening, God bless you, and have a great day," I concluded. "You do the same cap'n, congratulations on your son's graduation, I hope you make it there for the ceremony, be proud," the woman said sincerely. As I came through the bridge, people in boats on the other side waved at me and gave me a thumbs up, while one of the young men called out "good luck to your son!" It occurred to me that they had heard everything I said to the bridge operator, and now my boat name and Christian emblem were right in their face. The Lord had given the hot tempered, impatient Italian man another valuable reminder. My patience and courtesy with the bridge operator at a time of extreme disappointment and frustration, was not only a Christian example to her, but also to the people listening in the other boats that I didn't even know were there. It made me think about how our actions and reactions as Christians (whether good or bad) can have an affect on people that we are not even aware of.

Charleston Harbor was a giant crescent of open water around a blunt point of land, with a narrow opening to the ocean that was far from the mainland. I could almost feel a strong sense of history and tradition as I passed the cobblestone break walls and stately Victorian homes. The older homes were close together and in my minds eye it was easy to imagine a horse and buggy clomping down this waterfront street past the well maintained brick structures in Civil War times or colonial America. Several miles off shore on a point of land guarding the harbor entrance was Fort Sumter, now a national monument. I tried to imagine what it must have been like for the men who manned it that day, to be fired upon by the cannons of ships, and the sad loss of American life and carnage of the Civil War. As I came through the harbor the wind picked up and I found myself pounding and spraying my way through two foot waves. In spite of the conditions and the late hour, there seemed to be a tremendous amount of boat traffic for a weekday and many boaters returned my wave and my smile as I passed them. The marina where I was staying was several miles up the Cooper River. I had to go all the way around the peninsula that was the city of Charleston and then under a large suspension bridge to go up that river toward the marina. In contrast to the beautiful historic homes were modern day naval ships and an aircraft carrier bristling with fighter planes on the far side of the harbor. Two huge towers of steel and concrete rose from the water in the mouth of the Cooper River. I found out later that engineers were replacing the current suspension bridge with a brand new one that was taller to allow the passage of the largest ocean going ships up the river.

Even though I wasn't going to make it to the marina before it closed, the enemy must have thought things were going too well, so he took one more shot at me with a brief but severe rain storm that hit right when I was in the middle of the harbor. Closing up the cabin and donning rain gear, I continued on undaunted, thinking: "I hate this, but I'm not going to let it get me down, because the Lord is with me and I'm gonna get to take a warm shower and sleep in a real bed tonight!" That short storm seemed like a minor inconvenience after what I had been through that week, and at seven forty-five I pulled through an opening in a steel break wall and found dock spot number C7. It was one of the few open slips visible among the fleet of impressive sail and power boats. After tying the boat securely and locking the cabin, I loaded my food, my garbage, and my overnight bag into a dock cart and headed toward the marina office and shower building.

Just as the young man promised, there were two large coolers packed with ice outside the office door. After I put my food in them and discarded my garbage, I took the greatest shower I have ever had in my life. When I came back out into the night air I was filled with a sense of adventure, and felt like I was twenty-nine again. Since the marina seemed to be deserted except for me, I put my bag down and walked toward the pay phone to call a cab for a ride to the airport. As I picked up the receiver, I noticed a balding, overweight, middle aged man sitting alone at a patio table on the back deck of the marina. He sat like a statue, staring off blankly at the boats in their slips. The sun was slipping behind the horizon across the river, and Charleston Harbor was just visible off in the distance. I didn't really want to disturb him, but something told me I was supposed to, so I put down the receiver and approached him. "Excuse me," I began, "I'm on a sailing trip from Florida to New York and I just tied up here. Do you know where I can catch a bus to the airport, or if there is anyone here who might be willing to give me a ride there?" I asked politely. "I'd be happy to pay for their gas," I added. "I could take you to the airport," the man replied, in a soft calm voice that fit his appearance. "I'm not very busy right now, as you can see," he said smiling. "Won't take any money though," he stated. He went on to say that he was just happy to have some company and help a fellow boater. Having traveled by boat for many years, he knew what it was like to need a ride, and how much it meant when someone offered one.

As we walked to his car in the marina parking lot he introduced himself as Donald. He was a retired Canadian professor, living in his boat and spending a few days in each major city along the east coast for the summer. I was impressed to learn that he had purchased his forty foot sloop in the Virgin Islands and sailed it back to the US. He likewise said that he admired my courage sailing a twenty-five footer from Florida to New York. He was open and easy to talk to, and when I explained why I was going to the airport to rent a car he seemed sincerely interested in my trip and my family. As he drove we talked and shared sailing experiences. I felt a bit of a bond developing, so I gradually worked the conversation around to how the Lord had been with me and protected me on this trip, and how he had given a man with little money such a beautiful boat. As soon as Donald heard me going in that direction, he quickly but politely stopped me by saying: "Those beliefs are fine for you, and you have every right to believe whatever you wish, but I respectfully ask that you not talk to me that way any more. I do not want to hear that kind of thing, and I was nice enough to give you a ride, so I hope you will respect my wishes." Shocked and disappointed, I quickly changed the subject back to the adventures and mishaps I had experienced on the trip from Amelia Island to Charleston. By the time we pulled into the airport, any awkwardness between us was gone and we were eagerly swapping sailing stories again. As Donald dropped me off, I was impressed that this stranger, who wanted nothing to do with God, seemed sincerely concerned for my safety and that I would make the connections I needed. I offered him some gas money, but he refused to take it, so I thanked him earnestly and managed to get in a sincere "God bless you" as I shook his hand and said goodbye. As he pulled away, it occurred to me that if I hadn't been held up by the "bridge Nazi" I would never have met or had the opportunity to talk to Donald. To this day I do not believe that I encountered him that night by chance. Although he did not allow me to witness to him, I hope that I will learn some day that meeting me that night somehow had an effect on his life.

As the headlights of the rental car sliced through the darkness on the empty expressway, my body relaxed for the first time in a week and I felt an overwhelming weariness wash over me. It was now ten o'clock, but I had been up and pushing myself for twenty one hours. It seemed like it happened days ago, but I realized it was just that morning that I had been "shipwrecked" on the sand bar, after staying up all night trying to cruise in the dark. As I drove, I thought about Donald and I prayed that God would touch his heart. He must have had a terrible disappointment or tragedy in his life to reject God so completely. It saddened me that it bothered him so much when I casually mentioned the Lord in passing.

I found a small, cheap motel that was close to the Army base and the Columbia airport named the Airport Inn. When I asked for the most inexpensive room, I smiled when the price dropped from $36.95 to $33.00. My room wasn't fancy, but after living in the boat for a week it was the Taj Mahal. I sprawled on the firm mattress, marveling at how good a real bed felt as I pulled the crisp coolness of the top sheet up to my face. "Thank you Lord!" I praised, as I lay there listening to the noisy air conditioner for a minute. Then I opened my eyes and it was eight o'clock the next morning. As the sun streamed into my face through an opening in the drapes, I realized that I had fallen asleep so quickly and slept so soundly, that I had slept nine hours in what felt like a few seconds.

After enjoying a basic continental breakfast that seemed like a king's feast, I returned to my room to gather up my things and head for the airport. Walking toward the room, I passed a cleaning woman coming out of the room next to mine. She smiled and nodded as I greeted her with a cheerful good morning. The chubby, older black woman had a work ethic, a gentle sweetness and a humble sprit that I admired. She worked every day, doing laundry, making beds and scrubbing people's toilets to support her family, while I was spending a month cruising through America in a boat. I felt a little guilty and I tried to think of some small way to bless her, encourage her, or reach out to her. I had thrown a few tracts into my overnight bag just in case I needed one, so I spread them on the bed and began to sort through them. Among them was a hard plastic card with a picture of Jesus on one side and daily prayers and reminders on the other. It wasn't much, but it was all I had with me and it was more of a keepsake than a paper tract that would probably end up in a trash can. I kept it in my hand as I brought my bag to the car, and then I sat in the car and waited until she went into my room. Once she was inside, I went in smiling politely so I didn't alarm her and said: "Thanks for cleaning my room, you do good work." Handing her the card I said: "Jesus told me to give you this, he loves you and wants you to know that he does." Then I backed out of the room with a smile and a wave saying: "God bless you, have a good day." It took her a second to comprehend what I said, and then I heard her shout after me: "God bless you! God bless you child!" I could still hear her praising the Lord as I got into the car: "Thank you Jesus! Praise you Jesus!" It blessed me to hear her praise God in spite of her humble circumstances, and I smiled as I realized that I had brightened someone's day who was already a believer.

BRO 91
81A

Chapter 20

Private First Class US Army Aboard

The flight that my wife and daughters were on into Columbia was delayed, so I sat comfortably in the airport lobby, writing down everything that happened to me in my captain's log book. It felt good to relax, and after a week of fighting the elements and the clock I thoroughly enjoyed the feeling of no stress, no schedule and no worries. It was great to see them when they finally came down the crowded hallway smiling. As we embraced, my wife Mary teased me, saying she expected me to have a sailor's hat on, and a seaman's duffle bag slung over my shoulder. She thought I would be wearing Old Spice and whistling the tune from the commercial. My wife was a sight for sore eyes, looking tanned and attractive. Nicole was as tall and pretty as ever, and when I saw her eager smile I reminded myself that she wasn't my little girl anymore, but a grown woman. Although Lauren was eighteen, she still looked like a young girl. Her bright eyes and small cute face stood out in the airport crowd, and even though she wasn't known for expressing emotion I could tell she was glad to see me.

At the Army base, it was a joy for us to see Tom for the first time in almost ten weeks. He looked very much like a soldier in his camo fatigues and beret. It was fun sightseeing on the base with him and hearing about his experiences during basic training. After dinner we dropped him off at his barracks and Mary treated us to a room at the Embassy Suites Hotel. If I thought I was in the Taj Mahal the night before, I now felt like I had died and gone to heaven. The accommodations were luxurious and the all you can eat breakfast buffet the next morning really was a feast fit for a king.

The military pomp and pageantry of the graduation ceremony was touching and exhilarating, stirring patriotic feelings in everyone and making us very proud of our son. After the ceremony, Tom was a free man and I could tell he liked the feeling. We spent the rest of that day touring the area and trying to do things that Tom couldn't do during basic. When we returned to our room at the Embassy Suites, we let Tom order a pizza with whatever he wanted on it and we watched some TV. After breakfast the next morning, we took Mary and the girls to the Columbia airport where we said our goodbyes. Tom was going to cruise with me for a week up to Norfolk, Virginia. From there he would fly home and then be shipped off to advanced infantry training at the US Army school of music. The plan was to leave the boat at a marina in Norfolk for a few days, and Mary would join me again. We had an offer to stay at a time share resort near there in Colonial Williamsburg, in return for taking a tour of the property and listening to a sales pitch. Since she didn't really want to sail with me (and after the past week I didn't blame her) that would at least give us the chance to be together for a few days during my trip. After our three day get away, Mary would fly home and my sailing buddy Marty Douglas would join me in Norfolk, to sail with me up Chesapeake Bay, along the Jersey coast and into New York Harbor.

After we left the girls at the airport, Tom and I headed for the marina in Charleston, making a stop at Wal-Mart on the way, to pick up some things that Tom needed. When we arrived in Charleston we couldn't find the marina, so I called them on my cell phone. The owner stayed on the phone with us as we drove and talked us right into the marina parking lot like an air traffic controller. While we had the use of the rental car and dock carts, we decided to fill the fuel tanks at a gas station to stretch the fuel budget. I also bought the drinks and snacks that Tom wanted, and a few other staples we would need during the coming week.

Back at the boat, Tom put the groceries and his clothes away, while I pumped the water out of the ice box and stowed the fuel tanks below decks. I told him that it was great to see him and finally have some help, and that it was an honor to have a private first class in the US Army aboard as my crewman. Even though I owned the boat for a year, Tom had not been inside since I cleaned and refurbished the interior. He was impressed with how roomy, new and well equipped it was compared to other boats I had owned in the past. Once everything was aboard, I asked the manager if someone could follow me to the airport, to return the rental car and then bring me back. He asked Carolyn to do that favor for me in the marina pickup truck. Just to make sure I didn't get lost in Charleston again, I decided to follow her, and she led me right into the rental car return lot.

She was a tall girl with glasses, short dark hair and boyish features. As we rode back together in the pickup, I learned that she had just graduated from a Lutheran college and wanted to become a biology teacher. The marina was just a summer job, until she went back to school in the fall for her master's degree. The highlight of her week was going to a Loretta Lynn concert that night with a bunch of her friends at the stadium. I told her that I was a teacher at a Christian school and had a ministry for outdoorsmen. Then I told her how the Lord had blessed me with a beautiful boat and how he had guided and protected me all week. She said that she had been raised in a Christian home, but it was hard for her to believe that God was real and live as a Christian. I told her that what she just said was probably true for ninety percent of the people who called themselves Christians and the other ten percent were lying. My little joke brought a smile to her face as she nodded in agreement.

Seeing her openness, I used her knowledge of biology to convince her that a divine creator had to exist. I began to list the specialized equipment, perfect design and incredible instincts found in every plant and animal species (including humans). The miracles of eyes and taste buds, hearts and lungs, wings, paws, skin, fur and camouflage colors, were all proof that each creature was fearfully and wonderfully made. Living things were far too perfect and miraculous to have happened by random chance and refined themselves through millions of years of evolution. She nodded slowly as she thought about what I said, and then agreed that the makeup of living organisms was incredibly complex and sophisticated. "The farther you go with research, and the more advanced upper level courses you take, the more miraculous and awe inspiring the study of life becomes," She said.

As we pulled into the marina parking lot, I encouraged her to trust God and dedicate her life and teaching career to him. I told her that if she did, he would bless and use her beyond her wildest dreams. She thanked me sincerely, and as I got out of the truck, I said: "God bless ya Carolyn, thanks for the ride and good luck with that teaching career." As I walked to the office, I prayed that the Lord would bless her life and use her as a loving, godly teacher, to touch the lives of thousands of young people.

In the marina office I got a pleasant surprise, and I knew that it was the hand of God blessing me again. On that particular weekend, there was a special discount offer for twenty-five foot boats that stayed for three nights! It sounded way too coincidental and unbelievable to be true, but yet it was. That made my docking fee just seven dollars per night, instead of the eighteen dollars per night I was planning on. "Thank you Lord," I thought, as I paid the bill, thanked them for their help and headed down the dock smiling with my food and my ice. Tom was glad to see me back, and by five o'clock we were motoring smoothly down the Cooper River toward the historic port of Charleston.

Chapter 21

Scary Dreams and Scarier Situations

It was a calm sunny day, so it was much more pleasant crossing Charleston Harbor this time and I could tell that Tom was enjoying himself. We had to go several miles out into the harbor, almost to Fort Sumter and then turn left into a narrow canal to get back in the Intra Coastal Waterway. We only had four hours until dark that night, so we tried to go as far as we could. We passed a small older power boat that was stopped in the middle of the river. I hailed them and found out that they were dead in the water with motor trouble. The tiny craft contained a young black family with three children life jacketed up to the ears. The dad smiled at me helplessly and the mom looked scared. I quickly made a U-turn and slowed down as I approached them. "Throw us a line and we'll tow you back to your dock," I shouted. I was smiling on the outside to reassure them, but worried inside that their dock wasn't too far away, since there wasn't much daylight left. Even though we hoped to go as far as we could that night, those beaming smiles and relieved, grateful faces made it well worth losing an hour or two to help them. Just as we got close, a large power boat pulled up on the other side and also offered to help. His boat was a much better choice to tow them, with the power to get them to safety before dark, so we allowed him to be the hero. We were glad that they were in good hands and relieved that we could continue on and make a few more miles that night.

It was a clear night so we kept going until it was too dark to see (which proved to be a mistake). We were in a narrow canal, so I thought we could navigate by staying centered between the two shores in the darkness. But with no moon and no lights on shore, it got so black we couldn't see anything. It was too dark to keep moving forward, and the canal was so narrow, it was impossible to anchor there without at least partially blocking the channel. Using the spotlight, I got as close to the left side as I dared and put one anchor off the bow and one anchor off the stern to keep us close to shore. I had a highway trouble light with me that looked like the roof light on an old fashioned police car. It had magnets on the bottom and flashed a powerful yellow light that could be seen for miles in the darkness. I placed it on the highest point of the cabin top, and even though the magnets didn't stick to fiber glass, it seemed secure there. It was the best I could do in that situation, but I still felt like I had parked my "car" in the middle of the highway for the night.

As I lay on my cushion looking up through the open hatch, I worried that a boat load of drunks or a tug pulling barges would plow into us in the dark. Then I worried that we would be fined by the Coast Guard for blocking a shipping lane. I watched nervously as the mast and cables above me were lit by the eerie yellow light of the flasher and then plunged into darkness again. Because I was a nervous wreck, it was even harder to sleep than it normally was in the boat. The flapping of the Christian flag and the clanking of the ropes against the mast kept me awake for quite a while. When I did drift off, it was only for brief periods of fitful restless sleep. I found myself dreaming scary, crazy "Twilight Zone" dreams, as I drifted in and out of consciousness, not fully awake, but not sound asleep either.

I dreamed that I was sleeping in our hotel room in the Embassy Suites, but the hotel was floating down a river and had run aground and become stuck in some trees. Then I dreamed that I was lying there in the boat asleep, yet fully aware that Tom was out on deck steering in his Army uniform. I tossed and turned restlessly as I worried whether or not he was taking the right turns and forks in the river. I became deeply distraught as I saw that he wasn't paying attention and was about to crash into something, so I sat up quickly to warn him, only to find him sound asleep on his berth and the boat still safely anchored. For the rest of that night and the next two nights I had scary dreams like that, and they all seemed way too real. In each one I was asleep on my berth as the boat moved toward Norfolk with no one at the helm or with Tom steering carelessly. Then I would wake with a start just as we were about to crash, run aground, or make a wrong turn.

Even though I hadn't slept much, I was glad when my eyes opened to bright sunlight and blue sky at six thirty. Both anchors were dug in deeply in two opposite directions, so when I tried to pull them up neither one of them budged. That type of anchor was designed to release from the bottom when you were directly over it, so I had to untie one anchor rope from the boat to go get the other one. Then I could come back to grab the end of the loose rope and pull up the one I had untied. I disconnected my bigger anchor first, which proved to be a mistake. It had a fat rope on it that floated on the surface. I tied a boat fender to the end of it so I could pick up that rope again, then I motored over to the smaller anchor and pulled it up. When I came back to pick up the first rope, I forgot that it was floating just under the surface. The current had pushed it toward me and without thinking I motored right over it. Before

I realized what was happening, the heavy rope was tightly wrapped in the propeller stalling out the motor.

"Oh no, I can't believe it, how could I have been so careless," I cried out in total frustration. The motor had been running beautifully, and I hoped that my mistake hadn't destroyed it. Tipping it up and leaning over the side I unwrapped the tightly wound rope from the propeller, praying that the heavy rope had not sheared the pin or damaged the lower unit. To my great relief, it started right up and seemed to push the boat normally when I kicked it into gear. All the noise and confusion woke Tom, and he came outside bleary eyed wondering why I was praising the Lord and making so much noise.

After I pulled and washed the mud from the big anchor, I let Tom steer while I coiled and stowed both anchors and the emergency flasher. As I got out milk, cereal, bowls and juice for breakfast, I realized what a luxury it was to have another person aboard. I could move about the boat freely, doing whatever I needed to, and I didn't have to scramble back to the tiller to keep the boat on course. "Thank you Lord," I prayed, "for keeping us safe at anchor last night and for preventing any damage to the motor. Thank you for the early start, and for allowing me to have this time with my son. Thank you for the joy and freedom of having another person aboard, so I can begin to relax and enjoy this trip. Thank you for the beautiful weather this morning and the calm area we are cruising through right now. Speed us toward our destination; show us the way to go, and keep us safe, In Jesus name I pray, Amen."

It was a beautiful day and we covered a lot of ground smoothly and without incident. Although I steered most of the time, I really enjoyed the freedom of letting Tom take over when I wanted to fix food, use the bathroom or check the charts. As dark approached, we again found ourselves in a narrow canal with no wide area to anchor safely. I wanted to be anchored well before sundown, so we weren't groping in the dark trying to find a safe spot to spend the night. As we approached ICW marker number twenty-four, an idea occurred to me. The marker was mounted on a stout smooth wooden pole sticking up out of the water close to shore. If I could just get a rope around that pole and attach it to my bow ring we would be securely tied up for the night. My bow would point at the pole no matter which way the wind blew, and if I kept the rope short we would be out of the center of the channel and under a flashing light. That would mean not getting out anchors, pulling them up or putting them away in the morning. All we would need to do to get underway the next day was untie one knot and put the motor in gear.

I let Tom steer slowly toward the pole while I stood on the bow with a rope. As we got close I yelled: "kick it into reverse," but was stunned when his hand fumbled with the control lever, taking too long to pop it out of gear. As a result, we headed right at it way too fast! I reached out and pushed off the pole with all my strength, to keep the boat from plowing into it and felt a splinter drive deep into my hand. I breathed a sigh of relief as our starboard side slid past the pole missing it by just a couple of inches. Then I watched in horror, as I realized that the side cable that held up our mast was going to hit the corner of the wooden triangle that was mounted on the pole. "Bang, crack, boom, kersplash," were the noises I heard, as I dove to the deck with my eyes closed, hoping the mast didn't fall on me. I opened them to see Tom laughing hysterically and the large red triangle from ICW marker number twenty four floating face up in the water next to our boat. The force of the taught cable hitting the bottom corner of the triangle had turned it and pulled out the nails that held it to the pole. As it fell, it hit the edge of the deck with a loud boom and then landed in the water. Fortunately, the only damage we sustained was the wood splinter in my hand.

Watching Tom laugh, I realized that it would have been quite funny, if it wasn't such a traumatic experience. As I stared at the big red triangle floating slowly toward shore, I shook my head in disbelief. I knew that we could have popped our mast cable, wrecked the boat and been badly injured if the mast fell.

I decided that it was not a good idea to tie up to an ICW post, so we continued on down the canal. I felt that we could be in big trouble if the authorities knew we had damaged an official Intra Coastal Waterway navigational marker. My first instinct was to keep going and say nothing, since no one else saw what happened and nobody would know that we were the ones that broke it. Then the Lord reminded me that a Christian man had to do the right thing, even when it hurt or was inconvenient, and especially when no one was looking. I also thought about the bad example I would be setting for my son, if I left the scene without reporting the mishap and taking responsibility for my mistake. I reluctantly went to the radio and hailed the Coast Guard on the emergency channel. "This is the sailboat God Speed calling the U.S. Coast Guard," I started. "Come in Coast Guard do you read me?" I said, and then waited for a reply. "This is the United States Coast Guard," answered a confident young voice, "how can I help you?" I told him that we had gotten too close to an ICW marker post and that our mast cable had struck the red triangle, knocking it off the post and into the water. I said that we had no way to retrieve the large sign and that it was floating in the water near shore in the vicinity of that post. I went on to say that it was red marker number twenty four. Without sounding upset, he politely asked for the name of our boat again and our boat registration number. Then he thanked me for reporting the incident, and said that he would give the information to the proper authorities, so the marker could be put back up as soon as possible. I felt greatly relieved that we weren't in any trouble, and a deep sense of satisfaction, knowing I had done the right thing.

A little farther downstream, we came to an area where the canal got really wide and it was still daylight. It was an ideal spot to anchor for the night, so I motored in close to a gravel beach and threw one anchor off the front and one off the back. We were in about eight feet of water and more than a hundred yards outside the flashing red light that marked the edge of the channel so I felt safe there. There were fish splashing and swirling in the shallows, so we tried our luck casting with a couple of lures as it got dark but caught nothing. I put the flashing yellow beacon on top of the cabin and then sprawled out on my cushion, while Tom watched some TV using the headphones. Feeling more relaxed and secure than I had the night before I quickly drifted off to sleep.

Boooaaaawwwwp! I woke with a start and sat up so quickly that I bumped my head on the low ceiling above my berth. I had been awakened by the blast of a ships horn. Popping my head through the open hatch to see what was happening, I gasped in amazement at the unexpected scene around me. The beach was now three hundred yards away and our boat was right in the main shipping channel, close to the flashing red marker that had been so far away when I anchored. An ocean going tug was pushing two barges down the river right past me in the darkness. As I felt the low rumble of its engines and was blinded by the powerful spotlight that was aimed at me, I felt like a fool. The captain had given me a loud blast on his air horn, to warn me that he was going to pass me and that I was adrift where I shouldn't be in the dark.

The tide had come in, and when the water got deeper, both anchors pulled loose. I praised the Lord that I had floated out and not in to the beach and that I had missed drifting right into the marker post with the flashing light on it. I shuddered to think what could have happened if I didn't have my yellow flasher on and that tug captain didn't see us in time. If the tug hadn't come along and woke me when it did, I could have drifted anywhere while I slept, even across the channel into the docks and expensive boats on the other side of the river. Rousing Tom from a deep sleep we pulled the anchors aboard and went back in to the beach where we anchored again, this time in more shallow water. I was pretty sure we would stay put now, but as we re-anchored in the strong current, the floating anchor rope got under the boat again and became wrapped around the rudder. It was very frustrating, but at that moment I was too tired to deal with it. I decided to wait until morning and untangle the ropes when I brought the anchors up to get underway.

When my eyes opened again it was still dark. I tried to relax and fall back to sleep, but my active mind wouldn't let me. My watch told me it was after five, so I began to weigh the facts. It would be light in an hour and it would probably take that long to straighten out the anchor ropes and get the anchors aboard. There was a strong current flowing in the direction we were headed and there was no wind and no boat traffic. If I got up now and got started, Tom could sleep in. When he did wake up, we would be many miles down river and he could take over steering while I fixed breakfast or maybe even took a nap. Dressing quickly I went up on deck to begin the difficult chore of getting the anchors aboard.

The fat, floating anchor rope appeared to be wrapped around the rudder, as it stretched from the anchor to a point under the back of the boat, even though it was tied to the bow. I untied it from the bow ring and tied a floating boat fender to that end instead. That way I would not lose my big anchor if the rope came free from the boats underside. Reaching into the water with the boat hook, I grabbed the tightly stretched rope that was coming from the anchor and then dropped the end of the rope with the fender attached into the water. As I pulled on the "anchor" end of the rope, the floating fender was pulled toward the back of the boat and then underwater as the rope unwrapped itself from the rudder. I expected the rope to keep coming until the fender went around the rudder and came out, but it pulled only so far and then stopped. I pulled and jerked on the rope as hard as I could, but it would not budge another inch. The fender and rope were caught on something underneath the boat and the only way to get them free was to get into the water.

Donning a life vest and getting out the swim ladder, I prepared to go underneath the boat. As I hung the lightweight low budget swim ladder over the side, I swallowed hard as the powerful current picked it up and almost lifted it off the boat and swept it away. That's a lot of current down there, I thought. If the ladder comes unhooked from the boat or I lose my grip on it I will be swept away so quickly that I might be a mile from the boat in a matter of minutes. Since Tom was asleep in the cabin, he wouldn't even know I was gone for several hours, so I put a safety line over the side to hold on to while I was in the water. Once in the water it was hard to move as the rushing current pushed against me, lifting one side of the swim ladder up from the boat even with my weight on it. Hanging on to the motor for dear life, I wrapped both legs around the rudder as I felt for the rope with my free hand. The husky rope was wedged in the narrow slot between the steering rudder and the back of the keel. The weight of the boat in the current and the floating fender had pulled the rope all the way to the top of the slot and right against the boats bottom. On one end of the rope was the anchor, dug into the bottom by two tons of sailboat being pushed by the current, and on the other end was the floating fender, pulled tightly against the other side of the slot by the same weight and force. I needed to somehow push the rope and fender all the way to the bottom of the slot to free them, but feared that only superman would be able to budge them with that much force pulling on the rope.

To make matters worse, the steering rudder was turned sharply to the left pinching the rope even tighter in the slot. I had to climb back up the ladder and get aboard to straighten the tiller handle, and then bungee it in place to widen the slot. Then I had to climb back down into the current (in the dark) to try to free the fender and rope. Back in the water again, I pushed and pulled at the fender with all my strength but could barely move it. Before giving up, I tried one last idea. Using the motor, the motor bracket and the safety rope, I was able to pull myself up into a position where I was actually standing on the fender and rope with both feet, one on either side of the rudder. With both hands against the motor bracket, I used my entire body like a coiled spring, pushing down with my legs, my back and my arm muscles with all the strength I could muster. To my surprise, I felt the rope move downward in the slot and heard a thump as the fender came free, bumped along the bottom of the boat and then bobbed to the surface. I smiled as it raced away from me because the back of the boat now free from the anchor, pulled away as it turned quickly in the current. Dripping wet on deck, I praised the Lord as I put the swim ladder away and pulled and stowed the smaller anchor. Starting the motor, I went after the fender to bring the large anchor aboard. After what happened the previous day, I was careful to approach it so the floating rope could not get underneath the boat. Once the big anchor was aboard and the thick rope neatly coiled, I changed into some dry clothes. Soon I was making my way down the river, just as the golden rim of the sun began to show itself above the trees.

Voyage of the Heart

Chapter 22

Monster from the River Bottom

It was probably the best weather day we had so far. The absence of any wind left the water glassy calm, and the only boats I saw that early were the couple of crab fishermen I passed. "God Speed" slipped effortlessly through the silver green water and I took in the scenery as the rising sun brightened the world around me. I enjoyed the coziness of a dry sweatshirt and the sweetness of an orange, and I reflected once again on how precious the "little things" in life were, after coming through a series of traumatic events. As the day wore on, we made our way through tree lined rivers where the mangrove roots had been exposed by the rising and falling of the tide. It was interesting to see the unique shapes of the gnarled wooden fingers as they clung to the banks, or twisted their way grotesquely into the water. We cruised through forests, then upscale residential areas, passing beautiful homes and condos with large yachts as we made our way toward the outer banks. By midday we were in North Carolina and found ourselves to be part of a steady parade of boat traffic in both directions. People in other vessels, on shore, and on their docks waved politely as we passed. A few gave us a "thumbs up" sign, and one man even pointed heavenward, nodding with a big smile when he saw our boat name. When I asked for passage at a pontoon bridge, a sweet older man with a gentle voice responded very respectfully. After opening the bridge, he actually came out on the dock, winked at me and then saluted us as we passed the bridge house. I smiled and waved enthusiastically as I thanked him and shouted a hearty "God bless you."

That afternoon we stopped for gas and ice at an upscale marina, and I was happy to learn that we were now in fresh water. Trying to keep things fun for Tom, I bought some night crawlers and frozen shrimp so he could fish when we were safely anchored for the night. I caught myself smiling as I thought: "Is there really such a thing, as being "safely" anchored for the night?"

A nice young man named Doug who worked at the marina, helped us get fuel, bait and ice. Talking to him as he filled our tanks, I learned that the burly, blonde college student had played some high school football. He insisted on carrying both full tanks down the long dock and back to our boat himself, so we let him. As he handed them aboard I complimented him on his eagerness to help us and his respectful attitude. I told him that I sensed he was a Christian, because he was so considerate and had a servant's heart. He admitted that he didn't attend church much, so I encouraged him to really get to know God, and handed him a couple of tracts. I told him that I knew many Christians who attended church regularly that did not have the same willingness to serve others that he did. I said that the Lord would bless his life, and use a strong young man like himself to do many great things. I thanked him as I shook his hand, and said "God bless you Doug," as he untied our ropes and helped us push away from the dock.

As darkness approached, I found a wide spot in the narrow canal and anchored outside of the main channel close to some cattails. I promised myself that I would throw both anchors off the bow from now on, because I had so much trouble bringing up anchors that were off in two different directions. Tom was eager to try his luck fishing, so he lowered a hook covered with night crawlers to the bottom as soon as we were stopped. Knowing that we were in a muddy, fresh water river in the south, my instincts told me he might catch catfish, bullheads, or carp. To increase his chances of catching something, I took a zip lock bag full of whole kernel corn out of the ice box, and dumped its contents over the side to attract bottom feeders. He got a bite right away, bringing a nice channel catfish aboard and I congratulated him for catching something so fast. I showed him how to handle and unhook it as we admired the size and long whiskers of the fat, sleek gray brown fish. Telling him I would clean it in the morning and we could have fresh fish for breakfast, I put it on a rope over the side to keep it alive. To my amazement, he caught another one just like it as soon as he put a worm back in the water. He was having so much fun he resigned himself to stay up all night fishing. I was an avid fisherman, but after being in the water at five AM and cruising all day, the softness of my pillow sounded more appealing than catching catfish, so I said good night to Tom and lay down inside the cabin.

Several hours later, I was startled out of a deep sleep by the sound of Tom's voice shouting loudly from the deck. "Dad, I've got something huge," he yelled frantically, "I need your help!" Running barefoot up on deck in my underwear, I saw that his rod was bent double and looked like it was about to snap. He said he had been hooked to something enormous for ten minutes, but couldn't get it up off the bottom. I watched as he cranked in several feet of line, only to have the gigantic "thing" on the other end sizzle his line back out much faster than he gained it. All he could do was hang on and hope the line didn't break, before this "monster" from the river bottom got tired and he could bring it up. I plugged in the spotlight and shone it into the water hoping to get a glimpse of his opponent, but the canal was so muddy, the powerful beam only penetrated a few inches below the surface. After what seemed like forever, he began to gain some line until finally we both gasped in amazement, as the biggest catfish we had ever seen became visible in the murky water below. "I can't believe it," I shouted. "I didn't know they got that big," Tom yelled, as we watched the huge shiny body writhe and roll beneath us in the beam of the spotlight. It was so big that when it splashed below us it sprayed us with water and we laughed when I said; "I'm not sure if I want that thing getting in the boat with me!"

As soon as I said that, I realized we had no way to get the huge fish aboard. I brought two lightweight, take apart fishing poles with us, but limited storage space didn't allow me to bring a landing net. I had to either climb down the swim ladder and grab it, or think of something else fast. I didn't have a gaff, but I did have the long handled aluminum boat hook that I used for coming into a dock. If I waited until the fish was really tired, maybe I could slip the rubber tipped boat hook behind the gill plate and lift it out of the water the same way I held a big fish with a finger hooked up inside the gill. It took many tries and a lot of patience, because the slippery gills of a catfish are close to the body. But, eventually, I was able to get the hook behind the gill plate, and then it took both of us to lift it straight up and into the boat. We stood there in awe looking at the slippery brown body of our "leviathan" as it lay on its stomach breathing heavily and taking in its new surroundings. We laughed, as we realized that it took up almost the whole cockpit floor, reminding us of the giant fish from the movie "Big Fish". Knowing that we could never use that much meat, and not having the heart to kill something that big and that old, we decided to keep it alive until morning so we could take pictures of it in bright sunlight and then release it. I carefully fished a sailing rope into the mouth and out one of the gills. Then I tied a large, loose loop in the rope so it could move freely and breathe normally. Lowering it gently into the water, I tried not to let its massive weight on the rope rip its gills or mouth. We watched it swim strongly next to the boat, even after being out of the water so long, and I was glad that the Lord designed those creatures to be so durable.

The next morning I awoke to brilliant sunshine and a beautiful blue sky. My first thought was that I had dreamed the whole episode with the giant fish, but one look over the side told me that it had all been real. The biggest catfish I had ever seen in person was still swimming normally on its rope. Looking even bigger and more impressive in daylight, it seemed big enough to tow the boat if I brought up the anchors. All five of its' smaller cousins on the other rope were also still alive and well. As I feared, trying to wake up Tom after he fished most of the night was like trying to wake the dead. After pushing, pulling and prodding him for several minutes, I somehow got him to stand erect. We shot a whole roll of film showing both of us posing with the smaller fish and the "monster". I really wanted to preserve that memory, and be able to show other people how big it really was. I talked Tom into releasing them all, since they were still alive. We agreed that it was a good idea, since it was so hot and we didn't really have a good way to clean things up and wash away the smell of fish guts. When we released them, I was happy that they all swam away normally and seemed to be fine. Praising the Lord that I could share an experience like that with my son, and thanking him for the beautiful day, I pulled the anchors and got underway while Tom went back to sleep. The bright morning sunlight helped me feel positive and I relaxed, knowing that I only needed to cover sixty miles each day to reach Norfolk on schedule.

CHAPTER 23

Twice Aground in Two Days

Everything went well that morning. So well that I began to feel that things were too good to be true, until I remembered who I was sailing for. I approached a bridge at eight fifteen that was scheduled to open on the hour and I thought I would have to wait for forty-five minutes. But to my surprise, it opened as I approached without me having to say a word, as though it had been waiting for me. I hit the next bridge at exactly nine o'clock just as it was opening for other boats that had been waiting. Then I arrived at yet another bridge just before the top of the hour as it too was preparing to open. I was so elated that I used God's perfect timing as a way to witness to the third bridge operator. "Thanks for opening," I began, "The good Lord's really been with me today!" "This is the third bridge in a row that was opening just as I approached it", I stated honestly. Then I left him with: "Well, God bless ya and have a good day now."

You may think I'm a little crazy, fanatical, or over zealous, but I firmly believe there is nothing the enemy hates more, than someone openly witnessing to other people with a heart filled with joy and faith. I also believe that when he hears someone doing that, he will rush in to knock you down, steal that joy and cause something to happen that could shatter that child like faith. To put it in sailing terms: Just when you're "sailing along" with your "sails" filled with the joy and fresh "wind" of the Holy Spirit, Satan loves to make something happen that takes the wind out of your sails, and leaves you dead in the water wondering if God is really there at all. With that in mind, read on to see what happened as I approached the next bridge.

For the fourth time in a row, I was approaching a bridge just as it was preparing to open, and the bridge operator had already given me the word to keep coming and she would open for me. As I got within fifty yards of the bridge, a loud electronic voice crackled through the radio saying: "Surf City Bridge, Surf City Bridge, we are a north bound vessel about a mile from you and closing fast. Would it be possible for you to delay your twelve O'clock opening for a few minutes until we get there?" It was the captain of another boat coming behind me, asking the bridge operator to wait for them to get there before she opened. "C'mon along, captain, we'll wait for you," replied the bridge operator. It was no problem for me to wait a few minutes, since I had been making great time, and I would have wanted the bridge operator to do the same for me, if I was still a mile away. I would make a couple of circles in front of the bridge to kill time until the other boat got there. Then we could both pass through the bridge together and be on our way.

I should have circled to my right and into the center of the channel, but the river was wide there, so I circled to my left and toward the shoreline so I didn't block the entrance to the bridge. My depth alarm began to beep wildly and Tom yelled: "five feet, four feet, three feet!" Before I could even react or turn, the boat stopped moving forward and I felt the heavy immovable weight of the tiller in my hand, telling me the rudder was buried in the bottom. "Sailboat God Speed are you stuck?" came the voice of the bridge operator over the radio. "Yes ma'am, I believe I am," was my sad reply. "I wish I had seen what you were doing sooner," she said regretfully. "Everything on your side of the bridge is good deep water, except for a shallow area on the left side of the river where you are now. "Thank you," I replied. "I guess I still have to get used to the idea that wide water doesn't always mean deep water," I told her, trying not to sound as disappointed as I felt.

Gunning the motor to full speed in both forward and reverse, I tried to rock the boat free, but it would not budge, in fact I may have got myself in deeper. To add insult to injury, the large power cruiser that I circled to wait for now appeared, motoring smoothly toward the bridge which began to open as it approached. I hailed the captain on the radio to ask if they would be willing to pull me out if I threw them a line. The woman at the helm responded that they were on a tight schedule and did not want to miss this bridge opening, since the operator had waited for them. She said they would motor right by me as fast as possible as they headed for the bridge. That would send a series of big waves my way. If I gunned my motor right when the waves bounced me up and down, I might come free. As they sped by, I realized that their cruiser didn't produce the same type of waves as the ones that tossed me so violently last week. Although I lifted and rocked for a few seconds, and revved the motor to a high pitched whine, I was still stuck. I was disappointed that the people aboard that boat weren't willing to stop to help me. I was sure they could have pulled me free with that much power and I knew that if our roles were reversed I would have missed the bridge opening to help them.

I sadly resigned myself to wait for the tide, and accepted the fact that I had just gone from too good to be true, to hopelessly behind schedule. Right then, as if on cue, a very average looking couple pulled up in a small, older power boat and asked if we needed help. If they were angels the Lord sent our way, he certainly disguised them well. Short, dark and overweight, they were dressed in out of style clothing, and I was sure that their humble runabout cost less than the small life boat suspended from the back of the yacht that just passed me. They sat there proudly smiling up at me from their low budget vessel with the flaking paint, ready, willing and eager to help.

When I answered that we did need help, the man said they were new to boating, but they would try to help us. Without hesitation, they swung around and came toward us, like the cavalry coming to the rescue in an old western. Before I realized where they were going, they motored between us and the shore and right into shallow water. As I cried out to warn them their boat slowed to a stop. I groaned as their old style outboard tilted up and began to spew mud, as they too became stuck in the shallows. Now I really felt bad, not only had I gotten our boat stuck, but I also caused someone else to be stranded in the shallows.

The man at the wheel gunned the throttle forward and backward and raised his propeller almost out of the water attempting to rock the boat free. As their motor churned the water into chocolate milk, the older boat slowly began to move forward and somehow the skipper was able to steer his way through the mud and back into deep water. "Come around to the front and I'll throw you a rope," I yelled, happy that at least they were now free.

Connecting two of my longest ropes together, I tied one end to my bow ring and tossed them the other end. After making it fast to his stern the man pulled forward slowly, tightening the rope and then revved his engine. The back of the powerboat swayed back and forth, but it stayed put as the motor roared and boiled the muddy water behind it. Tom and I stood on the outermost point of the port deck, leaning out as far as we could. We hoped that by tipping the sailboat to one side, we would lift the keel out of the mud a little, so it didn't dig in as we were being pulled forward. As we leaned the boat to port and rocked it up and down I felt us begin to move forward, slowly at first and then much faster as the man steered for deep water. In a matter of seconds I was praising the Lord as we came free from the bottom and were moving rapidly behind the powerboat. The man said that he was new to boating, and what happened next told me that he didn't know anything about sailboats. When he saw that we were free he came to a sudden and complete stop, not knowing that once in motion a sailboat will keep gliding through the water for quite a distance. As he turned with a smile to give us a thumbs up, his expression changed to one of panic, as he realized that *we* were still moving rapidly forward, and that our much larger boat was about to plow into the back of his. I could have steered to avoid them, but we were tied to their boat with a rope so I had to act fast. My only hope was to use my body as a shock absorber between the boats, pushing off with my feet and leg muscles as hard as I could to lessen the impact of a collision that could damage both vessels.

Diving to the bow, I wrapped my arms around the bow pulpit, held on for dear life and braced myself for the impact, determined to protect both boats from damage. I reached out for his boat with both feet and as they touched I let my knees bend and then straightened them as I pushed off with all the strength I could summon from my fifty-two year old body. "Lord, help me," I cried, as I felt the force of two tons of fiberglass bending my knees and back. I tried to push off with all my might, but I could feel that there was too much force for me to stop the boats from colliding with my body. I pulled my legs in at the last instant to protect them, but God was with us even in that frantic ordeal. Apparently his hand and my all out adrenalin charged effort took most of the force out of the impact, and my boat hit the other one gently and with a glancing blow. Miraculously the light collision didn't leave a mark on the polished bow of the "God Speed" and had no effect on the "fixer upper" power boat. "Thank You Lord," I sighed, as I thanked the couple for their help. I went below to grab a tract to give them, planning to pull along side, shake their hands and thank them properly. But when I came out, I was sad to see that they had already untied my rope, and were waving goodbye with a smile as they motored away.

As I watched the older couple disappear, I thought about how they had been the good Samaritans. Those who had so little, were willing to offer their time and humble boat to help, while those who had so much, had hurried past to make a bridge opening and stay on schedule. "Lord, bless that good hearted couple," I prayed. "Give them great joy and fond memories of times spent together in their boat. Lord, I pray that I will never get caught up in my schedule and my possessions, to the point where I would not be willing to drop everything to help someone in need. Thank you for sending help so quickly and allowing us to be floating free with no damage. Speed us on our way and travel with us the rest of this day, Amen."

After seeing the whole ordeal, the bridge operator was sympathetic to our situation and offered to open for us on the half hour. That took some of the sting out of getting stuck, and soon I had forgotten all about that minor inconvenience as we cruised smoothly along making great time on an otherwise perfect day. After driving the boat for thirteen straight days, I took advantage of the fact that Tom wanted to steer for a while. Bringing a cushion and pillows forward I sprawled comfortably on the fore deck with my back propped against the cabin front and my head cushioned by the cozy softness of the pillows. For a few hours I was in "heaven" as I relaxed completely, listening to the hum of the motor and the splash of the bow wave beneath me.

I may have looked foolish in my straw hat and "old school" sunglasses, but I felt like King Tut cruising on his royal barge. The boat sliced effortlessly through the water and the peace that passes all understanding filled me, as I was treated to a new and different scene around each bend of the river.

As evening approached, Tom began to complain about the sunburn on his shoulders and legs. I could tell by his grumpiness that several days of confinement in a small boat, not sleeping well and the relentless summer heat of the Carolinas was starting to take its toll on him. I decided that we would push hard until it was almost dark, and then spend the money to stay at a marina that night. We badly needed to walk around on land, take a shower and get a good nights sleep. The porta potty hadn't been dumped since Charleston and was starting to smell, and so was the large bag of garbage we had accumulated. We needed gas, ice, cold drinks and bait, but most of all we needed a break and a chance to start fresh in the morning, feeling rested, refreshed and positive.

My guidebook showed that there were two marinas ahead, so I got on the radio and did some comparison shopping to get the best price for a dock spot for the night. The first one I called sounded pretty upscale, and the woman got impatient with me when I hesitated to take the slip after hearing the price. The second one sounded more basic and the price was reasonable, so I took it and got directions from a man with a down home southern accent. A pleasant dark haired girl and a tall young man helped us come in to a weather beaten floating dock that ran parallel to the main river. After we were tied up I went to the office to pay for our stay, while Tom went to find the showers. On a porch outside the office, a large parrot was using its beak and gnarled feet to climb a rope. The striking bird with its brilliant red plumage looked like it had flown out of the pages of an adventure novel about pirates on the high seas. Once inside I learned that the birds name was Jasper, and that he was the pet of the marina owner. That down to earth marina catered mainly to fishing boats. The main building was like a giant "toy store" for fishermen, filled with enough mounted fish, rods, reels and tackle to excite even the most serious, well equipped angler.

After paying for our stay, I bought some cold drinks and ice, and also got permission to freeze two large jugs of water in their freezer overnight. I was happy to see that the marina had a canopy and gas pumps out front for cars. Large boats with built in tanks had to pull up to the gas dock and pay "marina" prices, but I could carry my small portable tanks to the self serve pumps and fill them for far less money. It was a long carry, but the savings was worth it, and I felt that this was one more way the Lord blessed us. After stowing the tanks, I threw our garbage in the dumpster, then I dumped and rinsed out the porta potty. Trying hard to make the trip more enjoyable for Tom, I planned a full sit down dinner using whatever we had aboard. Feeling refreshed and invigorated after a cool shower, I set to work to prepare a "feast". I opened the cabin top, set up the dining table and lit the propane stove. Even though we were tied to a grungy dock among beat up fishing boats, I tried to make things as appealing and appetizing as possible. We feasted on hamburgers, chips and carrot sticks in the boats cozy interior as we laughed and joked about the mishaps of the past few days. Dessert was Reese's Peanut Butter Cups and as I watched Tom inhale them, I was pleased to see that he was starting to enjoy the adventure of traveling and camping in the boat.

After dinner, Tom fished off the dock under a light, while I struck up a conversation with two men who were working on a fishing boat on the next dock. I told them about our trip and how the Lord had blessed us and brought us through some scary situations. They were friendly and seemed to be interested in what I said as they shared their plans for refurbishing their large vessel. Finding out that they were avid fishermen and hunters, I gave them brochures describing my videos and some tracts that featured famous hunters and fishermen. Wishing them good luck with their project and voicing a sincere "God bless you" I turned in at about ten o'clock, hoping to get an early start the next morning.

My eyes popped open at six and I was instantly wide awake. Retrieving the frozen water jugs from the marina freezer I cast off all lines and was pulling away from the dock just as it got light enough to steer. As I motored slowly northward in the pre dawn light, the calm silvery water stretched before me like a mirror, reflecting the fading moon. I smiled inwardly with a deep sense of satisfaction as hints of deep blue and warm pink began to appear in the east. As I thought about what a great start we were getting and how many miles we could make on such a perfect day I lifted my free hand skyward to thank the Lord as my heart filled with joy. Just as the first words of praise came from my lips, the boat hit something and stopped moving so suddenly I lost my balance and almost fell to the deck. The outboard raced as it tilted up and the propeller came out of the water for a second. Then it went back down and began spewing mud. Startled by the impact and the noise, I cried out in shock as I tried to figure out what had happened.

"I couldn't have hit anything, I'm right in the center of the channel," I thought, looking quickly at the marker buoys. Then my heart sank as I realized what I had done. There was a little green buoy just twenty feet to my left. That small floating marker indicated the right side of the channel. As I praised the Lord in the dim light before sunrise, I hadn't seen it and had passed to the right of it. The depth alarm would have saved me, but in my eagerness to get underway, I rushed away from the dock without checking to make sure that it was turned on. "I can't believe this happened," I thought, shaking my head in disbelief and fighting back tears of disappointment. It was almost as if the enemy heard me passionately praising the Lord and said: "Oh yeah! Lets see how long you praise him if I stop you right there, just ten minutes out of the marina, take that."

I tried to back up, but could not budge and when I tried to go forward; the rudder buried itself and wouldn't turn at all. Tom woke up and came out on deck shaking his head. Checking the tide chart he reported that it was going to get shallower for the next three hours. This was serious, if we didn't get free right away, not only would we be stuck there for eight hours, but at low tide the boat would be laying on its side on dry land! In desperation I called the marina to ask for help. I noticed several fishermen in the office when I got the water jugs. They were having coffee and swapping stories as they shared their plans for the day. I asked the manager if one of them could stop to pull us free, as they headed out for their day on the water. "Sorry Cap'n," came a curt reply, "we can't control any of the fishing boats, or interfere with their schedules." He suggested that I call "Sea Tow" or "Boat USA" and asked if I was a member of "Boat USA". He then went on to say that if I was, free towing was one of my membership benefits. "Thank you," I answered quietly, with my heart in my shoes as I hung up the microphone.

Just then a large powerboat came toward us at high speed. I waved my arms frantically, hoping they would see our predicament and stop to help, but they flew right by without even looking our way. When the big waves produced by the speeding boat hit us, our boat lifted up as it rocked and rolled to one side. Seeing an opportunity, I gunned the motor to full speed as I yelled to Tom to jump up and down on the outer edge of the deck. I also put all of my weight on the starboard side, hoping to tip the boat as much as possible. The combined lifting and tipping forces of the waves and our bodies must have brought the keel up just enough because we began to move slowly forward. "Rock her as much as you can while we have the waves!" I yelled to Tom as I steered for deep water. Keeping the motor revved to full throttle I felt the tiller move and jerk in my hand as the rudder dragged on the muddy bottom. "C'mon baby, just a few more feet and we'll be free!" I cried. "Please Lord, keep us moving forward," I pleaded, shouting to Tom to keep jumping up and down. As we inched forward I imagined that there were two angels in the sky ahead, pulling us with golden ropes, while two more stood in the water behind us and pushed.

With a sudden lurch, the boat righted itself and sped up as the keel pulled out of the mud. I could feel that the rudder was now free as I steered for the center of the channel shouting praises with all my heart. As I slowed the motor and corrected our course a red sliver of sun was just visible above the horizon, lighting the hillsides to the west. We were approaching a bend in the river, and as I lifted my eyes to the hills I gasped, when I saw what was right in my face at that moment. Directly ahead of me, on a hillside where it could be seen for miles, stood a huge white cross that had to be thirty feet tall. As it was lit by the first rays of the morning sun, it shone out across the valley with an almost heavenly glow. I began to weep, as the words from a Psalm came to mind: " . . . I will lift up my eyes to the hills - where does my help come from? My help comes from the Lord, the maker of heaven and earth." He had helped me again, and I believe that cross was his way of reminding me that he was always there, no matter what the enemy sent my way.

"Thank you Father," I whispered. "Thank you Lord, for yet another reminder that you are always with me." As I motored toward the distant hills with the rising sun warming my shoulders, I thought about other verses that remind us of his presence:

> ***...Do not be afraid, but be strong and have courage, for the Lord your God goes with you...I will never leave you nor forsake you; lo I am with you always, even unto the end of the age...***
>
> ***(KJV)***

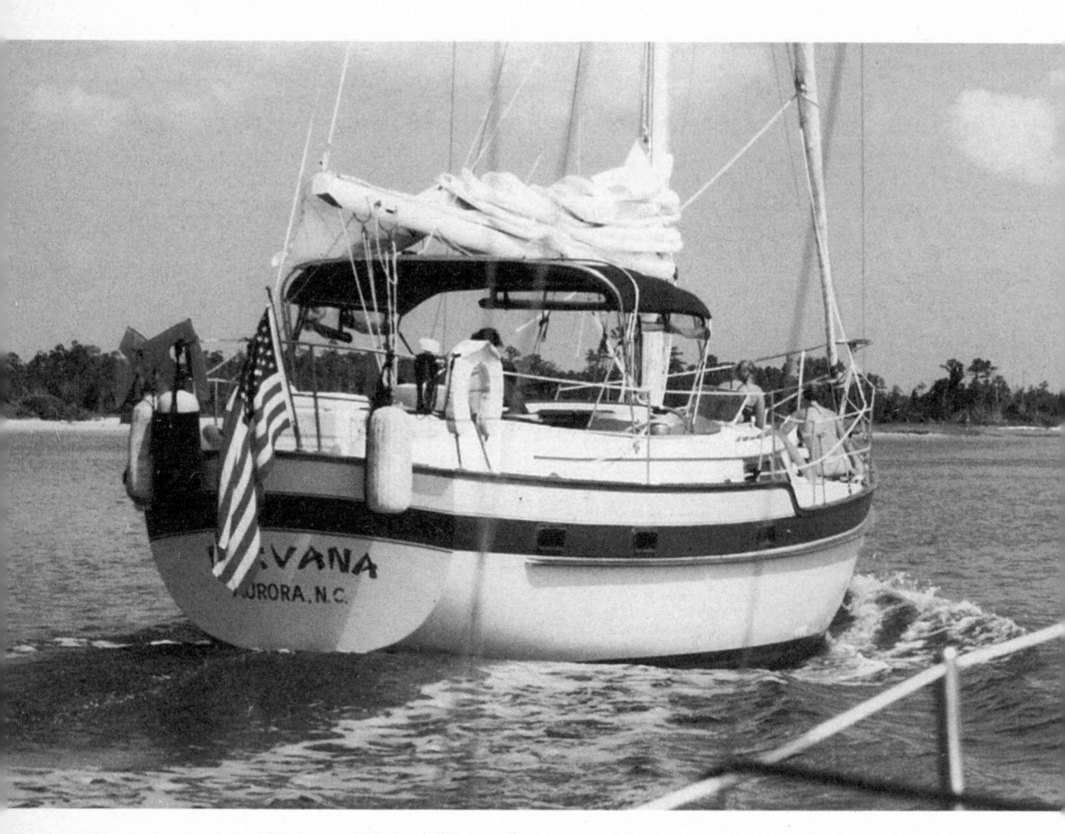
VANA
URORA, N.C.

Chapter 24

A Three Hour Tour

Morehead City, North Carolina, was a small industrial city with a busy active harbor, located on the Intra Coastal Waterway. It was a port of call for ocean going cargo ships and tug boats pulling barges. I was surprised by how much boat traffic we encountered there, and by how many fishing trawlers and pleasure yachts called the small harbor their home port. As we reached an intersection where waterways went in all directions, it was hard to tell which fork in the river to take. Without my charts I would have been lost, and even with them I needed to ask directions to make sure we were going the right way. A man and a woman fishing from a skiff pointed toward an open railroad bridge to indicate the ICW northbound. I thanked them and asked if they had caught anything. Grinning proudly the man held up a small flounder that had been dead for a while. Nodding approvingly, I thanked them again and called out a hearty "God bless you" as I motored away in the direction they had pointed.

The route was harder to follow now. Thin winding rivers, had given way to wide, shallow areas, where the deep channel was not well marked, and other rivers branched off in all directions. Every so often the river would split to go around an island and then come back together again farther upstream. The fact that the tide was going out, made that stretch even more shallow and harder to navigate. At one point we came upon a huge power yacht that had taken a wrong turn and run aground. Now at low tide, it looked sadly absurd parked there almost on dry land. I smiled, as I watched the children from that expensive vessel, wading, splashing and tossing a football as they played around it in ankle deep water. I could see that the adults on board were embarrassed and disgruntled as they sat in lounge chairs waiting for the tide to come back. I felt sorry for them, but that sight helped to heal my wounded confidence. I didn't feel as foolish having run aground three times, now that I saw that it happened to the biggest, most impressive boats on the waterway.

A few hours later, a beautiful sailing yacht named "Nirvana" caught up to us, and slowly passed us in the narrow channel. There was a woman at the wheel and several pre teen girls aboard who appeared to be having a great time. The woman smiled and the giggling girls waved eagerly from their life jackets as Tom and I returned their waves. I was pleased that the large sailing vessel was ahead of us, and I wanted to believe that the Lord had sent an "advance scout" to guide us through that treacherous area. I knew that a sailboat that size had a keel that went deeper than ours. Wherever "Nirvana" went, we could also go with room to spare. By following directly behind her, I was able to stay in the deepest water. At first I wasn't sure that it was God's hand that sent "Nirvana" to lead us, but after the next incident I was almost positive that it was.

The bigger boat was able to maintain a faster cruising speed than we were, so she gradually got farther and farther ahead of us. After an hour or so, she was about to go out of sight around a bend. Just then a group of dolphins appeared, swimming alongside "Nirvana" and the woman brought her boat to a stop so the girls could watch and photograph the playful creatures. She stayed there long enough for us to catch up to them. As we approached, the girls were still eagerly pointing and snapping pictures and the Good Lord had given us another hour of being able to follow our "guide". By the time we finally lost sight of "Nirvana", we were well beyond that shallow stretch, and the tide was coming in again.

The rest of the day went pretty well, but we lost some time and had a disagreement crossing a large sound with the compass. I made a miscalculation and figured the heading wrong. Tom tried to show me my mistake and give me the right heading, but I didn't believe that he was correct. I stubbornly went the wrong way for an hour, until it became apparent that I was off course and he was right. My stubbornness cost us two hours of daylight, and a back track of seven miles. Tom spent the next two days reminding me of my mistake, and saying that I should have listened to him. To this day I still feel bad about the incident, as I remember the verse that says not to exasperate your children. Tom has never forgotten about that time when he was right and I wouldn't listen, and he reminds me of it often.

That night we anchored among the crab pot buoys in a small swampy bay just off the main river. Dinner was Ramen noodles and hamburgers. After dinner, Tom did push ups on the cabin floor and then fished on deck in the moonlight, while I watched a little TV before turning in. Before going to bed, he baited both poles with shrimp and left the baits on the bottom during the night. He was hoping to find a big fish on one of the lines in the morning. We awoke to find both lines leading off into the swamp. When he reeled them in, we saw that the bait and all tackle was gone from both rigs, and the lines were cut off as cleanly as if they had been snipped with a scissors. We were both puzzled as we wondered what kind of underwater creature had cut the lines, but I was glad that it was gone.

The Good Lord gave us another early start on that calm windless morning. That allowed me to cross a large sound at daybreak while the water was still glassy smooth. I cruised easily on the still waters, saying my morning prayers while Tom slept. As the sun rose higher, I praised the Lord for the cloud cover that protected me and the slight breeze that kept me comfortable. As noon approached I remembered that I hadn't filled the fuel tanks in a while, and when I checked them I realized that one was empty and the other was quite low. We were entering a narrow land cut that ran through uninhabited forest land and swamps. My guide book said there were no marinas ahead, so I was thrilled when I saw a sign for one, and I called them to get some directions. To my dismay, I learned that we had passed that marina an hour ago and that it was seven miles behind us. If I turned back, I would be giving up twenty one miles of distance. I would lose the seven miles I had gained since I passed the marina. Then I would go seven miles in the wrong direction to get back there. After refueling, I would still need to go seven more miles just to get back to the point where I was. Figuring in the time it would take to tie up, fill the tanks and get going again, I knew that it would be at least three hours before I could hope to get back to that point. I asked the marina if they could deliver some gas to us with a boat. They said that would be fifty dollars, plus the cost of the gas, and they couldn't get to us for at least an hour.

I weighed my options carefully, knowing that if I gambled on finding a back country marina ahead, and ran out of gas, I would lose a lot more than three hours. Then I thought about what being towed would cost, so I reluctantly swung my bow around, increased my speed to full throttle and set off toward the marina. Upset with myself for an oversight that would waste fuel, mileage and time, I shook my head as I tried to understand how this happened, and vowed that it would not happen again. It occurred to me that God wanted us to stop at that marina for a reason, and maybe I had missed an important stop on his schedule. I resigned myself to the fact that I had to take this "three hour tour" and began to hum the theme music to "Gilligan's Island" as I sped along, trying to get back to the marina as quickly as possible.

Motoring through an opening in a crumbling break wall, I headed for the Texaco sign that marked the gas dock of the small marina. The high dock was crooked and the weathered boards were warped and rotting. As we approached, a pleasant young black man came out on the dock to help us come in and get tied up. He introduced himself as Charles, the dock master, and said that he would be happy to help us with whatever we needed. Since we were there anyway, I decided to make the most of a marina stop, so we could push for quite a distance before we had to stop again. After filling the tanks, Tom and I used the boaters shower and then I asked if there was a "Radio Shack" store nearby, where I could purchase more minutes for my cell phone. Charles gave me directions and allowed me to use the marina's golf cart to drive to the business district of the small town. Down the street I passed another marina that was closed and boarded up. Although it was abandoned, I thought to myself that it was in better shape than the one where our boat was. As I motored down the waterfront streets of that village, I felt like I was taking a trip backwards through time. The weathered bay front homes were humble yet stately, silently looking out over the water as they had done for generations. The quaint streets reminded me very much of Mayberry in the old TV show. I almost expected to see Andy and Opie come around the corner whistling, with fishing poles slung over their shoulders and Aunt Bea waving from a nearby porch.

As I pulled up in front of the local hardware store, no one seemed surprised to see a golf cart on Main Street. One look at the store told me it wasn't a "Radio Shack", and I sensed they didn't sell minutes for cell phones. When I asked inside, I found out that

I had sensed right, so I hopped in the golf cart and headed back to the marina, wondering what Charles was thinking when he sent me there.

The marina was located on the grounds of an old style hotel, and both facilities seemed to be part of one jointly owned operation. A sign told me that the hotel lobby was also the marina office, so I parked next to the large Victorian structure and went inside to pay my bill. The sprawling white building looked like it had been a waterfront mansion in the old south, which was converted into a hotel sometime after the Civil War. I could tell by the peeling paint and loose boards on the porch that the grand old house was no longer what it was in the days of Rhett Butler and Scarlet O'Hara. In the musty smelling lobby, a dirty glass chandelier hung over a spiral staircase with an ornate wooden banister that must have been beautiful in its day. The dusty velvet draperies, antique woodwork and ante bellum furniture were relics of a time and a culture that no longer existed. When I rang the bell a heavy set black woman appeared, wearing an ill fitting satin dress. I felt sympathy for the small town woman, whose clothing, makeup and jewelry made her look as outdated as her surroundings. I sensed that the hotel didn't host many people from outside the area, so I tried to think of something nice to say. Trying to be as polite as possible, I complimented her on her "pretty" dress and that almost brought a smile to her face. After paying for my gas and ice, I thanked her with a sincere "God bless you" and then went outside to say good-bye to Charles.

As I headed for the boat, I saw that a large sailing yacht was trying to come in to one of the rickety old docks. There was an elderly man at the helm and a nervous older woman on the bow trying to throw a rope to Charles. I could see that things weren't going well as the big boat moved in the current. Racing toward them, I got there just in time to grab the stern pulpit, and help Charles bring the forty footer gently in against the dilapidated dock. When the woman found out that I was another boater and not a marina employee, she couldn't thank me enough for running down the dock to help them. I told her that I had been in their shoes many times, and that the Good Lord always put someone on the dock at just the right moment to help me, so I tried to return the favor whenever I could. Seeing the perfect opening, I introduced myself to the upscale couple. I pointed to my boat at the end of the gas dock, and I was glad that her name and my Christian flag were clearly visible from their boat. I told them about my videos and my voyage, and how the Lord had blessed us and delivered us from danger so far. They listened with great interest and nodded approvingly as I shared my story and my plans. After thanking me again they shook my hand and wished me good luck on my trip. I wished them the same and added "God Speed" as I headed off down the dock with Tom and Charles.

As we walked to our boat, Charles asked me about the hunting videos I had mentioned to the elderly couple. I told him that the Lord had given me a ministry, sharing the gospel with outdoorsmen through my videos and my personal testimony. To my surprise, Charles told me that he too, was an avid hunter. Hearing that, I knew that I had to give him a couple of hunting tracts before we left the dock. Once aboard, I went below to get out the tracts and one of the brochures that described my videos. As I shook hands with Charles, I handed him the pamphlets and said: "There are some great tips in here, written by famous hunters. Tips for hunting and tips for life. Please read them over when you get a chance, you'll be glad you did." Then I ended with: "God bless ya Charles, it was good meeting you, thanks for everything and take care." Charles untied our dock lines and threw them to Tom while I started the motor. As I gave him a final wave and pulled away, the last thing I remember seeing was Charles, walking slowly down the dock, with his eyes glued to the open tract in his hand that he was reading.

Once we cleared the break wall and were pointing north again, I noticed a strong wind pushing us from behind. We had lost three hours backtracking, but now I had a crewman aboard to steer while I hoisted sails. With sails up and a strong wind behind us, God Speed leaned left and began to plow aggressively through the small waves. "Whoa, were moving now," Tom yelled with a smile. The boat surged ahead as we were caught by a strong gust, and our speed gauge shot up to nine miles per hour. "He was enjoying this," I thought with a smile. For the first time ever, my son realized what a joy it was to feel the lifting, pulling power of sails in a good wind. He sat there mesmerized by the power of the wind and the speed of the boat as the motor hummed and he steered a good straight course. When I had the sails secure, I asked if he wanted me to take over, and to my further delight he said that he was fine and would steer for a while. I smiled inwardly, happy that he was maturing and experiencing something that he would remember for a long time. At that speed it wasn't long before we were back at the point where we turned around to go back to the marina. When we headed for the marina it had taken well over an hour to get back there. Under sail power with Tom at the till, we got back to our starting point in less than forty-five minutes.

As I praised the Lord for the wind and for getting us back quickly, I thought about his reasons for making us go back to that marina. I thought about the elderly couple on the beautiful yacht, and I thought about Charles walking down the dock, earnestly reading one of the tracts. Did that stop make a difference in their lives? I guess I wouldn't know the answer to that until I was in heaven. As a feeling of peace and a deep faith in God welled up in me, I thought to myself:

. . . Not My Will Lord But Thine . . . (KJV)

Chapter 25

Courage in the Darkness

Because we lost several hours back tracking, it was impossible to reach the point we needed to get to that night before the sun went down. Forty miles ahead of us lay the deep open water of Albemarle Sound. It was by far the largest and most treacherous inland body of water I would have to cross on that trip. Almost comparable to one of the great lakes in size, it had been the graveyard for several commercial vessels. Infamous for its sudden storms and big waves, the only thing I feared more than crossing it, would be going up the New Jersey coast on the open Atlantic and into New York Harbor. Our best chance to cross it safely would be to start across very early in the morning, just before sunrise. That was the time of day that wind and water were usually the calmest. If we started at first light, we would be almost across and in sight of land by the time the midday winds began to whip up the big rolling waves that the sound was known for. Since the weather report for the next day sounded good, my plan was to push hard and find a safe anchorage at the end of the Alligator River, close to the entrance to Albemarle Sound. There was a swing bridge that would need to open for us, two miles before the river entered the sound. If we made it through that bridge tonight, we would have been able to head right out into the sound at daybreak.

Since we had to go back for fuel, it was now impossible for us to reach that bridge and get through it before sun down. That meant we wouldn't reach the sound until almost noon the next day. If we started across then, we could be in for a rough and dangerous ride, far from the sight of land on that big, open body of water. As we raced along at good speed on the wide waters of the Alligator River, Tom said it was fun manning the tiller with the sails up. Watching the speed indicator, he made a little game out of trying to see how often he could get the boat going faster than nine miles per hour. He said that we should just keep going when it got dark, and get through that bridge no matter how late it got to be. The thought of doing that was pretty scary at first, but the more I weighed the options the better it sounded. That river was wide and very open. The colored markers made a straight line right down the middle of it as far as we could see, and the chart said it would be that way all the way to the bridge. The chart also showed us that all of the markers in that section of the river were lighted, and they would begin to flash at sundown. If there was ever a time when we needed to keep going after dark, that was certainly it. Tom began to tease me, saying I wasn't truly a "man of the sea" if I didn't have the "guts" to sail after dark, and he reminded me that we had done it many times on Lake Ontario. We were moving at a fast clip, and the straight route gave me confidence, so I told him that if he had the courage to fly through the darkness at that speed he could keep going.

The day had been cloudy, dark and damp so dusk came early. As daylight began to fade, I dug out my trusty spotlight and plugged it in. Then I positioned myself at the bow pulpit, where I could scan the water ahead with the light once it got dark. A mixture of excitement and fear filled me as I sat there staring at the muddy brown water. We sliced through the rolling waves aggressively with both sails up and the motor at full throttle. I knew that Tom didn't realize how black it would really be on that cloudy night once it got dark, and I hoped he hadn't talked me into something that we would both regret later. As twilight came, we could still see for a short distance over the black water, but eventually all light faded and we found ourselves in complete darkness. I had sailed and fished on moonlit nights when you could see for quite a distance over the shimmering water and make out the dark outline of the shore. But that night we were surrounded by absolute and total blackness. We could not see ten feet in front of us yet we were clipping along at our fastest possible speed. Although I tried to scan the water ahead for obstacles, the waves and spray made it difficult to see anything, even with the spot light. What we were doing took either great courage, or great stupidity, and was definitely not for the faint of heart. Although it was a scary, heart pounding experience we certainly were making great time!

Eventually I just accepted the fact that we couldn't see, and trusted God that there wasn't a floating tree in the water ahead of us. Shining faintly through the blackness ahead was a tiny point of red light that flashed on and off. Far beyond it a second one also flashed in sequence. Without flinching, Tom lined up the flashing red lights and steered for them confidently. They were our only point of reference as we continued to plow our way through the darkness. We were secure in the knowledge that if we kept steering for the red flashers and didn't hit anything, we would eventually come to the bridge. A tug boat pulling a string of barges approached us from the opposite direction. It was also following the red flashers and we made it a point to give it a wide berth as it passed to our left. We were thankful that it was well lit and was also scanning the water ahead with a spotlight. It was a blessing that the wind and waves were coming from behind us, which increased our speed even more. In fact the farther up the river we went the bigger the waves got.

Soon we were being lifted and pushed along by the waves as we rode their crests and surfed down the front of each one.

Tom pointed out and identified each flashing marker as it became visible in the distance. He called them by number like old friends, and thanks to the chart, we knew exactly how far we were from the bridge. I was thrilled when we spotted a group of lights in formation ahead and knew that they were the lights of the bridge. When we were about three miles away, I tried to raise the bridge operator on the radio: "Sandy Point Swing Bridge . . . Sandy Point Swing Bridge . . . this is the captain of the "God Speed" we are rapidly approaching you from the south . . . can you read me," I asked urgently. My heart soared as a loud clear voice answered almost immediately:

"Yes cap'n, this is the Sandy Point Swing Bridge, I read you loud and clear and I have already spotted your lights. I believe I am seeing a mast top light," he went on, "are you a sailboat?" "Yes sir, we are indeed," I replied happily, pleased that I now had contact with the bridge. The pleasant, helpful man said he was equipped with powerful spotlights, capable of lighting up the whole bridge so it could be seen by approaching vessels in the dark. When we got closer he would turn them on, and then open the bridge as we approached.

"Thank you Lord!" I praised loudly, as I hung up the microphone. Things were going so well, I couldn't resist saying to Tom: "See, I told you that God is my navigator on this trip." He smiled and nodded, and then laughed at my exuberance. "You're the man, Tom," I shouted with a smile, "You got us here in the dark, and that took guts. Thanks for talking me into going for it," I continued, "if you weren't here; I probably would have anchored back there, three hours ago."

I don't think the enemy was happy about us making it to the

bridge, because he threw a few more obstacles in our path as we covered the last two miles. A tall shape appeared in the beam of the spotlight, and I yelled: "Turn right, turn right quick!" A telephone pole was sticking up out of the water dead ahead. It had no marker and no light on it. As it came at me out of the darkness, I shouted to Tom and he reacted to avoid it, but it was a very close call. After that, we passed through a "mine field" of crab pot buoys. The small floating markers attached to crab traps on the river bottom seemed to be everywhere. The colorful Styrofoam buoys are tied to each trap with a stout rope so crab fishermen can find their traps and pull them up. It was hard to see them in the dark even with the spotlight. But we miraculously got through them, without one of the ropes tangling in the rudder or worse yet in the motor.

"Sailboat God Speed, I'm going to turn on my spotlights now," chimed the voice of the bridge operator. "Let me know if you can see the bridge," he continued. The next moment, the bridge appeared out of the blackness ahead, bathed in light. "Sandy Point Bridge Operator," I barked, "I see the bridge lit up dead ahead, and it sure is a beautiful sight!" "Okay cap'n," he replied, "I'll begin to open as you approach, so you shouldn't need to slow down." "Thank you Lord, for this wonderful man, who is making this so easy for us," I said softly, as I hung up the microphone. I brought the sails down and wrapped them up as Tom approached the bridge. Then we heard the clanging of the drop gates, and saw the flashing lights warning traffic on the highway above, as the bridge began to open. As we passed beneath it I thanked the bridge operator for being so helpful. I told him that his help was heaven sent, and that he made our day and probably the next one, too. Thanks to him we were now in position to start across Albemarle Sound at first light. I left him with a fond God Bless you, and wished him a good night as the bridge grew smaller behind us.

As soon as we cleared the bridge, I began to look for a safe anchorage because it was so late. We anchored in the corner of a small bay close to the marsh. We were within sight of the bridge and the highway that passed over it. I put both anchors off the bow so the boat could swing and point into whatever wind blew that night. Since we were in fresh water again, Tom wanted to fish because he remembered the giant catfish from the other night. I rigged and baited two poles for him and then sprawled on my berth. With two anchors off the front, the boat moved and rocked gently in the small waves. It was the perfect motion to make me feel like I was being rocked to sleep in a baby's cradle. The gentle rocking motion was just what I needed to lull my worn out, stressed out body into a state of unconsciousness and I soon drifted into a deep sleep.

It seemed like only a minute later that I was startled awake by Tom's loud cries: "HELP, this is gigantic!" he shouted frantically from the back deck. I scrambled back to the cockpit, but was not fully awake until I saw that Tom was indeed hooked to something huge out in the darkness. It was easy to see by the bending and pulsing of his rod and the way his line was screaming out, that whatever was on the other end was very big and very much alive. Still exhausted, I collapsed on the cockpit seat and watched for thirty minutes as he gained several yards of line only to lose it again plus more when the giant thing on the other end decided to pull. I could see that whatever it was, it was larger, stronger and more aggressive than the catfish from the other night. After watching the tug of war stale mate for forty-five minutes, the "thing" was still no closer to the boat. Dead tired, I told Tom to call me if he gained some line, and I lay back down on my berth. After ten more minutes, Tom came below and slumped on the seat shaking his head sadly as he told me that the line broke. I felt bad for him, but it was pretty clear that whatever it was, it was way too big to land with the light tackle we had with us. To this day, Tom still talks about the giant "thing" from the Alligator River that we never saw and never landed.

The next morning my eyes popped open at five thirty, and it worked out to be the perfect time. The anchors came up easily and I was on my way out into the sound before six o'clock. When I realized how glassy calm the infamous sound was at that early hour, I praised the Lord and began my morning prayers as I started across. Even though the weather was clear where I was, I saw dark threatening clouds to the south, and I could tell that it was raining hard there. I praised the Lord for Tom's courage the previous night, which allowed me to be out on the sound at that early hour, moving away from the bad weather that was now behind us.

CASTILLO DE BUTRON
NASSAU
NORFOLK SOUTHERN
COAL PIER 6

Chapter 26

The Docks that Were Built Just for Us

Even though it was a calm windless morning, Albemarle Sound was so big and open, that by the time we were two thirds of the way across, we were in some good sized rolling waves. That didn't phase me, because by then the opposite shore was in sight and within reach. I continued to rejoice, that it was a calm day and that we had started across as early as we did. As I rocked and wallowed my way through the rollers, I didn't even want to think about what it would have been like out there on a windy day, and I was glad that another obstacle to getting home was now behind me. As I approached the other side of the sound, I caught up to a tug that was slowly pushing a string of barges north. Thinking that he had to be heading up the Intra Coastal Waterway, I waited to see where he went. By watching him, I could see where the ICW left the sound, so there was no chance of missing it or turning up the wrong river.

Once we were beyond Albemarle Sound, the chart showed that we would be in narrow rivers the rest of the way to Norfolk. By now we had left any threatening weather far behind, and I cruised confidently under a bright blue sky. We stopped at a marina that had an easily accessible dock to get gas, ice, cold drinks and ice cream.

Apparently there were quite a few bridges and a lock ahead as we approached the city of Norfolk. According to the marina owner, all of them operated on very strict time schedules, so he gave us a printed bridge / lock schedule for the Norfolk area.

As we left the marina to cover the final stretch to Norfolk, we enjoyed the ice cream and cold drinks we had purchased. I could not believe how creamy, cool and delicious a simple ice cream bar tasted in that heat after not having ice cream for two weeks. Even a drink of cold spring water in a plastic cup with ice tasted too good to be true. We were making great time as we cruised past waterfront homes, marinas, restaurants and expensive yachts. Checking my watch and the distance to Norfolk, some simple math told me that if things went well we could make it there that night before sundown. We would then be there a day ahead of schedule, and I got excited about the possibility of having an extra day in "port" to rest and relax.

When we approached the first bridge, a look at the schedule told us that it opened at three thirty and my watch said that it was three thirty two. I had high hopes that the bridge operator would be flexible enough to open for us, but found out that the three thirty opening had already come and gone. While we waited for the four o'clock opening, a large fleet of boats began to accumulate at the bridge, as one boat after another came along and had to wait for it to open. I was amazed by the size, number and variety of boats that joined us there as we waited.

A large power yacht with a family of three aboard had the words New Zealand under its name, and I found it hard to believe that they had motored it halfway around the world. The next boat proved again that everything is relative as it made the one from New Zealand look small. It was an "ocean liner" from Italy with several uniformed crewmen, that was actually a private yacht. There was another power cruiser from Florida, and a marine research vessel from Old Dominion University. Last but not least was a small, average looking motor boat named "Peaches" with four "good ol' boys" aboard. The four husky men had beers in their hands and smiles on their faces as they laughed, joked and socialized with each other, and everyone else. They didn't seem to have a care in the world, and I sensed they had nowhere to be, and no time schedule. I was amused as I watched them greet and talk loudly to the people in the other boats, giving unsolicited directions to the New Zealanders and waving to an attractive Italian woman on the luxury liner. The self appointed "waterway superintendents" wanted to be everyone's friends and know everybody else's business. They were friendly but not obnoxious, as they carried on conversations with several boats at once, their dingy yellow runabout a comical contrast to the huge cruise ship next to them.

At four o'clock the bridge opened and the odd looking "armada" proceeded through and dispersed, as each boat headed down the river at a different speed. A few miles down the line we approached the next bridge at four twenty, only to see that the mismatched "fleet" was again waiting on our side of it. As we stopped, the "mayors of the river" in "Peaches" informed us that the bridge normally opened every thirty minutes, but did not open at all between the hours of four and six because of rush hour traffic. I felt the dream of making it to our marina that night begin to fade as I accepted the disappointing news. Since we had to wait so long, I decided to anchor, relax and fish for a while. As we threw out a couple of baited lines with bobbers, I thought about how busy and hectic my life was. It seemed like I was always rushing around to beat the clock, meet a deadline or stay on schedule. Even on this "pleasure cruise" I found myself racing the sun to be in a certain spot each day before dark, and the only times I really relaxed was when the Lord forced me to stay put, as he was doing right then. At the other end of the spectrum were the men in "Peaches" who did not seem to have a schedule, a plan or a care in the world. Even though I knew that the Lord had created this energetic over achiever for a purpose, I reminded myself that I needed to slow down and be a little more like the men in the other boat (without the beer).

While we fished there at anchor we drifted close to the family from New Zealand, so I struck up a conversation with them. I learned that the middle aged couple had transported their large yacht to America on a cargo ship, and that they were spending a year seeing as much of the U.S. as they could by boat with their teenage son. I told them about the trip we were taking and how the Lord had been with us and protected us so far. The man nodded thoughtfully with a smile and replied that we certainly needed him with us, in a boat that size. One of the men in "Peaches" asked if we were having any luck fishing. I told them about the catfish Tom had caught the other night and about the giant "thing" last night that fought with Tom for an hour before it broke the line. They were down-to-earth types so I asked if any of them were hunters. When two of them said they were, I told them about my hunting videos and asked them to come along side so I could give them some brochures. As they pulled up close and grabbed our boat I gave all of them video brochures and some hunting and fishing tracts. I told them that the tracts contained some great "tips" and were written by famous outdoorsmen so they needed to be sure to read them.

The bridge opened promptly at six and the large group of boats again hurried down the river. The next bridge was Great Bridge and right beyond it was the Great Bridge Lock. The lock raised boats a little over two feet, bringing them from the water level of the river up to the level of Chesapeake Bay and the Atlantic. We reached Great Bridge in about twenty-five minutes, and then found out that the bridge and lock only opened on the hour. That meant that our ill fated "flotilla" was again dead in the water until seven. Frustrated, I headed for a long wooden dock on the right side of the river. I thought that it would be easier to tie up than to anchor again, and I would need my fenders out anyway when I entered the lock.

The sturdy dock looked like it had been put there for boaters waiting for the bridge, and there was a young black man fishing from it. He quickly gathered his equipment and began to slip away as I approached, but I asked if he could grab a rope and pull me in. Putting down his fishing gear, he willingly caught my lines and brought me gently against the dock. I sensed that he had a low self image because he apologized for fishing from the dock then quickly walked away. I told him that he had just as much right to fish there as I did to tie up there, and that he wasn't bothering anyone or in anyone's way. He stopped and smiled at me, then walked to the edge of the dock, put down his tackle and started fishing again. I felt bad that someone had made him feel like he couldn't fish there, or that he was less important than a person who owned a boat, so I tried to reach out to him. I asked if he had any luck fishing, and then I told him about Tom's giant catfish and the big one that got away. Before we left the dock, I gave him a fishing tract, and voiced a sincere "God bless ya man," as we pulled away and headed for the bridge.

Great Bridge and the Great Bridge Lock were located almost back to back and operated on the same time schedule. After all the boats cleared the lift bridge, the gates of the lock were dead ahead and already open to receive us. As we entered the lock, Tom and I talked about whether or not we should try to make it to our marina near Virginia Beach that night. Once we cleared the lock, it would be almost dark, and we would still be nine miles from downtown Norfolk. From there we had to go another five miles to reach Chesapeake Bay. Once in the bay we would still have to travel four miles down the shoreline and find the entrance to Little Creek in the dark, winding our way up the creek until we reached the marina. If things went perfectly, the best we could hope for in the dark was to cover the remaining eighteen miles in about three hours. If things did not go well, we could be lost on Chesapeake Bay for most of the night.

If I knew for sure that it would be calm and moonlit on the Chesapeake, I would have been tempted to keep going, knowing the advantages of getting there that night. We could eat at McDonald's and get a motel room so we could sleep in real beds! It also meant an extra day in "port" to relax, so we would have the luxury of sleeping in as late as we wanted to the next morning. Tom was so excited about the idea, that he offered to buy me anything I wanted at McDonalds, if I kept going and made it there that night. As I weighed the pros and cons it began to rain. It was a cold rain, and within minutes it was raining as hard as the worst rain I had ever seen. I was startled by the flash of a lightning bolt as it sliced through the dark sky ahead. It was followed by a loud boom of thunder that sounded like a cannon going off up the river. As I stared at the sky, several more flashes of lightning cut through the black clouds followed by rolling thunder. The lightning was ahead of us and appeared to be right over the city of Norfolk. The heavy rain, accompanied by thunder and lightning quickly settled the debate about pushing for the marina that night. I had done some foolish things in my boating career, but I wasn't about to head out on an unfamiliar stretch of Chesapeake Bay in the dark in a thunder storm. Much to Tom's disappointment, I made the decision to anchor for the night in the first safe spot we could find.

As soon as the water in the lock reached the level of the water in the river ahead, the heavy steel gates began to open. Without wasting a moment the odd collection of boats went their separate ways as they sped down the river to get out of the rain. As the other boats disappeared, we were left alone in the cold downpour, trying to find a safe place to anchor for the night. Now close to a major city, we found ourselves in an urban, industrial area. We could no longer pull into a pocket in the marsh grass to anchor, because we were surrounded by factories, coal yards and concrete walls covered with graffiti. The river narrowed as it passed next to railroad tracks, steel mills, refineries and rusty barges. The cold rain pelted me so hard that I felt like a fool standing out in it, and I was glad that Tom had things closed up and was staying dry inside the cabin. The sky was so dark it seemed like nightfall, even though sundown was still an hour away, and lightning continued to streak through the sky ahead.

I desperately needed to find a place to hunker down soon, but I sensed that there was very little chance of finding one in that area. As I rounded a bend in the river, I saw something so amazing, that it took me several seconds to realize that my eyes were not playing tricks on me. There on the right side, was a large vacant lot completely surrounded by chain link fences. The only thing on the property was a bulldozer, which led me to believe that the muddy open space was a construction site. Extending out into the river from that vacant piece of property, was a large floating dock complex that appeared to be brand new. It looked like someone was building a marina or riverfront condos with boat slips, and they had already put in the docks. I was blown away by all the factors that made the set up too unbelievable to be true:

1. The brand new docks were located among factories, refineries and coal yards in an industrial area.

2. Not one of the long, marina style, floating dock fingers was occupied by a single boat.

3. The vacant property had tall security fences around it, so no one on land could get to those docks.

4. Whoever was developing the property had put in all the docks before starting to build any buildings.

5. One dock already had two large boat fenders attached to it that were positioned perfectly for a boat our size!

"Thank you Lord, for again providing our every need," I shouted loudly, as the cold rain poured down my face and trickled down my neck and back. Without wasting a second, I headed for the one that had two round red boat bumpers attached. I smiled as I thought to myself that angels had hung them there in preparation for our arrival, knowing that I would not want to spend much time getting out fenders in such a downpour. I marveled that they were exactly the right distance apart for a twenty-five foot sailboat, as I tied us there securely and went inside. As I shed my rain gear and wet clothes, Tom teased me, saying that I wasn't a true "man of the sea". He called me a "wimp" because I was unwilling to push for our marina that night, but I knew I had done the sensible thing. As I lay on my berth in the darkness listening to the raindrops, I felt secure, and knew that I could relax and would sleep well there. Waiting for sleep to overtake me, I praised the Lord again for guiding us to docks that seemed like they had been built just for us.

Voyage of the Heart

Chapter 27

Buzzed by a Navy Helicopter

When my eyes opened the next morning I was still in awe of the way that God provided a dock spot and led us to it. I swallowed hard and fought back tears, as I thought about how his timing had again saved us, from a very bad experience. We had been held up at every bridge we approached, missing one of them by only two minutes. All in all, we spent a total of two hours waiting with the other boats for bridges to open. If we hadn't been delayed, we would have passed these docks two hours earlier, when the weather was good and we weren't even thinking about tying up for the night yet. Then we would have been out on Chesapeake Bay when the downpour and severe thunderstorm hit, instead of safely tied up here.

Since it was seven o'clock and daylight, I got underway and continued to wind my way toward the city of Norfolk. I said my morning prayers, and praised the Lord again for his timing, as I steered past box cars and loading docks. The dreary dampness of that gray, foggy morning made the factories and train yards seem even dirtier than they were. A shiver went through me, but I wasn't sure if it was caused by the cold damp air, or the bleakness of my dismal surroundings. As I passed ocean going ships tied to wharfs and huge warehouses, I was reminded that Norfolk was a major industrial center and busy international seaport. Soon the dirty factory yards and coal piles gave way to gleaming high rise office buildings and luxury hotels as I passed through the center of downtown Norfolk.

As I followed the main shipping channel away from the city and out into Chesapeake Bay, two ocean going cargo ships came out of the fog and passed me at close quarters. My boat seemed like a tiny toy below them as the overwhelming size and mass of the floating "cities" rumbled slowly by and I rocked and bounced in their wake. To my right was a United States Naval Base. I was impressed by the large number of ships riding at anchor, including several aircraft carriers. I found out later that over half of the U.S. fleet was based in Norfolk at that time. Security seemed tight, as large chains of buoys formed an impassable barrier around the ships to keep unauthorized boats out, and heavily armed Navy gun boats patrolled back and forth. A Navy helicopter spotted me crossing the bay and flew right at me, dropping down low to check me out. As it hovered above my mast I put on my best smile and waved eagerly, trying hard not to look like a terrorist. Not far behind it was a large naval vessel coming across the bay from the Atlantic. On the foredeck stood a large group of uniformed men, staring across the water as they headed into port. I was touched as I saw them; thinking that they might be coming back from Iraq and this could be there first look at America in two years. The ship was heading for the Navy base, and I guessed the chopper was escorting it in and scanning the water ahead for any possible threat to the vessel or the troops aboard. The helicopter pilot must have decided that I was too funny looking to be a threat to anyone, and buzzed off toward the base, as I continued down the bay toward the Little Creek inlet.

I was impressed by national security in post nine eleven America, as I saw that there was a Coast Guard cutter anchored off the mouth of Little Creek inlet and guarding the entrance to it. Our marina was located a short distance up that creek, and the Little Creek Amphibious Base was also located on that inlet. The joint military base is the home of the landing craft that are used to land troops from a ship onto a beach, as was done in the D-Day invasion. The U.S. Armed Forces School of Music is also located at the Little Creek base. It was there that members of bands from different branches of the military came for advanced musical training. Tom would be reporting there soon for advanced Army Band training, so I wanted to point it out to him. But as we cruised past the amphibious landing craft, he was still sound asleep in the cabin. Just as we hailed the marina on the radio it began to rain again. A nice lady told us where our slip was but we couldn't find it, so she came out on the docks waving to guide us in. It was raining hard and we were wiped out, so we just locked the boat and left it, taking only personal items, clothing and perishable food as we headed for the marina office. The marina manager was nice enough to put the few perishable food items we had left in their freezer, and give us a ride to the airport to rent a car.

As we headed for Colonial Williamsburg in the rental car, my stressed and weary body finally began to relax. The wipers slapped back and forth as the heavy raindrops pounded the windshield, but in the security of the warm dry car with four wheels on solid ground I felt as snug as a bug in a rug. In fact, I was so relaxed I could have nodded off in the blink of an eye if I wasn't driving a vehicle at sixty miles per hour. We had been given one of those complimentary stays at a timeshare resort, in return for taking a tour of the property and listening to a high pressure sales pitch. My wife Mary and daughter Lauren had flown in earlier that day and were already waiting for us there. It was very good to see them as they opened the door to our room, and Mary said that I was so tanned, I looked like Juan Valdez. After some badly needed kisses and hugs, I collapsed into the softness of the queen sized bed without even bothering to undress, and felt like I could lie there for a month.

I believe that it was God's timing that during those three days in Williamsburg, the remnants of Hurricane Charlie moved through the Norfolk area. We watched through windows as wind gusts of forty miles per hour shook the trees and it rained sideways for two days straight. As I watched the biting winds hurl torrents of rain into everything, I shuddered to think what it would have been like out on Chesapeake Bay, and praised the Lord that I was indoors and the boat was safely tied up at a marina. I called the marina to ask if they would be willing to put a couple of extra ropes on the boat to keep it from slamming into the dock in the high winds, and they said they would be happy to do that for me. On the third day we awoke to cloudy skies but the rain had stopped, so we made plans to spend our last day there at Busch Gardens. Soon after we entered the park it began to rain again and never stopped or let up. Although we tried to enjoy the indoor attractions and Tom and Lauren rode a few rides, we were drenched and miserable after just two hours, even though we were wearing official Busch Gardens rain ponchos. The rain got so intense that many of the rides stopped operating and the park announced that anyone who wanted a rain check to come back another day could have one. We took them up on their offer, and as we drove back to our hotel I could not stop thinking about what a blessing it was to be there and not on the boat in that weather.

First thing the next morning we saw Mary and Lauren off at the airport. Then I took Tom to the train station and helped him get a ticket and find his train before I headed back to the marina. My sailing buddy Marty Douglas would not arrive at the Norfolk airport until five o'clock that evening. At first I was disappointed that he couldn't get an earlier flight, because I would lose travel time sitting at the dock that day. But then I reminded myself that I was on God's time schedule, as I remembered how many times frustrating delays had turned into big blessings. Returning to the boat, I used that time to get everything ship shape, so we could leave the moment Marty arrived. I bought groceries and ice and filled the gas tanks, and then I thoroughly cleaned and vacuumed the boat. After that, I organized equipment, stowed canned goods, reloaded the cameras and put all perishable food and some cold drinks on ice. When I felt that she was fully rigged and ready, I went to the office to settle my bill and then drove to the airport to turn in the rental car and wait for Marty.

As I waited at the airport, I used the time to study maps and charts of Chesapeake Bay, trying to calculate distances and come up with a float plan for that week. We would be staying close to land as we headed north along the western shore of the bay. I tried to estimate which small harbors and inlets were a day apart, and would be the most logical places to spend each night. As much as I liked to fly by the seat of my pants, Marty liked plans, details, facts and figures. If I had a concrete plan to offer him, he would think I had my act together and feel more secure as we headed out into that large open body of water.

Marty's plane landed a few minutes early, and I spotted him right away as the passengers from his flight came down the ramp. Small in stature, yet feisty and muscular, he was in great shape for being my age, and still had lots of energy and drive. He smiled broadly as he saw me, and as I shook his hand I could sense how excited he was about the adventure that lay ahead. "This is good," I thought to myself. I needed some new blood aboard to motivate me to keep going, and keep me energized. I rushed Marty out of the airport and into a cab, as I eagerly shared my plan for the rest of the evening with him. There was a hook of land with an inlet and a small harbor called Poquoson about two hours north. If we could get underway quickly enough to find our way in there before dark, we would be in a good safe spot, and well beyond the wide, treacherous mouth of the Chesapeake where it opened to the Atlantic. On a previous trip to Virginia Beach, my son and I had been in six foot waves near there in a small day sailor. It would be great to get across that end of the bay while the water was flat, knowing that the farther north we went, the less chance we would have to encounter ocean caliber waves. If we could get into Poquoson that night, we would be in position to make it all the way to Annapolis in just two days, and when we got there, most of Chesapeake Bay would be behind us.

The work I did that day, getting the boat rigged and ready really paid off. When Marty and I came down the dock all we had to do was throw his bag aboard, untie two ropes and shove off. As we started down the inlet and passed the amphibious landing craft, he smiled and shook his head in wonder, as I shared some of the incredible experiences I had in the past two weeks. Soon we were passing the lighthouse that marked the entrance to Little Creek inlet, and heading out into the open waters of the Chesapeake. Marty smiled as he scanned the water ahead, and I could tell that he was enjoying himself. That night it looked like God's time schedule was the same as mine. Marty's flight had arrived early, and we had gotten back to the marina and underway faster than I could have ever imagined. Even though it was hard to believe, we were heading north across Chesapeake Bay, just forty-five minutes after Marty stepped off the plane!

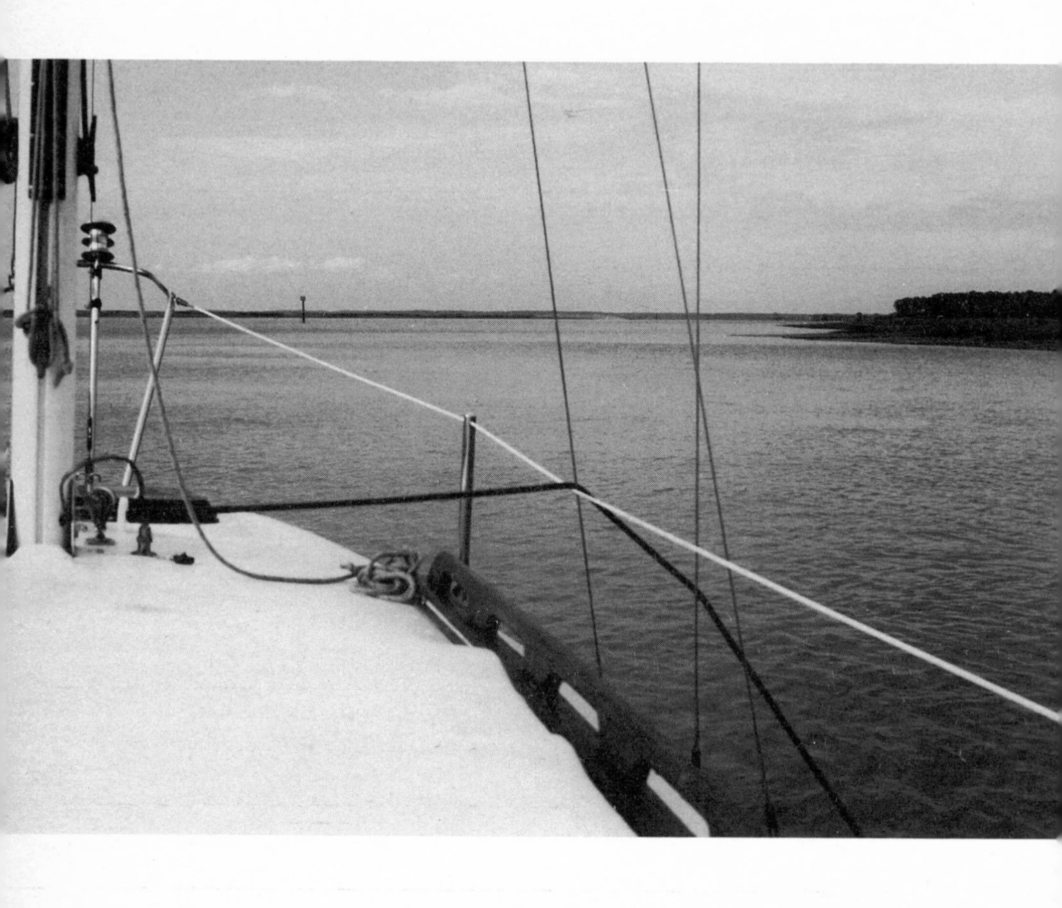

Chapter 28

No See Ums and Young Lovers

It was a cloudy gray night on the Chesapeake, but it wasn't raining. The sky ahead was the color of old weathered steel, which gave the water a cold foreboding appearance. As I quartered into a rolling chop, I praised the Lord that it wasn't windy that night, shuddering as I remembered my experience out there with my son two years before. I set a course diagonally north toward the western shore of the bay, hoping I would approach land just south of Poquoson. Once I could see the shoreline well, I could follow it northward until I saw the entrance to the inlet. The time passed quickly as we talked, and soon we were moving northward along the western shore. It wasn't long before we noticed a line of numbered markers, curving in toward an inlet behind a large point of land. Lining ourselves up with the markers we followed them in until we passed through a narrow channel between the sand dunes and found ourselves in a small bay that was surrounded by sea grass. On the far end of that sandy "lake" was a marina that looked like it catered to fishermen. A line of closely spaced red and green markers zig zagged their way across the bay toward its docks. Noticing how many markers there were and how carefully they were placed, I sensed that there was only one way in or out of that marina. As we picked our way across the little bay from marker to marker, our depth finder showed that the whole area was quite shallow, and that there was little margin for error. Straying even a few feet to the right or left made the alarm beep, showing us how narrow the channel really was.

Just beyond the marina was a boat launching ramp, with a large parking lot for vehicles. Next to the ramp were several sturdy docks that were just as empty as the parking lot. There was a young couple on the docks, and a motorcycle parked nearby that appeared to be theirs. At first I thought the launch ramp and docks were part of the marina, but when I asked the couple, they said it was a state owned public boat launch. When I inquired further, they told me they had often seen boats tied up there for the night, and that no one would bother us there. I was thrilled that the Lord had led us to such a perfect spot to spend the night. Marty and I had a running joke that started on one of our previous sailing trips. He always teased me that I had a way of finding a free dock spot, no matter where I was. In fact we often joked that I should publish a book called: "1,000 Free Dock Spots and Anchorages for Cruising Sailors". We both laughed about it as we approached the docks, but quickly got serious when we saw how shallow the water was. Moving slowing and carefully with an eye on the depth finder, we found a spot next to one of them that was seven feet deep. We tied up there, but made a mental note that we had to be very careful getting out of there in the morning.

As I got out fenders and ropes, I felt like I was being bitten by hundreds of mosquitoes all over my face, scalp and neck, yet there were no bugs visible in the air around me. "What's biting me?" I yelled in a panic, as I saw that Marty was also swatting his head and face. We were being swarmed by "no see ums" a type of biting insect so small that they are barely visible to the eye, yet they bite more fiercely and aggressively than mosquitoes. I had read about them, but never had the displeasure of experiencing them first hand as I was right then. I brought insect repellent with me, but stowed it away, because I hadn't encountered a fly or a mosquito in two weeks (even in the swamps). Now I dug for it frantically in the storage compartments, still swatting myself with my free hand as I did. After a generous dose of bug spray, I secured us to the dock. Since they were not floating docks, and didn't rise and fall with the tide, I left several feet of slack so the boat could move up or down during the night. After using the "Johnny On The Spot" porta john near the launch ramp, we turned in, hoping that our keel wasn't touching bottom in the morning.

I slept poorly there, knowing that someone who was up to no good could pull into the parking lot, walk out onto the dock and step aboard our boat as we slept. I lay there nervously, listening to all the things that go bump in the night. Every time a set of car headlights swung into the lot, I sat up quickly and popped my head out of the open hatch to look around, just like the plastic rodents in the carnival game "Whac-A-Mole". At one point, a young couple pulled into the lot in a pickup truck and parked there close to the water for several hours. Apparently, that parking lot was a favorite romantic spot, where couples sat by the bay in the moonlight.

I don't think sleep ever came that night, but morning and daylight finally did. We were still floating free, but we were much farther below the dock than we had been the night before. Eager to get out of there, we used the portable john on shore one more time and then got underway. We were very careful maneuvering in the shallow water, and made it a point to line up with the colored markers, as we made our way across the sandy bay and back out into the Chesapeake. To make sure we didn't have a problem, we followed the long curving line of markers far out into the bay, and did not turn or cut any corners until we had passed the last one.

The west side of Chesapeake Bay was calm that morning and

the sky was blue. The sun was well above the horizon and many sea birds filled the sky as we pointed our bow northward. Since I hadn't slept at all, I lay on the bow with a cushion under my body and a pillow under my head. Marty steered, and I was in heaven, as the calm water slipped beneath me. As I began to relax, a smile crept over my weary face as random thoughts came to mind: "What a beautiful day it is . . . thank you Lord, this is more like it . . . this is nice, very nice, I could get used to this . . . I hope things keep going this well . . . this is going to be a great day on the water"

Voyage of the Heart

UBC BOSTON
U B C

Chapter 29

"Big Waves Sink Small Sailboat on the Chesapeake"

By early afternoon our first fuel tank was empty. We would need to fill both tanks before dark, because we planned to push all the way to Annapolis the next day. Our depth finder encountered shallow water almost a mile out, so we were holding a course two miles from shore as we made our way north. At that distance we couldn't see the inlets and navigational markers that would lead us into a bay that had a marina. From Florida to Norfolk I had a detailed navigational chart of the Intra Coastal Waterway, and a guide book that listed marinas and facilities. Now that we were on Chesapeake Bay, my only guide was the state highway map from my North American Road Atlas. The boats odometer told us how many miles we had traveled up the shoreline, and where we were in relation to waterfront towns. But we had no local knowledge of where marinas were located. Without charts, we had no way of knowing when to approach shore, so we could see the markers that would lead us into a harbor.

I made a call on the radio to see if anyone could help us with some directions. A boat captain answered, and politely tried to help, but was limited because I couldn't give him our exact position. As I spoke with him, the confident voice of another young man broke in, saying that he would be happy to help me get in somewhere for fuel. The first man turned me over to him, and I thanked him very much for responding as he signed off. The young man was a fishing guide and the "Captain" of a small charter boat that took people out on the bay to fish. There was something special about his gentle, caring voice and his eagerness to help, that made me think I had either a Christian, the world's nicest guy, or a guardian angel on the other end of the line. Calmly and patiently he gave me directions, and made them so clear that even I could follow them. He told me what compass course to steer, and gave us visual landmarks to guide us in. All together he stayed on the radio with me for over an hour, checking in with us every so often to monitor our progress. At one point he didn't like what he heard, so he actually stopped fishing, and came our way until he saw us, just to make sure we were going the right way. He even called the marina for us when we got closer to let them know we were on our way in. As we talked, I learned that he had a small boy aboard that day who was deaf. The youngster was the child of a friend, and he had promised to take him fishing for some time. Apparently the little guy was having a ball, and I found myself wishing I could also be aboard his boat to see that. As I thanked him, I asked if he was our guardian angel, because it seemed like the Lord put him there to watch over us. I also told him that he had a better heart for others than most of the "Christian" men I knew. He laughed heartily, saying that he was happy to help, and that it made him feel good to "come to the rescue" of other people when he could. I ended the conversation with a hearty: "God bless ya, and have a great day fishin," and he thanked me as he signed off.

As we approached the marina, I could see that it was pretty old and run down, but I was just happy that we got in there safely, and that they sold gas. The woman who filled our tanks said that she was the owner's wife. She told us that her husband had taken a group of friends out fishing and would be back soon. When I told her where we were headed, she urged us to wait for her husband to get directions and a weather report, before going any farther north that day. When her husband returned, he warned us that it was supposed to get very windy and rough out on the bay, especially north of there. He recommended that we spend the night, saying that we could stay tied right where we were, and he would only charge us twenty dollars. Although it was a good offer, it was only three o'clock. My goal was to make it across the mouth of the Potomac River, where it emptied into Chesapeake Bay about ten miles ahead. If we made it across that river before dark, we could then reach Annapolis the following night. If we quit now and stayed there, it would be two more days before we reached Annapolis, and we would get there around noon. Marty and I were looking forward to seeing the sights of that historic harbor, and spending the night there. I also knew that Marty's vacation only allowed him to be with me for seven days. Stopping now, meant that Marty would have to go home before I ventured into the Atlantic to head for New York Harbor, and that was where I would need him the most. We were a little uneasy about it, but we made the decision to push on, and try to get across the Potomac that day. The marina owner raised his eyebrows and shook his head as he looked again at the size of our boat. I also noticed a couple of smirks among the fishermen on the dock, but they helped us untie and wished us well as they pushed us away. "God bless ya men, thanks for everything," I said, waving nervously over my shoulder as we headed back toward the bay.

Right before we reached open water, a cruise boat loaded with tourists passed to our right. They were coming in from a day on the bay, and heading into the same small harbor we just left. The captain gave a friendly blast on his horn to acknowledge us, and many of the people on board waved eagerly as we passed them. Returning their waves, a nervous fear gripped me, as I hoped those people didn't read about us the next day in their morning paper. "Big Waves Sink Small Sailboat On The Chesapeake", the headline would read, and the copy below would say: "Due to windy conditions and six foot waves, a twenty-five foot sailboat capsized and sunk near the mouth of the Potomac River last night . . . the two men aboard are still missing and are presumed to have drowned." I swallowed hard as I pictured that headline in my mind, and then got more nervous as I saw the whitecaps and big rolling waves on the open bay. "It wasn't this bad out here before we came in for gas," I thought. But I kept that thought to myself so I didn't alarm Marty. As we began to plow and slosh through the three foot rollers, I almost decided to turn back and take the marina owner up on his offer. I was way too tired to fight waves again, but the thought of facing the Atlantic Ocean without Marty aboard sounded much worse, so I kept going.

The Potomac River was the width of an average sized river where it passed through Washington, but it widened dramatically as it approached the Chesapeake. Where the mouth of the river opened into the west side of the bay it was actually twelve miles across. We had been following the western shore all day, and the sight of land gave us confidence and direction. But once we started across the Potomac, we would not be able to see the other side, or any land to our right or left for a while. During that time while we were steering "blind" it would be very important to hold a course that would bring us to the other shore quickly. Directly across from us, on the opposite corner of the river, was a point of land with a lighthouse, called Point Lookout. When we did see land again, we wanted to be heading right at Point Lookout and continue up the western shore of the bay. If we set a course too far to the left, we would be heading up the river toward Washington. If we steered too far to the right, we would be heading away from land and out into the middle of the bay. If that happened, we wouldn't see land for hours, and we would be lost in the center of Chesapeake Bay after dark on a very rough night. With the waves building to five footers, a dark threatening sky ahead, and three hours of daylight left, it was no time to steer the wrong course. We needed to get across the Potomac quickly and get in somewhere for the night as soon as possible.

Marty and I were both tired and grumpy, and we disagreed about which compass heading would take us straight across to Point Lookout. My instincts told me to keep steering the course I was on, because it kept me roughly parallel to the shore all day. Marty, who was a firm believer in technology and electronic equipment, loved playing around with the global positioning unit or GPS. I had a small hand held one aboard that plugged into the boats cigarette lighter, but I had no idea how to use it. Marty, on the other hand, knew how to use the GPS, and swore by it. He was able to calculate the approximate compass bearing to Point Lookout, just by looking at the state road map. Then he programmed it into the GPS unit, which translated it into a direction to steer from our current position. I was too tired to argue with him, so I gave in to technology, and steered the course that the GPS told me to. We were in some serious five foot rollers as we pointed our bow at nothing except the dark water and gray skies ahead. Our only consolation was that the wind and waves were coming from behind us. As I looked back, it was chilling to see a parade of ominous dark waves rising up and sweeping toward our stern. Each one looking like it was going to come right over the back of the boat. But the well designed vessel simply rose up on the crest of each wave, and rode it for a few seconds as it pushed us forward.

Since the wind was behind us, I had Marty steer while I got our sails up. With the pull of the sails and push of the following waves we practically flew across the Potomac, and in less than an hour I gave a shout of joy as the shadowy outline of land began to materialize ahead. As we got closer, Marty was able to make out a large lighthouse through his binoculars and we knew we were heading right at Point Lookout. His calculations had been right on, and I was thrilled that I listened to him. I told him that I would never doubt the GPS again. If I had followed my instincts, we would have been in the middle of Chesapeake Bay, in five foot waves as darkness approached.

The highway map showed that there was an inlet and small bay seven miles past Point Lookout, called St. Jerome's Creek. I hoped to somehow find our way in there to anchor for the night. As we approached it, we were happy to find channel markers that led us right in and up a wide creek. Following the markers, we went up the channel as far as we could and came to an apparent dead end. The channel ended abruptly as a narrow strip of sandy beach stretched across the wide creek blocking it off. On the other side of the sandy "isthmus" was a shallow bay or small "lake," similar to the one at Poquoson. That calm protected body of water would have been the perfect spot to anchor for the night, but there didn't seem to be any way for a boat to get in or out of it. That surprised us, because there were navigational markers on it and boats anchored there with people fishing.

There was a tiny creek that cut through the narrow strip of beach. It ran from the dead end channel (where we were) into the calm shallow "lake". The little "creek" connected the two bodies of water, but was not much wider than our boat and appeared to be six inches deep. Certainly the boats we saw in the "lake" couldn't have gotten in there by way of that narrow trickle of water. Since we could go no further, we decided to anchor as close to the strip of beach as possible. It was choppy there, and we would rock all night, but at least we were out of Chesapeake Bay and safely anchored.

Thirty minutes before dark, a fishing boat that was slightly bigger than our boat, came down the channel, and didn't look it was going to stop at the dead end. I wondered if he knew something about the small creek that we didn't, so I flagged him down and motioned for him to come over. He told us that what appeared to be a tiny little creek was actually the main boating channel in and out of St. Jerome's Bay. It was twelve feet deep and dredged out every week to give large boats access to the well protected harbor and marina on the other side of the bay.

As we pulled anchors and followed the fisherman through the narrow channel, I praised the Lord for sending him our way before it got dark. I also praised him for allowing us to be safely inside that calm, protected area that night. We anchored close to the creek opening, so we could get back out to the bay quickly the next morning. I positioned the boat just outside the main channel, yet close to a lighted marker, so other boats could see us in the dark. We slept well in that secure spot and were back out on the open water of Chesapeake Bay at first light.

Chapter 30

In the Wrong Place at the Right Time

Having slept well, it almost felt good to be back on the open water of Chesapeake Bay pounding and rolling our way north toward Annapolis. By seven thirty, we had already left St. Jerome's Bay far behind and I smiled as I thought about the blessing of being underway so early. Wind and waves were still behind us as they had been the night before, so we had our sails up. The weather radio said that things would calm down, and we could tell that the waves were already getting smaller and the force of the wind had diminished. We were less than sixty miles from Annapolis, and if things went well we could be there by late afternoon. That would give us the luxury of a whole evening, to relax and enjoy the sights of that historic harbor town. Marty and I had both been to Annapolis before, and enjoyed the quaintness of that bustling upscale seaport. We enjoyed seeing the beautiful yachts, and were impressed by the way the city catered to boaters, so we really looked forward to stopping there.

We motor-sailed our way north under gradually clearing skies, staying about a mile from shore on that blue bird day. Things calmed down so much that I switched to our biggest jib and later wrapped up both sails because there was no wind at all. As we approached

Annapolis the wind picked up again, but we were so close to being there, it wasn't really worth uncovering the sails. About a mile from the entrance to the harbor, we passed a unique and amazing structure. There was a full size house, high above the water right out in Chesapeake Bay. It had been built on tall, stilt-like pilings that had been driven into the bottom. There was a tower on the roof with a beacon, which told us that it was a light house. In the water below, a small skiff with a motor was tied to one of the pilings and a ladder led up to the base of the structure. "Look Marty, the lighthouse keeper is there," I said with a smile, as I thought about what an unusual job and how much solitude that person had.

As we entered Annapolis harbor, our eyes widened as we admired the beautiful sailing yachts, like two little boys in the worlds biggest toy store. Before we found a slip, I pulled in to a gas dock to fill our tanks and get ice. The young blonde man who worked there was friendly and very helpful. As he filled our tanks he told us how to contact the harbor master to get a spot for the night. We told him about our trip, and that the Lord had really blessed us so far. He didn't seem the least bit uncomfortable when we mentioned God, and said with a smile that "God Speed" was the perfect name for a boat owned by Christians taking a voyage like that. I sensed that he had a lot of experience with sailboats, and as we talked, he told us that he and his wife lived on a twenty-eight footer as their permanent residence. They had made the trip up and down the ICW many times, living at a dock in Florida all winter and Annapolis Harbor in the summer. After we paid for our gas and ice, he let us call the harbor master about a dock spot from his small office. Boating was a major source of revenue for Annapolis, and the city controlled the transient dock spots and moorings. The harbor master told me that a dock spot for the night was fifty dollars, and tying up to a mooring buoy was twenty-five. Trying to be a good steward of the cash I had left, I took the mooring buoy and he gave me the directions I would need to find it. When we said good-bye to the young man, he shook our hands and smiled sincerely as he told us that we were a breath of fresh air, and that he enjoyed meeting us. I thanked him and added a hearty "God bless you", while he was untying us. As he pushed us away, I shouted: "Maybe the good Lord will let you and your wife move up to a forty footer soon!" He laughed and nodded, giving us a thumbs up as we moved away to look for our mooring buoy.

God's hand of protection continued to be with us that afternoon. We found buoy number twenty-seven and tied the heavy mooring rope securely to our bow just minutes before a passing thunderstorm with high winds hit the harbor. We holed up in the cabin until the storm passed and then I called the harbor master on the radio. "Annapolis harbor master, this is the captain of the sailboat "God Speed" can you read me?" I asked. "Yes, captain, this is the harbormaster, I read you loud and clear," was his reply. "We would like to come into town, could you have a water taxi pick us up at mooring buoy number twenty-seven?" I asked politely. "Yes sir, we have a pickup at a yacht right next to you, the water taxi will be at your boat in just a few minutes," he answered respectfully. Marty and I looked at each other smiling and nodding. Without saying a word to each other, we knew exactly what the other guy was thinking. Even though we had to fight big waves in a small boat to get there, this was pretty cool, and at least for the moment, we felt like "big time" yacht owners.

Two water taxis moved in and out of the anchored boats in Annapolis harbor throughout the day. Each one was driven by a man in a white, navy style uniform wearing a boat captain's hat. Their sole purpose was to pick up boaters at their anchored vessels and bring them into town, or bring people from town back out to their boats. Our mooring fee gave us access to the boater's rest rooms, laundry room and showers. We hoped to freshen up, wash clothes and then spend the evening in town, taking in the sights and enjoying dinner in a restaurant. We gathered up everything we would need for our evening ashore, and were just closing the cabin when the water taxi pulled along side. Eagerly climbing aboard we thanked the "skipper" who smiled politely in his crisp white uniform as he motored over to pick up a family from the yacht at buoy twenty-eight. The main canal went right into downtown, and dead ended in the heart of the business district. Expensive boats were tied to the concrete walls on both sides of the man-made waterway. Boat traffic was intense as boats of every size moved in and out of the downtown area on that watery "Main Street" of Annapolis. The water taxi dropped us off in the center of town, right across from the harbor master's office and boater's facilities.

When I saw where the fifty dollar dock spot was, my heart sank. Our boat would have been parked right there in the center of that busy downtown area, with hundreds of locals and tourists walking by it. My Christian flag would have been flying proudly above the sidewalk, right in the middle of the most heavily populated city the boat had ever been in. Instead, it was in the wrong place at the "right" time, anchored in the middle of the harbor where only the sea gulls and a couple of yacht owners could read her name. Trying to save twenty-five dollars, I had missed a huge ministry opportunity, and I felt really bad about it. I wished I had thought about the visibility of the more expensive spot, before making the "frugal" choice. I knew that whatever God orders he pays for, and money invested in his work usually comes back multiplied many times over. There was nothing else I could do about it at that point, but I did learn a powerful lesson.

After we showered, did laundry and paid our mooring fees,

we began our evening in port by window shopping on the main street near the boater's canal. The upscale harbor front shops were quaint looking and very appealing to tourists. We enjoyed browsing in a bookstore that sold sailing books, boating charts, model ships, and nautical gifts. In the local ships store, we were again like two little boys, smiling and pointing at everything on display. That place had everything you could think of to outfit any boat, and many items you would never think of. We were reminded that Annapolis is the home of the US Naval Academy when we passed several uniformed naval officers on a cobblestone street. Marty offered to treat me to dinner in a very nice Italian restaurant. After living out of the boats ice box for so long, he didn't have to ask me twice. As we enjoyed the pasta, seafood and gourmet desserts, the negative experiences of the past two weeks seemed like they had happened only in a dream, as waves, storms and shallow water were now light years away.

After our decadent feast, we treated ourselves to large ice cream cones which we enjoyed while sitting on a bench near the canal. As we watched the parade of boats come and go, the sound of jazz filled the air as a local combo presented a waterfront concert. We lingered there as long as possible, but when darkness came, we reluctantly agreed that we should get back to the boat so we could be awake and on our way at first light.

Back aboard "God Speed" we stood quietly on deck, admiring the peaceful harbor scene in the darkness. The crescent moon had moved out from behind a cloud and gave the rippling water the appearance of liquid silver. The yachts swung slowly with the gentle breeze, all moving in unison to face the same direction, like silent watchmen staring out to sea. The peace that passes all understanding fell over the harbor and filled our hearts that night. Even though I felt like I had failed him, I could feel God's presence and his love all around us. "Thank you Father," I prayed, "for the relaxing, enjoyable time ashore, the good food and this safe anchorage. Lord, tonight you really did lead us beside the still waters and restore our souls. We thank you and praise you for your unfailing love and your blessings." When I finished praying we went below, and as I lay on my berth reviewing the events of the day, I knew I would treasure the memories of our time in Annapolis for a long time.

Voyage of the Heart

MISS CAISON
CAPT NC

Chapter 31

The Royal Treatment in a Hidden Harbor

The next morning we were awake and on our way out of Annapolis harbor before six. Once we pointed north, large swells came diagonally from behind us, hitting the right side of our stern. That made for a rough, unpleasant ride as we rocked and pitched our way up the bay for the first few hours. I felt positive in spite of the big waves because I knew that we were rapidly moving toward the calmest and most protected part of Chesapeake Bay. There was only one highway bridge that spanned the Chesapeake, and it was located just north of Annapolis. Now that we had passed under that bridge, the bay would continue to get narrower, until it became just a wide river at its northern end. To our left and slightly behind us we could see the city of Baltimore in the distance. Located just a few miles up the Patapsco River, it was positioned slightly inland from the bay. As the sun rose above the eastern shore, the low angle of its rays lit the city brilliantly, making it sparkle with a beautiful golden glow. As we admired the "golden city" I asked Marty if he thought heaven would look like that, but we both agreed that heaven would be much more breathtaking.

By mid morning, I saw that the prediction I made about the north end of the bay was correct. The farther north we went, the narrower and the calmer the bay got. I could now see both shorelines clearly and I began to move toward the eastern shore, because I would need to bear right when the bay forked in two different directions. Elk Neck State Park was on a large point of land that came down the center of the bay, splitting it into a right and a left fork. About ten miles up the eastern fork, the Chesapeake & Delaware Canal entered Chesapeake Bay. That narrow waterway was an integral part of the ICW, connecting the northernmost end of Chesapeake Bay to the Delaware River. Boats heading for New York, New Jersey or Philadelphia had to pass through the seventeen mile long canal to continue north. I was excited when we entered the C&D Canal, because it would bring us to New Jersey, and that meant we were finally getting close to New York.

There was no breeze on the protected waters of the narrow canal, and it was a ninety degree day. We had been up and cruising since five thirty and the midday heat was sapping what little strength we had left. At three o'clock Marty asked if we could stop for a minute so he could dive into the water, and right about then that sounded like a good idea. I slowed down and kicked the motor out of gear while Marty took off his shirt and emptied the pockets of his shorts. Without hesitating for a moment, he made a graceful dive from the highest point of the bow into the deep green water below. "Wow," I thought, "he must have really been hot, he didn't even wait for a life jacket or a safety line." Putting the swim ladder overboard, I threw him a rope and as he climbed back aboard he was grinning from ear to ear. Being more conservative and not as strong a swimmer as Marty, I flopped a clean bath towel overboard and dragged it through the water until it was soaked. Then I brought it aboard and wrung it out over my head, so the water ran down my body and completely saturated my clothes. I repeated the process a couple of times until I was just as wet as if I had gone for a swim fully dressed. We looked ridiculous but felt great. Perked up and refreshed, we headed out into the Delaware River to begin the next leg of our trip.

There was a small marina right where the C&D canal opened into the Delaware River. We could have called it a day, and stayed there that night, but it was only four o'clock in the afternoon. I wanted to get through the New Jersey section of the ICW quickly, in case we had to wait a day for perfect weather to venture out into the Atlantic. That short stretch, traveling on the "outside" and into New York Harbor, was the part of the trip I dreaded and feared the most. It would be critical to choose a time when wind and waves were at their calmest, to cover the most dangerous thirty miles of our voyage. I decided to go as far as possible that day, using every minute of daylight, and hoping that we would find a cove or inlet somewhere along the Delaware to spend the night.

As we turned right into the wide river, we were heading southeast toward the Atlantic. The river widened dramatically ahead into the large body of water known as Delaware Bay. The wide, yawning mouth of the bay opened directly into the ocean, so waves coming from hundreds of miles at sea could march right into the bay and twenty miles inland during a south east wind. A large point of land that was the southernmost tip of New Jersey protruded almost fifteen miles out across the opening of the bay. The Intra Coastal Waterway ducked back into the mainland just behind the tip of that point, and then made its way north, safely inland through most of New Jersey. That point (Cape May) sheltered the Jersey side of Delaware Bay from the wind and waves of the Atlantic. To stay in the calmest water, my plan was to hug the New Jersey shoreline, staying behind Cape May, all the way to the ICW entrance.

The Jersey side of Delaware Bay looked nothing like I expected it to. After we passed a large power plant on a point, we saw nothing for miles except wilderness. There was no sign of civilization, not even a highway, as trees, grass and swamps extended down the shore ahead of us as far as we could see. I felt uneasy, as I wondered if we would be able to find a marina, or even an inlet along that marshy uninhabited side of the bay. The chart showed that the Cohansey River entered the bay about twelve miles ahead. It appeared to be a good sized inlet and we would be there easily before dark, so it seemed like the logical place to spend the night. Our depth finder showed very shallow water close to shore, so we found ourselves moving farther and farther from the shoreline to stay in deep water. That made it more difficult to spot buoys or markers that would show us the mouth of the Cohansey. When we reached the area where it should have been, we saw only more of the same marshy, desolate, unbroken shoreline. We became more nervous as sundown approached, expecting to see it any time, as we continued eagerly down the shore. A couple of times we got false hope, as we spotted small groups of cottages on secluded beaches, but a close inspection showed no markers and no inlets there.

Now very frustrated and almost frantic, I tried the radio to see if another vessel could help us find the Cohansey, but no one responded. Finally in desperation, and as a last resort, I switched to the emergency channel and called the Coast Guard. A young ensign answered and was polite and respectful, but couldn't really help us, because we didn't know our exact position. He told me that red floating buoy number ten marked the entrance to the Cohansey River, about half a mile from shore. Then he gave me a gentle reprimand for using the emergency hailing channel for something that was not a life threatening situation. He went on to say that the "Captain" of a vessel should have navigational maps and charts of that area aboard, and was amazed that I didn't. He then reminded me that I was responsible for the safe navigation of my vessel, and for knowing where I was. I felt pretty foolish as I hung up the microphone, still having no idea where we were, or where we would spend the night.

Fear and dread set in, as we encountered more shallow areas and shoals with rip currents. We had to stay so far out that we could barely see shore, let alone a small protected cove or inlet to spend the night. Daylight was fading fast, when we spotted a small runabout anchored in an open cove near shore. The boat was so far away, that it was little more than a white speck on the water. *A boat that small had to be docked nearby,* I thought. If we could just get close enough to hail them, I knew they could point us to a place where we could spend the night. As I turned and headed for them at full speed, two thoughts haunted me:

1. It would take quite a while to get to them and it was almost dark, what if they pulled anchor and took off before we got there?

2. I was barreling at full speed into an area that could be very shallow and they were anchored right along the marsh grass.

"Marty, keep an eye on the depth," I yelled over the roar of the motor, "This could be our only chance. Lord, please get us in where that boat is without hitting something, and please make them stay put until we get there," I asked fervently, as the boat grew larger.

There was only four to five feet of water in the marshy cove, so we approached the group of fishermen in the small boat cautiously. They were happy to help, and we were greatly relieved when they told us there was a state marina just a mile down the shore. They pointed us in the right direction, and told us how to find the channel markers that would lead us up the small, well hidden inlet. They also said to call the marina on channel twenty three, to ask for a dock spot while we were on our way in. When I hailed the Fortescue State Marina, a Coast Guard officer responded. The small facility was closed for the night and the Coast Guard monitored their calls after hours. To my delight, he contacted the president of the boaters association, and made arrangements for us to have a slip for the night. The channel markers that would lead us into the "hidden harbor" were small, faded and oddly placed. I slowed down and hesitated, as I tried to figure out which side to pass them on, but God's guiding hand was there again. A voice boomed through the radio so loud and clear that it startled us. "Sailboat God Speed, follow me in," hailed a deep friendly voice with a New Jersey accent. Looking behind us, we saw a large fishing boat coming our way as it headed into port for the night. Apparently the captain had been listening to our conversation with the Coast Guard, and knew who we were and where we were going. He was only too happy to be our "guiding angel" and lead us up the winding channel to the marina.

As we approached the docks, an older man pointed to an open spot next to another sailboat so I headed there. A small handful of people had gathered, right above the spot where we were coming in. It looked like the word had gotten out that "new comers" had arrived, from "a far away place" and curious onlookers had gathered to see us. It must have been low tide, because the docks and the sidewalks were way above our heads. Once we were tied up, we had to climb a ladder, to get up to the docks and the people who were waiting there to greet us. The friendly older man introduced himself as the president of the boaters association. He was the one who had talked to the Coast Guard and reserved a spot for us when we called. The small group of people was made up of loveable senior citizens. They were warm, friendly and almost too helpful, as they welcomed us to their small, quaint seaside village. They gathered around us, eagerly asking questions, introducing themselves, and offering help and advice. They all talked at once, telling us the best place to have breakfast, buy supplies and fish from the docks. They wanted to know our names, where we had come from and where we were going. When they found out that we had come all the way from Florida in the small sailboat, there eyes widened, and I felt like they thought of us as "celebrities" from that point on. I got the feeling they didn't get too many boaters in there that didn't live there, and seeing how hard it was to find the entrance channel, I wasn't surprised.

They told us that the sailboat next to ours also had two men aboard, and had arrived just an hour ago. They were on their way to Atlantic City to do some gambling in the casinos. When I looked at it, I realized that it was also a Hunter 25 and almost a carbon copy of our boat with a different color scheme. Our new friends asked if we were hungry, and heartily recommended an Italian restaurant about half a mile away that overlooked the bay. The two men from the other sailboat were already there having dinner, and it sounded like a great idea. A sweet woman insisted on calling the place on her cell phone, because it was almost closing time. She told them emphatically that they had to stay open a little longer that night, because there were two hungry sailors in town who wanted to have dinner there. She talked like she was the owner of the restaurant, and insisted that they give us the "royal treatment" since we had come all the way from Florida by boat. A short, stocky man offered to take us there in his car. As we got in, I smiled as he proudly shared more information about the area, in his classic New Jersey accent.

At the restaurant, our "chauffeur" took us inside and introduced us to the restaurant owners, waitresses and the two men from the other sailboat as though we were VIPs who had graced their small town with a visit. The other sailors insisted that we join them for dinner. We sat down eagerly, because I had all kinds of questions about their boat, their trip, Delaware Bay and the New Jersey section of the Intra Coastal Waterway. Doug, the owner of the boat was a round faced, jovial, gray haired man about my age. He seemed mellow and pretty laid back about everything, and loved to talk about sailboats. Mark, his sailing buddy, had dark hair and was younger, thinner and lacked the warmth and people skills of Doug. Their wives had allowed them to take a week long, "guys only" boat trip from Baltimore up to Atlantic City to gamble. We were surprised that they planned to go right out into the ocean, and sail up the coast on the "outside" in the open waters of the Atlantic. They were impressed by our long trip from Florida, but equally surprised that we chose to stay in the ICW, where we were slowed down by bridges, winding rivers and boat traffic.

It was interesting to me, how the voyage of those two men was such a study in contrasts to our own, even though their vessel was almost identical:

» Their boat had no name on it, and they were heading into dangerous waters where few people would see them to get to their destination quickly.

» They hoped to spend as much time as possible, surrounded by people who were also focused on the pleasures of this world, in a colorful, provocative, noisy, smoke filled environment.

» The purpose of their spur of the moment trip was simply to have fun, get away from their wives, and try to win a lot of money.

My Heavenly Father had given me yet another object lesson that was powerful yet sad: Even though our bodies or earthly "vessels" might appear to be the same from the outside. The heart of someone living for God is filled with purpose, joy and rewarding satisfaction. While the heart of someone who does not know him; is empty, unfulfilled and lonely. Desperately seeking, but never quite finding, fulfillment and joy in the pleasures, distractions and accomplishments of this world.

As we enjoyed our pasta, I gradually worked God into the conversation. Since I had a captive audience that loved sailing stories, I told them how the Lord had given me my boat, saved us countless times and navigated our trip. Then I told them about his incredible timing, as even that night the fishing boat had appeared on cue, to lead us safely into that quaint friendly place. I worked in a little bit of my testimony and also mentioned that I had a ministry sharing the gospel with outdoorsmen through my videos. I probably said too much, but I sensed that those two men might not hear those things anywhere else, and I knew where they were going the next day. They didn't seem turned off by what I shared, and took in everything I had to say, nodding politely with a smile. Not one of us was eager to leave the luxury of the restaurant for the small confines of a boat, so we lingered there, swapping sailing tips and information for quite some time. As we stood to leave, the man who drove us there "magically" appeared at the door, to give us a ride back to the marina.

Back at the docks, a small group of fishermen had gathered above their boats to socialize and plan their strategies for the next day. Two of the men, who had welcomed us earlier, gave us some valuable information about crossing Delaware Bay. They said we should follow the shoreline only as far as Egg Island point. Then they gave us the exact compass heading to steer across the open water of the bay. If we followed that course, we would be right at the entrance to the ICW in Cape May when we saw land again. That was a better strategy than hugging the shoreline, because it was a much shorter distance. The weather report looked good for that morning, but they cautioned us to be careful, because ocean going ships had been lost on Delaware Bay. Doug and Mark were also planning to leave at first light, so they offered to follow us across the bay. That idea made both crews feel more secure, since the small sailboats would be far from the sight of land during the crossing.

While Marty took a walk to explore the town, I dumped and rinsed the porta potty and washed down the boat. As I worked under the light of a street lamp, a black crowned night heron landed on a dock piling close to me. As the large white bird stared at me, I remembered the one that had watched me on Amelia Island. "Lord, I don't really believe that this is the same bird I saw on the dock in Florida, but he sure looks the same," I whispered. "Has this bird been following me eight hundred miles?" I asked. "Are you using him to remind me that your Holy Spirit is always with me, and his crown to remind me of your sacrifice? Whether this is the same bird, or his New Jersey cousin, I thank you and praise you, for the ways that you remind me of your presence. Thank you Lord, that we are here and safe, and have been treated so well. Please continue to travel with us and protect us, in Jesus name I pray, Amen." With that I turned in, knowing that everything was ready for an early start the next morning. All we had to do was fill the tanks when the gas dock opened at six, and we would be on our way across Delaware Bay.

Voyage of the Heart

Chapter 32

His Majesty's Ship Surrenders to the Enemy

By seven o'clock the next morning the unlikely "armada" was well on its way across the open waters of Delaware Bay. The two men on a sailing "mission" were followed close behind by the two men on a gambling excursion. We started across before sunrise, and made quite a few miles in the dead calm of early morning. The sky was blue and the huge body of water had been almost like a mirror for the first hour. As we moved out of sight of land and the wind picked up, it was comforting to see our sister ship plowing confidently along behind us. We stayed in radio contact with the other men during the crossing, and when we saw them put up their sails we followed suit. With sails aloft and our Honda outboard purring smoothly, "God Speed" sliced aggressively through the rolling chop, gradually opening the distance between the vessels as we pulled away from the other boat.

For their safety and ours, we stayed in visual contact with them, but by the time we sighted Cape May and the entrance to the ICW they were over a mile behind us. As we headed for the channel and they turned toward the Atlantic, I said goodbye to them and thanked them for following us. I also voiced a sincere "God

Bless you" and wished them "God Speed" and good luck on their voyage. As we headed into the mouth of the river, a massive vessel with many decks came from the bay and followed us up the channel. As we moved up the inlet, we passed a dock where hundreds of vehicles were boarding and waiting to board another vessel that was identical to the one that was following us. The lettering on its side told us it was the Cape May Ferry. Apparently the two large ferry boats shuttled vehicles back and forth across the bay from Cape May, New Jersey, to Lewes, Delaware.

It felt good to be safely across the big water of Delaware Bay, and on the inland waterway that would take us through most of New Jersey. As we cruised through the commercial and residential sections of Cape May, we moved into "another world", finding ourselves in an area unlike anything we had seen before. Homes, apartments and businesses occupied every available foot of waterfront space. Every so often a marina, a store, or a restaurant interrupted the solid wall of two story residential dwellings. Houses and condos were built so close to the river that many porches and decks were built on pilings that rose from the water. Deeply tanned people were everywhere, fishing, sunbathing, and sipping cold drinks on almost every dock and balcony. As we passed waterfront restaurants, well dressed couples waved from dockside tables topped with tall exotic drinks.

Almost every residence had an expensive looking boat tied up outside, and most of them were powerboats. For every boat that was sitting at a dock, it seemed like there were three more moving up and down the crowded waterway around us. I felt like I was on the busy interstate again, now surrounded by a steady stream of boats moving in both directions, instead of vehicles. As we passed under a fixed bridge our motor sputtered, coughed and died without any warning. I was in shock as I pulled the start rope, because it had run flawlessly for three weeks straight. It took me three hard pulls to get it started again, but it ran really rough. Dead ahead on a bend in the river was a restaurant with some outdoor tables. It had a large dock along one side for patrons arriving by boat. Since the motor sounded like it was about to quit again, we headed there hoping they wouldn't mind. The motor stopped running about ten feet from their dock, but we were able to glide the rest of the way in and get tied up. Before we could even look at it, a big power boat slowed its engines and also headed for that dock. There was a large older man aboard with three women of about the same age. The man was steering, and the women seemed clueless about coming in to a dock, so Marty and I ran down to help them get in.

They had the same New Jersey accents and loveable "grand-parent" ways as the kindly retirees in Fortesque, and they made a big fuss as they thanked us for helping them come in. When we told them about our motor problem, they offered their cell phones so we could call a marina. They also offered to take us and our outboard to any marine repair shop in the area, by boat, or in a vehicle if necessary. Using the restaurants yellow pages, I called several Honda dealers and finally got a live mechanic on the line. When I told him the size and year of our motor, he told me to check the water outlet nozzle to make sure that water was spraying out of it. If it wasn't, he said to clear the nozzle with a paper clip or a pin, and if that wasn't the problem to call him right back. Before we could check it, an expensive looking speed boat approached the dock and started to pull in behind our boat. Marty and I ran to catch their lines and pull the large racing boat gently into the dock, being careful not to scratch the brand new vessel. The attractive, well tanned "with it" young couple aboard didn't appear to be married, and had the looks of Hollywood celebrities. Dressed provocatively in designer swimwear, and cruising in a boat that took more money for gas in one summer than my boat cost, they seemed to have everything the world could offer. They thanked us for helping them come in and glanced at the emblem and name on our boat, as they made their way to a table near our new "friends". As I pulled the start rope on our motor, I wondered if the Lord had stalled us there, just so we could meet the four retirees, and help that young couple.

The motor started right up, but still ran rough. The mechanic on the phone had been right; it wasn't spraying water out of the outlet jet, so Marty dove into the muddy river with a paper clip. Once he cleared the nozzle, it began to spray water normally and soon settled into the smooth hum I had grown used to. Overjoyed that the repair had been so simple and cost free, I praised the Lord loudly, hoping that our friends had heard me. Walking to the table where the man and three women were having lunch. I thanked them up and down for the use of their cell phone and their kind offer to take our motor to a repair shop. Then I told them that the Good Lord got our motor going again, so they wouldn't need to. Deliberately speaking in a loud voice, I went on to tell them how God had blessed our trip so far and provided our every need. As we said our goodbyes, one of the women hugged me and the large man offered his big burly hand. They wished us "God Speed" on the rest of our trip, and I voiced a loud "God bless you" as we left them. I was pleased to see that the young couple had been watching the whole exchange, and that they were still watching us from their table as we headed off down the river.

Things went smoothly for the next few hours. Surrounded by the heaviest boat traffic we had ever seen, we wound our way through densely populated areas lined with dwellings. As we moved along a section of the river that had condos on one side and a large swamp on the other, the motor died again. I pulled it repeatedly as we drifted toward the marsh grass, but it made no sound at all, so we threw an anchor and sat there shaking our heads as we tried again and again to restart it. After Marty took the cover off and tinkered with it for a while, it started up and seemed to run okay, so we pulled the anchor and continued on our way, only to have it quit again thirty minutes later. This time we began to drift toward people's docks and expensive boats, so I got the anchor out again and threw it over the side. By now our nerves were shot and our patience was gone. The motor had been spraying water fine before it died, so Marty thought we bought some bad gas that had water or rust particles in it. He disconnected the fuel hoses and bled some gas from the carburetor and then put things back together. The motor started right up, so we upped anchor and got underway again, hoping that everything would now be fine.

The motor seemed to run okay for the next hour or so. During that time we went under three fixed bridges. Each one appeared to be too low for our mast to pass beneath it. We approached each span at a dead slow glide, ready to kick the motor into reverse and rev it hard before the mast could make contact. But each time, the top of the mast just cleared the bridge, missing it by as little as six inches. After that, we approached a bridge that had numbered lines on the walls above and below the water line. That told boaters exactly how much clearance there was at any given time, based on how high or how low the tide was. Some quick math told me that our thirty-two foot mast, resting on the cabin top five feet above the water, would not clear that bridge until the tide went out. Checking the tidal chart, we found that we would have to wait at least an hour to have any chance of clearing it. Since we had time to kill, we decided to pull into a dock and work on the motor some more, hoping to get it back to being one hundred percent dependable. We pulled into a floating dock section that was close to a large marina. Marty thought that if he could install a new squeeze bulb and a fuel filter in the gas line, our motor problems would be solved. He went to work on the motor taking things apart, while I walked to the marina to buy the parts we would need.

As I walked along the docks, I admired the charter fishing boats, ski boats and cruisers that were tied there. A very nice fishing boat with two men aboard was trying to back into a slip as I passed. Going quickly down the steps, I grabbed a line and pulled the boat gently into the dock, holding it away and steady while the owners positioned some fenders. The captain couldn't thank me enough for helping, and I sensed that people there weren't used to having strangers rush to help them. Seeing an opportunity, I said: "The good Lord always sends someone to help me when I need it. I wouldn't be much of a Christian, if I didn't help someone else in need." With that I moved on, calling out a hearty "God bless you" over my shoulder as I continued down the dock. As I crossed through a boat yard, I encountered a tall black man in mechanics coveralls. I asked him if there was a place nearby where I could buy some fuel line parts, and he sent me in the right direction. Thanking him, I headed for a gas dock with a small "ships store" that sold boating accessories. Finding what Marty needed there, I headed back, hoping that the water had gotten low enough for us to fit under that bridge. When Marty had everything put back together, we got underway and headed for the bridge. It was low tide, so if we didn't fit under it now, we would be stuck there. Then we would either have to back track and go out into the ocean, or spend several hours putting our mast down and then back up again. Neither one of those choices sounded appealing, so I prayed hard that we would slip beneath it as we approached the bridge.

The closer we got, the more it looked like our mast wasn't going to clear it. If it hit the bridge, even at a slow speed, the impact could pop one or more of the cables that held it up. If the mast fell, one or both of us could be seriously injured and the boat would be damaged. Even if it didn't fall, it would be unsafe to use sails without the taut opposing cables that held the mast in place. As we closed to within a few feet, it still looked like it was going to hit from where we stood. I slowed the motor and kicked it into reverse, but the current and our forward motion kept pushing us toward the bridge and apparent disaster. Giving the motor full throttle in reverse the boat slowed almost to a stop but not quite. "Marty, stand on the port rail!" I yelled, as both of us put our weight as far to the left side as possible. The boat leaned left, which gained us a couple more inches at the top of the mast. As the mast top reached the bridge I cringed and then breathed a sigh of relief as it passed beneath it, missing the steel girders by just a couple of inches. "Thank you, Lord!" I repeated over and over as I steered for the tallest point of the bridges underside. "Stay there man!" I said nervously to my sailing partner, who now sat on the edge of the deck with his feet dangling over the side. Now that we were under the bridge, a frightening thought occurred to me. If the mast bobbed up or the bridge was lower on the far side we would really be in trouble. If it somehow got stuck between two beams and I could not get out from under the bridge the boat would be destroyed. As the tide came in the rising water would push the top of the mast up into the steel and concrete. As the boat continued to rise the bottom of the mast would be driven downward into the boat collapsing the cabin roof, or holding the boat underwater as the water rose enough to fill it and sink it. Needless to say, I breathed much easier when I saw the top of the mast come out into blue sky on the other side of the bridge. I praised the Lord that we got beyond that one, and that there was nothing but marsh ahead, so we wouldn't have to worry about bridges for a while.

After another hour we were well beyond the last docks, dwellings and marinas, and had left all signs of civilization far behind.

We were winding our way through marsh lands again, where swamp grass and water went as far as the eye could see. We had not seen any boats or people for quite some time, and there was less than an hour of daylight left. We talked nervously about the motor, hoping that Marty's last repair had solved the problem. But thoughts continued to haunt me that it could die again out there in that desolate area, miles from any help. The river got narrower as it wound its way through the swamp, and the thought of anchoring out there all night didn't sound very appealing. Pushing the motor wide open, I was trying to make it to the next town before dark, hoping we could find a lighted public dock or other safe place to tie up. Just after I rounded a sharp bend, the motor died again, in one of the narrowest stretches of the river. "No, not here, not know!" I cried out, in absolute frustration, frantically pulling the start rope again and again. Dead in the water, we drifted toward the riverbank. As I desperately pulled the silent motor, I yelled to Marty to get an anchor over the side before we got stuck in the mud, but the river was so narrow there, we didn't have to drift far to be in shallow water. As soon as the words "stuck in the mud" came out of my mouth, my heart sank, as I felt the keel drag bottom and the boat lean toward shore. A few more pulls told me that the motor was not going to start this time, and now to add insult to injury, we were aground in the middle of the swamp. We were miles from civilization, hadn't seen a boat in an hour and it would soon be dark. I slumped on the seat crushed with disappointment and buried my face in my hands, as Marty lowered his gaze and simply shook his head in disbelief.

At that moment, the Christian Flag that had been flying so proudly at the top of the mast broke loose and slid down the mast cable all the way to the deck. It really spooked us, because it looked like we were defeated by the enemy, and had lowered our colors to surrender. It was as if Satan wanted to show us that we were beaten, and that our trip was over. With my vivid imagination, I could almost hear his voice telling me:

"Let's see if you still tell people how God blessed and protected you, after you spend the night aground in the blackness of this swamp. Especially after you wake up tomorrow with no motor power and have to spend the rest of your money to tow your broken little boat out of here, and get it home. You are done telling people how real God is, and flaunting his emblem in their face, and I have brought down the flag of Christ to let you know that I am here, and that I am not happy with what you have been doing."

I'm not sure if I started to shiver because Satan felt so real at that moment, or because it was getting cold and damp out there in the swamp as it got dark. I told Marty that I felt like the enemy was trying to stop us from completing our "missionary trip", and he nodded solemnly in agreement. We sat there staring out over the swamp as the light faded, too tired and depressed to move or even speak. We felt defeated and completely exhausted, both physically and emotionally. As I told myself that this was the end of the trip, a still small voice reminded me of all the times that God had blessed me, protected me, and provided my every need. In spite of the devastation and weariness I felt, there was a peace and a quiet confidence deep within me, that told me the trip was not over. The still small voice told me that the Lord didn't give me that boat and bring me so far, only to let things end this way. As I felt his presence, even at that moment of great disappointment, I chose to believe what the still small voice was saying.

Chapter 33

A Bridge Too Low and a Mast Too Tall

As we sat there in the silence, I told Marty that I thought I heard a noise. He said I was imagining it, so we both listened again. Ears that had been deadened by thirty years of teaching drum lessons strained eagerly for a sound other than the frogs and insects of the swamp. Suddenly, Marty grabbed my arm and whispered: "Wait, I do hear something, I think it's a motor." A minute later, hopeful smiles came to our faces, as the low rumble of a powerful motor broke the stillness of the marsh. There was a boat winding its way down the river toward us. It was coming from behind us and heading the same way we were. As it came around the bend, we saw that it was a sleek, sporty, racing boat, similar to the one that the young couple at the restaurant had. The muscular young man driving was sipping a beer, and the attractive woman with him looked bored as she stared off across the swamp. Marty and I stood up and began to wave our arms frantically, motioning for them to come over. But I sensed from their expressions that they really didn't want to be bothered. He was reluctant to slow down, and when he did stop, he made no move to come toward us. There was a hardness and lack of warmth about the couple, and they seemed annoyed that we had interrupted there evening cruise.

"We're dead in the water with motor trouble, and we really don't want to spend the night here," I shouted loudly. "Could you tow us in the direction you're going, and drop us off at the first marina or dock you come to?" I asked politely. "I really don't wanna tow anybody with this, it's brand new," replied a deep, inner city, tough guy voice. "There's no way I would bring this baby into water that shallow anyway," he stated firmly, "the motors on it cost ten grand apiece." We hadn't seen a boat in an hour, and it was almost dark. I knew his boat might be our only chance to get in somewhere that night, so I made up my mind that I wouldn't take no for an answer. "A sailboat's the easiest thing in the world to tow," I told him, "Once you get one moving, they just glide along on their own. You won't even know we're behind you," I assured him. Hoping to "close the deal" I added: "I can tie several ropes together to make a really long tow rope. Then I can throw it out to you, so you don't have to come into shallow water. I'd be happy to pay you something toward your gas. Please help us get in somewhere, if you don't, we're gonna be stranded out here all night!" Still looking annoyed, but softening a little, he reluctantly swung around and came as close to us as he could while staying in deep water. The woman caught the rope I threw on the third try, and made it fast to the ski ring on the back of their boat. I remembered that our keel was in the mud, but had drifted into it slowly. *It shouldn't be buried the way it was when I ran aground at cruising speed,* I thought. "Go real slow until we start moving," I yelled, knowing that a boat that powerful would either pull us out of the mud, or pull our bow ring right out of the fiberglass. They started ahead slowly taking the slack out of the rope, then "God Speed" turned sharply, leaned to starboard and was free of the bottom.

Overjoyed, I praised the Lord, as I steered to stay centered on their boat. If I held a straight course and steered with them, we really would glide effortlessly behind them and they would hardly know we were there. As the man sped up, I noticed a wisp of smoke and a red point of light in her hand as the woman lit a cigarette. While they were towing us, I tried to think of a way to witness to them, if only with our attitude and our actions.

We moved very well behind the large powerful boat, reaching faster speeds than we could have on our own. After being towed for about thirty minutes we rounded a bend and I was happy to see the lights of civilization ahead. A main road passed over the waterway, just before the river widened to become Peck's Bay. The long fixed bridge that took the highway over the river had three large openings for the boat traffic below. The center opening appeared to be tall enough for our mast but it was going to be close. The openings on the right and left were smaller, with vertical clearances that would allow the passage of powerboats, but not a sailboat with a mast. There was a big marina on the left, just beyond the bridge with a long fuel dock that ran parallel to shore. The young couple seemed to be heading there, so I quickly got out the fenders while steering and told Marty to put them on the port side. I was so preoccupied watching Marty hang the fenders; I didn't even realize where we were heading. "Oh no," I gasped, at the horrifying sight ahead. The couple was heading straight for the opening on the right side of the bridge, as they always did. Not being sailors, they had forgotten all about our mast. It didn't even occur to them that our mast would never pass under the bridge opening on the right side, even though their boat always did. To make matters worse, we were heading for the bridge at a much faster speed than we could under our own power. I couldn't even imagine the kind of damage that would occur to the boat and our bodies as the middle of the mast made contact with the bridge at that speed. Marty and I began to yell and shout wildly, waving our arms to get the couple's attention. I prayed that they would hear us over the rumble of their motor and look back before it was too late! The woman looked back, and we pointed frantically at the top of the mast and then at the bridge ahead. She tapped the man on the shoulder, who also looked back. When he saw us pointing and yelling he got the message, and headed for the center opening of the bridge.

We always approached bridges that were a "close call" very slowly, but this time we had no control over our speed. As we raced toward the bridge, it didn't look like the mast was going to clear this time. It was hard to tell, because when you looked up from the deck, the mast always looked taller than it was. Watching the top of the mast fly toward the steel beams at ten miles per hour, I yelled to Marty to save himself and he dove into the cabin below. At the last second I stepped to the left so the mast wouldn't fall on me, covered my head with my free arm and dropped to my knees to wait for the disastrous impact. "Three, two, one . . . nothing, just silence," I thought, with my eyes still closed. "It should have hit by now," I told myself, so I opened my eyes. Looking up, I was thrilled to see the top of the mast moving just inches below the concrete and steel of the bridges underside. "Thank you, Lord Jesus," I shouted. "Thank you Lord," Marty chimed in, coming out of the cabin with a smile and looking straight up to watch the mast top pass under the bridge.

Now the trick was to have them drop the tow rope at just the right moment, so we had enough forward glide to make it there, but not come in too fast either. Since we had no motor power, and no way to slow ourselves down, the thought of hitting the dock at ten miles per hour was even scarier than not quite making it there. It was clear that our reluctant towers didn't know sailboats, so I had a bad feeling about what was about to happen. The man never slowed down as he approached the dock, and the woman waited too long to untie the rope and drop it. As a result we headed for the dock too fast. They circled, waved goodbye and left, which meant that we only had one chance to grab that dock. Since it was a long dock that ran parallel to shore, I steered for the far end of it, hoping we would have slowed down by then. On that end was a pair of round red fenders like the ones on the dock in Norfolk. I headed for them but we were still moving too fast to bump against a dock. "Marty, we're coming in too fast, but we can't miss this dock!" I shouted. "Be ready to jump off with the front rope, and do whatever it takes to stop her and bring her in."

As soon as we were close enough, we jumped to the dock holding the front and back ropes. The boat bounced off the big round fender and almost pulled both of us in the water as it rebounded away from the dock. Its forward motion pulled us down the dock as we dug in our heels for a tug of war with two tons of fiberglass moving at three miles per hour. Somehow with God's help we brought her to a stop before we ran out of dock, and tied her securely against the big red fenders. Greatly relieved after that ordeal, we sat there on the dock panting, smiling and shaking our heads. I teased Marty about diving into the cabin, and he kidded me about the way my face looked before the mast cleared. Even though we were exhausted, it felt good to be able to laugh about the mishaps and close calls of the day, now that we were safely tied up where we could get mechanical help.

As we sat there, a young man came down the dock carrying a couple of fishing poles. With a smile and a handshake he introduced himself as Chris. That dock was his favorite night fishing spot, and he had caught some nice ones there under the dock lights. As I talked to him, I learned that we were just across the river from Ocean City, New Jersey. When I told him about our motor problems, he said his friend Paul was a mechanic, and that Paul was staying there that night on his boat. Without being asked, he went off to look for his friend to see if he could take a look at our motor. He returned a few minutes later with a freckle faced, sandy haired young man that looked like a little boy in a grown up body. Paul listened carefully to all the symptoms, as Marty and I described how the motor acted that day. He nodded thoughtfully, evaluating everything we said, and then he pronounced his diagnosis. "It sounds like you got a really bad tank of gas somewhere," he said. "All you need to do is dump your tanks and fill them with good fresh premium gas," he stated confidently. "After that, I bet she'll purr like a kitten. If she doesn't, I'd be happy to tear it apart and work on it for ya," he added helpfully.

We continued to make small talk, and I shared our trip plans with them. I told them how the Lord had blessed us so far, even sending a boat our way that night, just before it got dark. When I described the young couple and their boat, Chris said they were friends of his. He told me that the muscular young man who helped us was an off duty police officer named Josh. When I said they had been reluctant to help, Chris found that hard to believe, since Josh and his girlfriend had been stranded in the swamp themselves just last week with mechanical trouble. Chris also said there was a party at the marina that night, a couple of docks over. A group of the younger boat owners was getting together to play cards and have drinks on one of the house boats. Josh and his girlfriend Mindy would be there and Chris and Paul were going over there now. As they prepared to leave, I asked if either of them were hunters and I told them about my videos and my ministry to outdoorsmen. Chris said that he was a hunter and Paul said he had a good friend who was. I gave them hunting tracts and brochures, and as I shook their hands and said goodbye they both promised to read them and pass them on.

After they left, Marty and I took a walk around the marina. I wanted to thank the young couple who helped us, and we needed to check out the facilities so we knew what was available to us the next morning. After we found the shower building, main office and ship's store, we took a walk on the docks to admire the boats. Half way down one of the docks, we found the party that Chris and Paul had told us about. Attractive, well dressed young people were crowded aboard one of the larger boats smoking and sipping drinks as loud music boomed. Chris and Paul saw us and waved with a smile. When I spotted Josh and Mindy (the couple who towed us) I waved at them to get their attention and then yelled a sincere thank you in their direction. "I can't thank you guys enough for getting us in," I began. "We'd still be out there in the swamp, if you hadn't come along to save the day," I added, as they nodded with a forced smile. "God bless ya now, have a good time." I concluded, as we moved off down the dock.

The next morning I awoke before the sun and took a quick shower. Then I prayed and worked on my Captain's Log in a gazebo, while I waited for the ships store to open. When it did, I bought a navigational chart that showed the New Jersey section of the ICW and the Atlantic coastline. I also purchased hose clamps and a large fuel filter from the helpful man who worked there. Marty and I dumped the gas tanks into the sandy soil of a parking lot, and then we refilled them at the gas dock. After he bled the carburetor and installed the fuel filter, the motor started with one pull. It seemed to run smoothly, but to test it we let it run at low idle at the dock for forty-five minutes. While the motor ran, Marty hoisted me up the mast using the main halyard rope. I was determined to restore our Christian flag to its rightful position at the top of the mast. I wanted to display it proudly, and show the enemy that he had not won. We used a heavy duty bosons harness that was designed for lifting someone up the mast to make repairs. The bay was choppy that morning, and the mast swung like a pendulum as the boat rocked and chafed at her ropes. With my weight near the top, the side to side swinging of the tall aluminum pole was much worse. Getting the tiny metal snaps secured to the mast cable without dropping them in the bay was quite a challenge as I swung back and forth. It was probably the scariest and most unpleasant job I have ever done, and I tried not to look down at the dock or the white caps thirty feet below.

Once the Christian flag was flying at the top of the rigging, and the motor had run for almost an hour without stalling, we felt that we could get underway with confidence. It was still early and Marty hinted that it would be nice to have coffee and breakfast in a restaurant. I was so happy about the motor and the flag I agreed that we should enjoy a good meal to celebrate our blessings. Getting directions in the marina, we walked to Pappy's Pig Roast and Barbecue. The man in the ship's store recommended it highly, and it was supposed to be just a short walk down the highway. The "short" walk turned out to be over a mile, but the breakfast smells that greeted us as we stepped inside made the long trek seem worth it. The cozy little restaurant was clean and appealing, and the woman who came to our table greeted us with a smile, even though we sensed that she had been a waitress forever. We feasted on pancakes, sausage, eggs, juice and coffee, and since meals like that had been few and far between, we both over ate. As we finished, we got into a conversation with our waitress. The short, blonde woman with the thick New Jersey accent was very open, and she listened intently as we told her about the voyage we were taking. She seemed sincerely interested in our story, nodding respectfully as I shared how God's hand had saved us several times. As she cleared our plates, she went behind the counter and began talking to the cook. It was easy to see that she was talking about us, since she pointed our way more than once. The large, dark haired man who was cooking wore an apron, but was built like an NFL lineman. He had the face of a tough guy, yet there was something in his eyes that told me he was a gentle giant. He seemed to be the boss or owner of the eatery. His eyes widened and he nodded thoughtfully, as he listened to the woman and looked at us. Taking off his apron he waved at us and said: "Adella tells me you've had quite a trip. It's pretty slow right now, so I'd be happy to run you guys back to the marina if you need a ride." "Wow that would be great!" I replied, thinking that right then, a nap sounded better than a mile walk back to the boat.

As we got into his SUV, we learned that his name was Tom, and that he was the owner of the restaurant. The soft spoken, down to earth, blue collar "Joe" had started the small family run business, and worked hard to make it a success. We shared the same stories with him (about how God blessed our trip) that we had with his sister Adella. He took it all in, nodding thoughtfully and then wished us a safe journey the rest of the way home. As we got out, we thanked him for going so far above and beyond the call of duty for his patrons. We left him with a fond "God bless you", and assured him that if we were ever in Ocean City again, there was no doubt where we would eat breakfast.

Atlantic City, New Jersey was ten miles farther north than the marina near Ocean City where we spent the night. To reach it, we had to make our way through a maze of winding rivers and man-made canals. The route was not well marked as it crossed a couple of shallow bays, so the chart I purchased turned out to be worth its weight in gold. We had been in heavy boat traffic all morning and as we entered the city we passed through residential areas, where crowded apartment buildings and boat houses rose right from the water on both sides of the canal. Then the route turned inland again and away from densely populated neighborhoods. When we spotted the tall, sparkling buildings that housed the casinos and beach front resorts, we were way out in the marshes again, and could see them only from a distance. As me moved away from the shiny buildings of Atlantic City, the only thing ahead of us was endless marsh grass and water, as far as we could see.

The sky darkened and it began to rain. Not a hard rain, but the kind of relentless drizzle that lasted all day. After we passed Atlantic City, Marty decided to take a nap in the cabin, leaving me steering through the swamp alone for several hours. As I wound my way down narrow rivers, I was surrounded by grass taller than the boat, and I thought to myself: *It feels like I'm cruising on a jungle river in the Amazon, or on the jungle cruise ride at Walt Disney World.* "Careful now ladies and gentlemen," I mocked, taking on the voice of a tour guide. "This stretch of river is home to some of the largest crocodiles in the world, so please keep all hands and feet inside the boat," I said smiling. If I didn't know where I was, I would have expected to see a hippo surface next to me, or round a bend to see a group of elephants spraying water as they bathed in the river. What amazed me the most was that I was not cruising through a remote jungle, but through our most densely populated state.

The depressingly dark sky made the empty desolation of the swamp even more dreary and foreboding. The cool, misty drizzle chilled me, so I donned my poncho but still shivered. The cold rain, dark sky, and remoteness of the area got me down. I began to feel an overwhelming sense of loneliness as I stood there steering my way through the swamp alone. To make matters worse, I was on the very shallowest stretch of the Intra Coastal Waterway at low tide. The depth alarm beeped constantly, showing less than five and sometimes less than four feet of water in the middle of the channel. Several times I braced myself for contact with the bottom, only to feel the boat keep moving as the keel dragged through mud. At one point I did get stuck momentarily, but was able to break free by backing up and then gunning the motor forward in a new direction. I wanted to get out a warm, dry sweatshirt to put on under my rain gear, but leaving the tiller in that shallow, winding channel was out of the question. Anchoring while I changed clothes was too much work alone, and we were barely going to make it to the next "port" before dark as it was. I thought about waking up Marty, but I could see that he was in a deep sleep. In fact as he lay there sound asleep, with his mouth and eyes wide open, he looked dead. My over active imagination ran wild as I asked myself, "What if he really was dead?" He was over fifty, and we had put a lot of stress and strain on our bodies that week, sleeping very little. I had heard of men much younger than we were having heart attacks in their sleep. Deciding that it was crazy to think like that, I forced myself to keep going, hoping to make it to a town before the blackness of night enveloped that cold, desolate place.

As I stood there shivering and moving my shoulders inside my damp clothes, I began to pray fervently. I prayed that Marty would wake up and relieve me, so I could put on something warm and dry. I prayed that the rain would stop, and that we would reach the end of that swamp soon. I prayed for the strength to endure the cold and keep steering through that dismal environment. But my most fervent prayer was that we wouldn't run aground and be stranded there with night approaching. I shivered as I thought about how absolutely black and cold it would be in that lonely place after dark, and those thoughts made me stare at the depth finder more intently than ever. That three hour stretch was by far the most unpleasant part of the trip for me. As I steered through that never ending swamp in the rain, shivering and in constant fear of running aground, I wondered how many people knew that there was that much remote, desolate, wilderness in the state of New Jersey.

After what seemed like forever, I spotted some houses and cottages in the distance. The route seemed to lead away from them rather than toward them which was disappointing, but I took it as a sign that we were getting close. The rain finally stopped, and Marty came back from the "dead", so I had him take the till while I changed into warm, dry clothes. My spirits brightened as things began to look better, and I praised the Lord for bringing me out of the "wilderness".

As we followed some green buoys through an opening in the shoreline, we realized that we were finally out of the swamp. We found ourselves at the entrance to two bays separated by a large mass of land. To the left, a wide channel led into one large bay that had houses along the far distant shore. That channel was bordered on the left, by a big island that had a deserted factory and a water tower on it. On the right side of the land mass was another wide open bay that seemed to go on forever. To make things more confusing, there were two other channels that led off in different directions from that spot. It was another one of those frustrating moments when the land and water around me did not look anything like my chart. Since there was less than an hour of daylight left, I had to figure out which one of those four choices was the ICW north, and I could not afford to be wrong.

The map showed me that on the correct route, I would pass close to a water tower that would be on my left. Since the water tower near the deserted factory was the only one visible, I thought that had to be the way to go. But it bothered me that the water tower on the chart was on the mainland and not on an island as this one was. Still unsure, I told myself that going that way would put us in the calm water ahead, moving toward the houses and civilization on the far side of the bay. As we passed the factory and water tower, it haunted me that there were no more ICW markers visible. They had been the only bright spot in the dismal swamp, standing out like red and green lollypops against the dark somber sky. Now their friendly presence was gone, and there was nothing to reassure me that I was going the right way. As we passed the island and moved into the open water of the bay my heart sank further as the depth finder began to beep loudly. It said that we were only in four and a half feet of water. I turned right hoping to find deep water and it got shallower, so then I turned left, but it continued to be dangerously shallow no matter which way I went.

As we looked at each other in confusion and disappointment, the enemy delivered another blow that should have been the knock out punch, to break my spirit once and for all. After running great all day, the motor started to run rough again and then died, just as it had the day before. Almost in shock, I pulled the start rope repeatedly but got no response. "This thing would make a good anchor," I said to Marty sadly, as I slumped on the seat devastated. Half a mile away in the direction of the houses, was a small fishing boat with people in it. We tried to hail them with our "air horn" (which was really just a small party noise maker horn I bought at Wal-Mart.) After three weak blasts it ran out of air, so I tried my band director's whistle. Blowing it again and again as loud as possible we got no response from the distant boat, so we gave up on that idea. As I sat there with my strength gone and my spirit crushed, Marty played with his favorite toy, the GPS, trying to figure out where we were, and what we had done wrong. I don't understand how he found our position, or why he was so sure of it, but he put a tiny dot on the chart to show me exactly where we were. I had seen the tower and turned to the left of the land mass, eager to head for the populated area on the far side of the bay. I should have turned to the right of that land, out into the big choppy bay that didn't seem to have a far side. If I held the chart correctly and oriented it with the compass, the way to go was very clear. The water tower we wanted was around the corner, on the other side of the land mass, and I was sure we would see it, if we could just get back out there.

At that moment, I felt a slight breeze in my face, coming from the direction of the fishing boat. Now that there was some wind and I knew where we were, a surge of new energy and passion filled me. "Marty, snap on the biggest jib we've got, while I uncover the main. I'm gonna sail her outta here," I shouted loudly. As the boat turned and responded beautifully to the wind, I stood proudly at the helm and yelled across to Marty: "Who needs a motor anyway! We're sailing men! Men of the sea, I tell ya! Just give me a breeze, a tall ship and a star to steer her by, and I'll get her home!" I bellowed heartily with a sense of false bravado, putting on a show in an effort to cheer us up, and make light of our sad situation. As I thought about what just happened, I was filled with awe and wonder. One minute I was absolutely crushed and ready to give up, with no strength left. Then moments later, I was filled with new strength and the determination to keep going. I knew that the Holy Spirit had rushed in to fill me at that deeply disappointing time. The words from a well known Christian song said it perfectly, and as I thought about them, tears came to my eyes.

. . ."His strength is perfect, when our strength is gone. He carries us, when we can't carry on. Filled with his power, the weak become strong. His strength is perfect, when our strength is gone.". . .

Deeply touched by those words, I praised him silently as the boat surged ahead under full sail power.

Then something else occurred to me, and I was blown away as I thought about it. As we came into that bay, we found ourselves in extremely shallow water no matter which way we went. When we turned around to sail back out of there (the same way we had come in) the depth finder showed the water to be from eight to ten feet deep in the same area. Had the tide come in that much in fifteen minutes? Had

I blundered into a deep channel that led out of the bay, and if so, was it blind luck or did I have help? Maybe with one stroke of a giant invisible finger the Lord parted the muddy bottom ahead of us, instantly dredging a deep channel to get us out of there. I never found out, and will probably never know what happened that day in "Wrong Way Bay". But in minutes, we were safely back where we started. Without missing a beat we tacked, rounded the corner of the land mass and saw the water tower just a few minutes later. It wasn't long before we were pounding our way north through the chop in the middle of the wide bay. Now that we were back on course, I asked Marty to take the till while I tried the motor again. To my surprise it started with one pull and ran fine, so we flew up the bay with motor and sails, following the widely spaced but clearly visible ICW markers.

Things were going well, but now we had to pay the price for our wrong turn and the time we lost to motor trouble. It was getting dark quickly, but we were in the center of a wide bay, where the deep water and lighted markers went right down the middle. Things were similar to the night on the Alligator River, when Tom got us safely to "the bridge too far" in the dark. We began to see a few lights on the eastern shore of the bay, but we were at least a mile from shore, as we made our way from one flashing marker to the next. From that far out, we had no way of knowing where a harbor, a marina or even a protected cove might be. Our only hope was to keep going, and trust that God would lead us into the place where he wanted us to spend the night. With Marty at the till, I scanned the water ahead with the spotlight, as we plowed along through the darkness. Eventually the wind died, but the motor was still humming, so I brought down and covered the sails on the fly, and we continued on at full speed ahead.

Chapter 34

Blessed with a Brand New Engine

Two and a half hours later the motor was still running great. As we approached one of the flashing markers we noticed that it looked different from the rest, so we slowed down to take a closer look at it. It was larger than the others and diamond shaped, having the letters LB printed on both sides. Marty looked at the chart, mumbling the number of the last ICW marker we had passed and then shouted: "Long Beach, LB stands for Long Beach. This flasher marks the entry channel that leads boats into Long Beach, New Jersey. If there's a marker like this, and a well marked channel leading you in, there has to be a harbor with marinas and facilities," he stated confidently. Looking toward shore, we saw a flashing red and a flashing green marker, that seemed to be the right distance apart to mark an inlet or harbor entrance. Moving slowly and watching the depth finder, we made our way toward them in the darkness, using the spotlight to find the unlit channel markers that led us in. As we got close enough to see shore, I headed for a long well lit dock that turned out to be the fuel dock of a marina. Our motor quit twice within the last hundred yards of the dock, but restarted each time and we were somehow able to make it in and get tied up. A red faced older man with liquor on his breath came out to greet us, and introduced himself as the dock master. He charged us fifty dollars for the night, but right then I would have paid a hundred. There was a slip available if we wanted it, but since we were so unsure of the motor, he gave us permission to stay at the fuel dock, as long as we were gone in the morning.

Marty and I decided to walk into the business district to stretch our legs, see the sights, and get something to eat. We learned that we were in a small waterfront town on the outskirts of Long Beach, called Beach Haven. Apparently that quaint, bay front village was well known as a tourist destination and Mecca for sport fishermen and boaters. As we walked downtown we passed marinas, boat dealers and a small midway with amusement rides. We ate in a bright, clean, crowded pizzeria that seemed to be a local hot spot, feasting on a large pizza with "the works" and ice cream sundaes. Maybe we had been on the boat too long and were starving, or maybe it was just a great recipe. But it was by far the thickest, juiciest, most delicious pizza I have ever had. It was so good, that Marty still reminds me about the pizza in Beach Haven, New Jersey, to this day. Back at the boat I turned in, while Marty went off to call his wife, take a shower and spend a little more time on shore.

It was a windy choppy night and the boat was tied to the outside of the fuel dock, where it was fully exposed to wind and waves. It rocked and lifted with each wave, grinding the fenders against the rough dock. As I lay there inside the cabin, the noise of the boat slamming and rubbing on the fenders was unbearable. After a while, it slammed so hard that I feared the boat would damage its fiberglass hull. The constant rocking, rolling and jerking motions, and all the noises made it impossible to fall asleep. I went to the office to see if the slip they had offered us was still available, but I was worried that we couldn't get into it with that much wind and no motor. The sign on the door read: "After hours, inquire at manager's apartment," and an arrow pointed across the driveway to a second story town house overlooking the docks. Through the glass doors I could see a middle aged woman in her bathrobe holding a small white dog as she smoked and watched TV from the couch. I really didn't want to bother her, but I thought about the boat slamming into the dock and rang the bell. When she answered the door still cradling her aged poodle, she introduced herself as Monica, the owner of the marina. She was polite and forced a smile as she tried to help me, but I saw a deep sadness and sense of loneliness in her tired eyes and care worn face. She said that I was welcome to slip number thirty-seven if I could get into it, but if not, I should drop anchor on the protected side of her docks and she would refund my money in the morning. As I walked back to the boat weighing my options, I thought sadly about the lonely woman who owned this thriving business, yet seemed so empty. She needed to know that God loved her and wanted to replace her sadness with joy. But she wouldn't be very open to the words of a stranger who was trying to strike up a conversation, while she stood in the doorway in her bath robe. *Maybe there would be a chance to talk to her tomorrow*, I thought, as I untied my dock lines.

The wind was sweeping down the long dock and diagonally out into the bay. I decided to tie one very long rope to the corner post of the dock and the other end to my bow ring as though I was on a mooring buoy. Then the boat would drift out and away from the dock and point toward the corner of it all night. I could do that easily without motor power, and when Marty came back I could pull the boat back to the dock using the rope. Once he was aboard we could let her drift back out, and then drop an anchor off the back in case the wind changed during the night. I had the bow rope secured and was drifting away from the dock when Marty came back. I started pulling on the rope to bring myself in, but the wind changed and I began to drift sideways around the corner of the dock and toward shore. With no motor power I began to panic. The still attached rope wrapped around the end of the fuel dock and caused me to swing in a circle. That made me drift sideways toward the sterns of several expensive yachts in their slips. "Untie that rope from the dock," I yelled across to Marty, just as I was about to make contact with the beautiful boats. Using my weary body as a fender, I grabbed the back railing of a huge power yacht and used all my strength to hold my boat away from it, as I rocked and moved in the wind blown chop. By then Marty had untied the rope and dropped it into the water, so I yelled to him in a panic stricken voice to find slip number thirty-seven. The slip was only five spots down the dock from where I was, so I decided to work my way along the other boats to get to it. It took everything I had left to push and pull my way down the dock a few feet at a time, as wind and waves pushed me aggressively into the boats I was trying to protect. At one point, a couple sleeping in their boat was roused by the commotion and came out on deck to see what was happening. I was amazed and thankful that they were not outraged, as they helped push me away from their big investment and farther down the dock with a boat hook. Miraculously, and with God's help, I was able to work my way down to our dock spot without scratching our boat or anyone else's. Marty ran out on the dock finger next to our slip and helped me bring her in bow first. Then he held the boat steady while I attached four opposing ropes to keep her suspended in the middle of the slip without touching anything. After that traumatic midnight ordeal, we collapsed on our berths wishing we could sleep for at least two days.

Exhausted and wracked with aches and pains, I did sleep until bright sunshine shone through the cabin window (which was rare on that trip). After I showered and started a load of laundry we walked to get coffee and donuts, stopping at a marine parts store on the way back. Eager to have the motor fixed once and for all, we asked the two men at the counter for their opinions about what could possibly be wrong with it. They both agreed that we should try two brand new spark plugs, so we purchased them and headed back to the boat, hoping we had finally found the answer. During all the craziness of getting into that slip the night before, the jib halyard had come loose and the rope got pulled, so the snap that hoisted the jib was at the top of the mast. I groaned deeply as I realized that Marty would have to raise me to the top of the mast again, a job I really hated. Before I could think too much about it, I had him do it right then and get it over with. It didn't take long, and I was relieved when he lowered me to the deck holding the end of the jib rope.

While Marty installed the two new plugs, I brought our fuel tanks to the end of the dock to have them filled. After stowing them, I walked to the shower building to get our laundry. As I passed below her balcony, Monica came out in her robe and called down to me, wondering how we made out with our motor problem. I wanted to somehow encourage her, or counsel her, but since she was yelling down from across the driveway, it just wasn't the time or place. I thanked her for asking and told her that my buddy was installing new plugs as we spoke. I told her we would be out of the slip soon, but she answered that it wasn't a problem, and that we could stay there as long as we needed to. Then I thanked her very much for being so flexible and accommodating. As I left her, I voiced a sincere "God bless you", and the wish that she would have a great day. Walking back to the boat, I prayed that God would touch the heart of that sad, lonely woman, asking him to help her find his love, and fill her with the joy and purpose that only came from knowing and serving him. Marty had already installed the plugs and said that the motor started with one pull and had been running smoothly for thirty minutes, so we made the decision to untie and get underway. It was the second day in a row that we headed out believing that the motor was fixed and I hoped and prayed that this time it really was.

I can't even describe how much boat traffic we encountered that day, as we moved away from Beach Haven and headed north toward Barnegat Bay. Huge power yachts weighing many tons swept by us at full speed, throwing five foot waves at us broadside. There were so many boats going both ways that it was the worst ride of the trip, with waves and chop coming at us from all directions at once. Just as we rocked and rolled from the impact of one big wave, another would hit us from the other side before we even had the chance to recover. There was so much boat traffic, it was hard for us to find an opening in the never ending parade of boats, and we had to constantly speed up and slow down to avoid a collision. It was a Sunday, and it seemed like everyone in New Jersey who owned a boat had them out that day, and were right around us. We caught up to another sailboat named: "Just The Three Of Us". The depth finder was reading very shallow water all through that stretch, even in the channel, so we thought it would be wise to follow another sailboat. I hoped they had a keel deeper than ours, and knew that area well. They were going a little slower than I wanted to go, but it was worth reducing speed to have an "insurance policy" against running aground right in front of us.

We only had to travel forty miles that day to reach Manasquan. That was our jumping off point, to go out into the Atlantic and up the coast to New York Harbor. I was excited, because the weather report for Monday morning looked ideal. It was supposed to be a blue bird day, sunny and fair with no wind. I hoped to head out into the ocean before first light, so I could cover the most dangerous thirty miles of the trip during the very calmest part of the day. As I moved through the sea of boat traffic, one nagging thought continued to haunt me. I could not, and would not head out into the open Atlantic, unless I was absolutely sure that the motor was running perfectly again, and was one hundred per cent dependable. Without any warning "Just The Three Of Us" got stuck in the mud dead ahead, right next to an ICW marker. I had to do some quick maneuvering to avoid her, and was glad she was leading the way and not us. Even though we were a little ahead of schedule, we couldn't waste much time, because it was critical that we made Manasquan that night. With that in my mind, it was very hard for me to say what I said as I passed the stuck sailboat, but it was the only thing I could say and I had to say it: "We'll turn around and come back, and stay with you until you get off or get help." I shouted loudly, to be heard over the drone of the motor. A relieved thank you came from the woman's lips, as her worried expression gave way to a hopeful smile. Her husband nodded and also smiled gratefully. If we turned back to help, we risked getting stuck ourselves, not to mention the time and daylight we would lose. But I thought about the old couple at the bridge, and the expensive cruiser that had zoomed by to stay on schedule. I also thought about the countless times the Lord had sent someone to help me, and how our Christian emblem was right in their face as we passed them, so I knew there was no other choice. To my great relief, as I came about and headed back, they rocked themselves free. "Are you okay?" I yelled across to them. "Yes we're free, thank you very much for coming back," was the woman's reply. I was thrilled that I had done the right thing, yet was not held up, or thrown off schedule by my offer. I gave them a thumbs up and a hearty God bless you, as they waved goodbye with grateful smiles.

As the narrow channel entered Barnegat Bay, I was pleased to see white sails dotting the bay everywhere. Sailboats considerably bigger than ours were sailing in all directions across the wide open waters. That led me to believe that the whole area was deep, and it wasn't as critical to stay in the well-marked channel. Marty and I admired the different types of sailboats as we cruised northward. But as we headed across the open water, what I had feared, but didn't even want to think about happened: the motor died again! To soothe the disappointment, I tried to think of it in terms of the good news - bad news principle. The good news was: It ran fine all morning and got us through that sea of boat traffic in the narrow channel. The other good news was: We were now on the open waters of Barnegat Bay and could use sail power to keep going. If the motor acted like it did the last two days, it would start up again after sitting idle for a while and cooling down. That meant we could at least use it intermittently, and save it for times when we had to have a motor. The bad news was: There was no way in the world we could even think about heading out into the open Atlantic, until it was fixed by an expert mechanic. Slowed down by the need to sail, we would not make it to Manasquan that night to take advantage of the calmness of the ocean the next morning. Even if we did make it that night, getting the repairs we needed would eat up most of the day tomorrow. That meant we would have to wait a day or two, for another "window of opportunity" when the ocean was calm again. Marty had to be in New York City tomorrow, to get home and back to work. If we couldn't head across to the "Big Apple" at daybreak, he would have to catch a train or a bus there from New Jersey. That meant I would have to face the north Atlantic alone.

We made it all the way to the Tom's River Bridge with sails, and then restarted the motor when we saw how much boat traffic was waiting there for the bridge to open. Just as I expected, after not using it for three hours it started on the first pull. Now I was concerned that it would quit while we were jockeying for position in all that boat traffic or worse yet, right when we were passing through the narrow opening of the bridge. We were surrounded by dozens of other boats, so I held my breath as it continued to run while we waited for the bridge to open. Once we cleared the bridge, I breathed a lot easier, and as we moved out into open water again, I shut the motor down. I thought it would be smart to save it for the end of the day, when we would need it to come into an inlet or a dock.

The winds died down toward evening and eventually we were barely moving. Far ahead of us the wide bay pinched off to a blunt point and ended. Right at the end of the bay we could see a lift bridge opening and closing even from that distance. The chart told me that it was the Mantoloking Bridge and as we approached the end of the bay we could hear other boaters hailing it by name and asking the operator to open for them. Once we were beyond that bridge, it was only seven more miles to Manasquan inlet where the ICW entered the Atlantic. With no wind, we were going so slow that it was almost laughable, and I knew we wouldn't make it past the Mantoloking Bridge that night. As darkness approached, we had to think about getting in somewhere for the night, so I decided to start the motor before it got too dark. It ran for about thirty minutes and then died, but by then I could see a fleet of anchored boats and masts on the right side of the bay. There was a slight breeze, so I headed that way using sails and tried the motor every so often to see if it would start. Every third or fourth try, the motor would start and run for a minute or two, giving us an extra burst of forward motion and bringing us just a little closer. It was getting dark fast, so I put on our running lights so other boats could see us. Then I noticed another boat yard on the opposite side of the bay and a little bit closer to the bridge. The one on the right, (that I was heading toward) looked more like a yacht club or a group of private docks. The one on the left had a Sunoco gas sign, a break wall and large storage buildings. It looked more like a commercial marina and seemed more likely to have repair facilities. "Which one do I want, Lord?" I whispered, and then went on to ask: "Which one would be a better choice for tonight, and the best place for us to be tomorrow." I was already leaning toward the one on the left, even though it was farther away. Then I felt a gentle off shore breeze against my right cheek and that settled it. Pushing the tiller hard over, I turned the bow to point right at the Sunoco sign. The sails filled from behind and we glided smoothly across the calm bay, looking pretty enough to be a sailboat painting. It would have been a great moment in sailing, and a great memory, if we weren't limping in on a sail and a prayer.

I was nervous about steering through the narrow opening in the break wall and into tight quarters under full sail, so I had Marty strike the main before we reached it. With a billowing jib, I took her right through the opening like I knew what I was doing, and then came the true test of a sailor. I had to bring the boat gently into a dock with a sail and no motor power. I had done it with a small day sailor, but never with something that big. I was worried, because you can't throw a sail into reverse. I picked out the most open and approachable dock spot and headed for it. It happened to be at the far end of the fuel dock right in front of the office. Marty had already put the fenders on coming across the bay, so at the right moment I yelled "strike the jib" hoping our forward motion would carry us the rest of the way. The boat glided smoothly toward the dock, slowing down just the right amount. Just before the bow hit, I pushed the tiller to the right and the boat nestled sideways against the dock. "See that Marty," I kidded, jumping to the dock with a rope. "We're sailing men, men of the sea I tell ya, we don't need no motors". We smiled through weary faces, but we both knew I was very lucky and very blessed to get us in there that easily.

Faded bold letters on one of the storage buildings told us we were at the "Winter Yacht Basin" and I felt good about the choice we had made. Standing on the dock, we walked the boat to the end of the fuel dock and around the corner to another dock section where it would be out of the way. I didn't think the manager would mind it being there until we made repairs, and it was parked with the back end close to another dock, so it would be easy to lift the motor off and back on again. Marty went for a walk to explore the area (he loved doing that) and took pen and paper with him, hoping to find a phone book. He promised to look up all the marine repair shops in that area and write down their phone numbers. It sounded like a good idea, and I told him to put a star by the ones that were Honda dealers. Soon after he left, a car pulled up and a couple began unloading bags of groceries and carrying them to a powerboat at the next dock. After they went aboard, the man saw me adjusting fenders and ropes, so he came over to say hello. "Did ya just come in?" he asked, in a Scottish accent so heavy it made me smile. "Just tied up about ten minutes ago," I said nodding, and then added: "The Good Lord must have really been with us, we somehow got in here with just our sails. We're on a trip from Florida to New York, and we've been having motor problems for the last three days. We're going to have to take the motor in to be fixed tomorrow; do you know of any good repair shops in the area?" The man nodded sympathetically, and then said that he wasn't from that area. He and his girlfriend had come down from New York City by boat for a three day get away. The short, dark haired, solidly built man sounded just like "Scottie" from Star Trek, but with a deeper voice. As we talked, I learned that he really was from Scotland and had only lived in New York for a few years. He said the owners of that marina were really nice, and I was amazed when he told me that the forty dollar docking fee included the use of a vehicle. As he said goodnight, he wished me luck with the motor, and told me to come and get him if I needed help lifting it onto the dock, or putting it back on the boat.

"Wow! Thank you Lord!" I whispered quietly, as I lay on my berth staring at the stars. "You really did put us in the right place tonight," I praised. With the use of a car, it would be easy to take the motor to be fixed, and I could bring Marty to any train station or bus depot in the area. As I thought about how calm the ocean would be the next day, I really wanted to head out there in the morning, and complete that dangerous phase of the trip when conditions were ideal. Once safely in New York Harbor I was "home free", and for all practical purposes had "made it". After that, the relaxing scenic ride up the Hudson and along the barge canal would just be a time to unwind and savor the memories of my successful voyage. The thought of calling repair shops, and standing around all day, while that window of perfect weather slipped away, was extremely frustrating, when I was so close to making it.

If there was only some way I could rent a brand new motor, just to get to New York City and home, then I ***could*** *leave the next morning,* I thought desperately.

Like a light going on, a great idea came to mind. There **was** a way that I could "rent" a new motor to get me home, and I could do it quickly and easily. All I had to do was go to the nearest Honda dealer and buy one, using my credit card. As soon as I got home, I could list it for sale on eBay. The ad would read: "Brand New Honda Outboard - Used Only Six Days - Still Has Original Manufacturers Warranty." The marina people could tell me which area Honda dealer had lots of motors and gave the best deals. Then I would be waiting at their door to purchase one the moment they opened. If things went well, I could have it on the boat and still be underway the next morning. I would be getting a later start than I had hoped for, but on such a beautiful day it shouldn't get too bad out there before I made it into New York Harbor. I had done extremely well buying and selling things on eBay, and I was sure I could resell a top of the line outboard for very close to what I paid for it. If I got a really good deal, and someone bidding on it wanted one bad enough, my "rental fee" could be very small.

When Marty returned with the numbers of several repair shops, he thought the idea of buying a new motor was an expensive gamble. But I was determined to go with it, because I wouldn't be at the mercy of some mechanics schedule, and I could still get underway in the morning. I awoke with the sun and dumped and washed the porta potty before the marina opened. Then Marty helped me take the outboard off the back of the boat, and lay it gently on the carpeting in the center of the cabin floor. A very friendly, middle aged man wearing glasses showed up, and welcomed us to the "Winter Yacht Basin". He introduced himself as Ken Winter, as he shook my hand earnestly. When I told him about our situation, and what I hoped to do, he offered us the marina pickup truck, and said that his daughter Kim in the office would help us with anything we needed. Kim was bright eyed with short blonde hair and a fresh, "girl next door" face. She smiled easily, and reacted well to our predicament. I praised the Lord for her sincere helpfulness and people skills. Ken highly recommended a Honda dealer in town that he had dealt with for many years. Kim looked up their number and Ken called them personally to put in a "good word" for us, only to learn that they didn't open until ten. That meant I wouldn't be underway until almost noon, and that would be too late for Marty to make connections in New York City to get home. I would have to drive him into town so he could catch a train that morning from

New Jersey. Kim drew a detailed map, showing us exactly how to get to the train station and the Honda dealer. As we left, Ken reminded us to mention his name when we purchased the motor, and they would give us a good deal.

"I still can't believe they let us borrow this," I said to Marty smiling, as we drove through the quiet streets in the "Winter Yacht Basin" pickup truck. We were in Point Pleasant, New Jersey, and it really was a beautiful morning just like the weather radio predicted. Stopping first at the train station, we learned that Marty's train didn't leave until nine thirty, so we had some time to kill. We located "Surf and Off Shore", which Ken said was the oldest Honda dealer in New Jersey. Then we got bagels and coffee at an appealing looking bakery along the main street. After I got Marty on the train, I headed back to wait for the doors to open at "Surf and Off Shore". Once inside, I was greeted by the manager, a tall, sandy haired fellow named George. When I explained my situation and my time schedule, he said he would do everything he could to expedite the transaction. He quickly introduced me to Merideth, a short, middle aged woman who was in charge of sales, and explained my predicament to her.

By now, I had come to expect incredible blessings, but it still amazed me when they seemed too good to be true. Almost hidden away, in the far back corner of the showroom, was a Honda 9.9 long shaft motor on an outboard stand. It was brand new, but a slightly older model, built three years before the one I owned. For whatever reason it hadn't been sold, and had been sitting there gathering dust, almost as if it had been waiting for me. Because it was older, and Ken Winter sent me over, Merideth said she could give me a really good deal on that one. A Honda 9.9 horse outboard, with a long shaft, usually retailed for about three thousand dollars. But she agreed to sell it to me at her cost: $1,825.00, and there would be no sales tax because I didn't live in New Jersey. As soon as the deal was made, George rushed it back to the shop to test it and tune it up. While I waited, I thanked the woman, and told her that finding that motor, was just another in a long series of blessings that the Good Lord sent my way on that trip. When George came back to say that my motor was waiting for me in the pickup truck, I thanked them both sincerely. When I looked in the bed of the pickup truck, I was thrilled to see that my new motor came with a gas tank. The new tank was smaller than the two already aboard, but it would give me an extra margin for error, and I could go even farther between fuel stops with three tanks.

At ten forty-five I was leaving "Surf and Off Shore" with my new motor. Back at the yacht basin, the brawny Scotsman helped me carry it to the dock, and we carefully lowered it into position on the bracket. In a few minutes I had it securely attached, and all electrical wires and fuel lines were connected. I thanked him very much, and gave him a couple of tracts and a sincere "God Bless you" as I shook his hand. Then I filled all three tanks at the fuel dock, and settled accounts with Kim in the office. I gave her the pickup keys, and thanked her and her dad again for their gracious hospitality. I assured them both that if I ever passed through that area again by boat, I would patronize their marina. I left a couple of my brochures and a fond "God bless you" with them, as I said goodbye and headed for the dock. At eleven forty-five, I was moving through the narrow opening in the break wall, powered by a dependable, brand new outboard. Although I was alone again, I now felt ready to do battle with the open waters of the Atlantic, and I knew that God would get me up the Jersey Shore safely. As I cruised quickly across the bay toward the lift bridge, I picked up the microphone, and finally got to say what I heard all the other boaters saying the night before: "Mantoloking Bridge, Mantoloking Bridge, this is the sailboat "God Speed" I am north bound, and I respectfully request that you open for me as I approach."

CHAPTER 35

Seven Foot Seas in the North Atlantic

Once I passed under the Mantoloking Bridge, I only had to go about seven more miles to reach the ocean. There was still a lot of boat traffic, but it wasn't as bad as it had been the day before on a Sunday. The stretch between Point Pleasant and Manasquan was made up of narrow canals that seemed to be man made. Big waves produced by other boats came at me from all directions on that short stretch, which made for an unpleasant ride. Ken Winter told me that the ocean was like glass at seven thirty that morning, when he was on his way to work. It would be after one before I got out there, but I was still encouraged and excited by that report. I hoped that conditions hadn't changed too much since then, and didn't get much worse during the five hours it would take me to get into New York Harbor.

After passing under several highway bridges and a railroad bridge, I arrived at the inlet in Manasquan where the ICW enters the Atlantic. Two long piers with a lighthouse at the end of one of them, stretched far out from shore to act as break walls for the narrow channel. It reminded me of the entrance to the Genesee River in Rochester, and several other ports along Lake Ontario. As I made my way down the channel, I saw that the piers were surrounded by octagon shaped concrete pillars that were fat in the middle and tapered at both ends. They had been dumped there haphazardly like boulders along both piers to prevent erosion. I rocked and bounced unpredictably in the narrow channel as I was hit by the random waves from other boats. But I told myself that once I was in open water and away from boat traffic I would be fine. A chart on the wall at "Surf and Off Shore" showed that this stretch of coastline was deep open water, with no shallow bars or shoals between Manasquan and New York. Once you were a couple hundred yards off the beach, the water was at least nine feet deep, getting deeper the farther out you went. Knowing that, I planned to hug the shore all the way up the Jersey coast to Sandy Hook. Then I would make a "bee line" toward the mouth of New York harbor, and would only need to cross eight miles of "open" water.

As I cleared the piers and headed straight out into the ocean wave conditions were a little worse than I hoped for, but still far from being scary. Winding through the narrow canals my flag hung like a limp dish rag, showing no wind at all. Out there, where I was exposed to wind and waves coming all the way from Florida, there was a light breeze of about ten knots from the south. Steady waves of two to three feet were sweeping up the coast and in toward shore. Although disappointed that it wasn't calm out there, I knew what a blessing a south wind was. Even though I'd be bounced around, the wind and the waves would be behind me, pushing me toward my destination all afternoon. The blue sky overhead gave me confidence, so I wallowed my way out to a point about a mile from shore. From there, the south wind and following waves would be directly behind me, pushing me northward and slightly toward land for hours. If Marty was still with me, I would have put up both sails while he held that course. Then we could have made it to New York in record time, using sail power and the motor. But he wasn't there, and I was alone, bouncing around in three footers. I was reluctant to let go of the steering tiller, but plagued by thoughts of how much faster I could go with a sail up.

Finally I gave in, and I kicked the motor out of gear and scrambled forward to snap on the jib. I tried to work fast, because I knew I was in for an unpleasant experience. Without steerage, the boat rocked and bobbed helplessly, as it circled and floundered in the three foot rollers. "One hand for you, and one for the boat," I muttered, remembering the advice I had been given by an old sailor years ago. It reminded me to hang on tight with at least one hand, when I was moving around on a deck that was bouncing and rolling in rough seas. The sail flapped wildly, and the jib ropes whipped me as I fumbled with the snaps. Hanging on for dear life, I worked quickly so I could get back to the tiller and get the boat under control as soon as possible. I knew that if I fell overboard out there, know one would even know I was in the water, let alone come to my rescue. Salt spray stung my face as I finally hoisted the sail and ran back to grab the tiller. Just as I breathed a sigh of relief my heart sank, as I saw that one of the jib lines was tangled and caught on the bow cleat. I had to go forward again to free it, in order for the jib to be useable. Once the sail was up and all ropes were free and clear, I pointed "God Speed" north, knowing there would be no turning back. The jib filled, lifting the boat forward, and soon she settled into an almost comfortable pattern of rolling and surging ahead with the push of each wave. Now that things were under control, I praised the Lord that I had the jib up, and that wind and waves were coming from behind me. I didn't even want to think about what it would have been like to plow into them bow first for five hours, if they had been coming from the north.

Things went pretty well as I made my way up the Jersey Shore, admiring the high rise hotels and beach front resorts from a distance. I had grown accustomed to riding the ocean swells, so I hardly noticed that the farther I went, the bigger they got as the day wore on. Eventually, I looked back at the endless parade of waves that marched toward my motor, and realized that they had to be at least five footers. I was about half a mile from shore when it occurred to me that the deep green water had changed to a muddy brown color as the big waves churned up the bottom. Shortly after that, something began to happen that could have spelled disaster. Even though I was a good half mile out, the depth finder began to beep loudly, telling me that I was only in five feet of water. Surprised and puzzled, I turned to angle away from shore, hoping to move out into deeper water. On that heading, the waves were no longer squarely behind me, so I rocked and wallowed more, and lost some forward speed. As I moved farther and farther out, looking for deeper water, I still didn't find it, and became very frustrated. "I can't believe this," I moaned.

The chart in "Surf and Off Shore" said this whole area was at least nine feet deep, but I'm two miles out and I still can't find deep water anywhere, I thought desperately.

"So much for hugging the beaches," I mocked. The shoreline was now barely visible and I passed two fishing charter boats that were anchored way out there. An army of people surrounded each vessel standing elbow to elbow on the deck. Each person was holding a fishing rod with a line going straight down into the water, and a few waved as I passed.

The farther out I went, the bigger the waves got, and then a light fog began to obscure the shoreline. Even way out there, the deepest water I could find was eight feet, but every once in a while it dropped to six feet or even five. I took a compass reading while I could still see the shore, to make sure I kept heading in the right general direction. The waves now appeared to be at least seven footers, and everything in me wanted to move closer to shore. I decided that the only safe approach was to keep my back end square to the huge waves, and hope that I didn't pass through water too shallow for my keel to clear the bottom. The view behind me was definitely not for the faint of heart, as gigantic walls of muddy water moved swiftly toward me. When I was in the valley between two waves, I wasn't able to see over the top of the next mountain of water that came rushing at me. Each giant wave looked like it was going to crash over the stern, sweep me off the deck like a rag doll and swamp the boat. But instead, each one lifted the small boat high in the air, pushing it along faster, as it rode the crest of the wave for several seconds like a surfboard. If I hadn't been so nervous about the shallow depth readings, that wild ride might have been fun. I shuddered, as I pictured what would happen if I ran aground out there in waves of that magnitude, so I tried not to think about it. I began to pray loudly as the depth kept dropping to five feet, and even to four a couple of times. I prayed that the water would get deeper, as I checked and tightened the snaps on my life vest. I also prayed that the Lord would point me toward the harbor entrance, and that I would get there as soon as possible. After I finished praying, I ducked down, so I could see the framed picture of Jesus with the young sailor on the cabin wall. It gave me quiet strength and reassured me. The valleys between the waves were so deep, that they made me think of the valley in the Twenty-Third Psalm. To pass the time, I mulled it over in my mind and rearranged the words a little to fit my situation:

. . . Even though I sail through the valleys of the shadow of death, I will fear no evil for you are with me; your rod and your staff, they comfort me . . . (KJV)

All I could see ahead of me was open water, so I began to fear that I wasn't going the right way. Then as if to reassure me, a passenger jet, that was coming in for a landing, passed low over my mast, heading the same way that my bow was pointing. "That plane has to be landing at one of the New York airports," I cheered. Then I quickly checked my compass and memorized the heading so I could stay on that course. "If I keep going that way, I'll eventually see the city, and then it should be easy to find the harbor entrance," I told myself. Soon after that, I spotted an ocean going cargo ship. I was thrilled to see that it was coming from the same general area where the plane seemed to be heading. The depth finder continued to show very shallow water, but as scary as that was, I had no other choice but to keep going straight and trust that the Lord would get me into the harbor safely. I was getting used to being lifted and thrust ahead by the monster waves, and even though the depth alarm beeped constantly, I never seemed to hit anything, so I began to relax. At one point I allowed my mind to wander, and wasn't focusing on holding a perfect course. The boat turned sideways to the waves for just a moment, and that was all it took. Before I could react, the boat rolled over onto its side, and then as the weight of the keel righted it, the mast swung wildly back and forth. As the boat rocked violently from side to side, I lost my balance and fell to the deck, recovering just in time to grab the tiller and straighten her out. Fortunately, I turned my stern to the waves, just before the next wall of water lifted me and sent me rushing forward again. I had learned a valuable lesson, and after that I was very careful to stay focused at all times. I sighed and nodded, as I recalled one of the favorite quotes of my elderly Irish mother-in-law:

....."A calm sea never made a skillful mariner".....

I had to strain my eyes to be sure, but finally I gave a shout of joy, as I spotted the tops of two stone towers rising out of the haze ahead. As they grew larger, I could see that it was the top of a suspension bridge, and my heart soared. "New York City, dead ahead," I yelled happily. I was sure that I was seeing the huge suspension bridge that spanned the mouth of the Hudson, so I steered for it eagerly. My depth finder still showed shallow water everywhere, but I miraculously hadn't touched bottom yet, and was starting to believe that I wasn't going to. As I got closer, a tugboat, pushing a long string of barges came out of the haze. It was heading out into the ocean, but was not coming from the suspension bridge, where I thought the harbor entrance was. Instead, it was coming from a spot two miles to the *left* of the bridge. I was confused and kept staring at the tug, until my eyes were able to make out what was behind it. As they did, a spontaneous cheer sprang from my lips as I filled with a deep sense of relief.

Behind the tug, was a large opening in the dark line of land that lay in front of me. High above that opening, and gradually materializing out of the haze, was an incredibly tall, two mile long suspension bridge, that dwarfed the first one I had seen. Without a doubt, that had to be the Verrazano Narrows Bridge, and the entrance to New York Harbor. The first bridge I saw was farther inland, and was probably one of the bridges between Rockaway and Brooklyn.

At first, I thought I was imagining it, but the closer I got to the Verrazano Bridge, the smaller the waves seemed to be. By the time I could see the rides of Coney Island, there was no doubt that the waves had gotten smaller, and it really looked like I was going to make it. Up ahead, I could see that when I passed the point on the west side of Coney Island, I would be in flat calm water. As I approached that calm area, I counted down the seconds as eagerly as the crowd in Times Square counts down to the dropping of the ball on New Years Eve. As I felt the boat stop rolling and glide smoothly across calm water, all the emotions that were pent up in my worn out, stressed out body were released at once. I cried, I laughed, I shouted and I cheered, but most of all I praised the Lord. "Thank you, Lord Jesus," I called out in my loudest voice. "Thank you, Lord, I praise your mighty name," I shouted again and again. Gliding across that calm water toward the bridge meant that I had conquered the most dangerous part of the trip, and now I would almost surely make it home.

As I cruised happily toward the bridge, my elation dimmed a little as I realized that it would be dark in less than an hour. I was in a small boat, about to enter the biggest, busiest harbor in the world, and I didn't know the waterfront at all. I had made a reservation for the night at a marina on the Hudson. It was located directly across from the Empire State Building on the Jersey side. Remembering how long it took to go a few miles by sailboat, I tried to figure out how far up river that marina actually was. I was at the mouth of the Hudson, but I still had to go two miles just to pass under the Verrazano Bridge. Once I did, it was at least five more miles to the southern tip of Manhattan. From there the Empire State Building was still several miles up the river, and my heart sank as I did the math. I realized that I was almost two hours from that marina, with forty-five minutes of daylight left. As I moved toward the bridge, there was a large bay to my right between Coney Island and Brooklyn. As I glanced toward the far back corner of it I saw some masts there. I headed that way to get a better look, and as I got closer, I saw that there was an inlet entering the bay in the opposite corner where it came to a point. Up that inlet, there appeared to be a group of masts, leading me to believe that there were docks or moorings there. I headed eagerly in that direction, because I had no desire to be poking around the docks of New York City after dark, looking for a safe place to tie up.

As I followed the marker buoys up the channel, I could see that it was indeed a marina or yacht club, tucked away in a very unique setting. Almost hidden from view up the inlet and behind a high point of land, it was a miracle that I had even seen it. Surrounded on three sides by cliffs and on the fourth by water it was located just across the river from Coney Island. In stark contrast to the million dollar yachts of Annapolis, many of the boats were older, average looking and within the price range of down to earth, hard working, blue collar Americans. The fleet of affordable, well used boats was protected from weather and vandalism by the natural cliffs, and tall chain link fences topped with barbed wire. "Brooklyn Basin Marina" the sign on a small building at the top of the cliff read. The place looked exactly like you would expect a marina in Brooklyn, New York, to look. The clean, well maintained floating dock sections made the place appealing, while the graffiti on a wall just outside the fences reminded you where you were. A long outer dock section that enclosed and shielded the docks of the "regulars" ran parallel to the channel. It had the words "Transient Dock" on it, so I pulled in there and tied up for the night. After I called the other marina to cancel my reservation, I walked to the office to pay for my dock spot.

Climbing the steps, I passed a young black couple coming down to the docks with a little girl. They carried a picnic basket, drink cooler, pillows and other items they needed to spend the night on their boat. The girl, about ten, had an eager smile and bright eyes. Her parents greeted me warmly, with a pleasant "good evening" and sincere smiles, as they passed me. The family had a gentleness and a sweet spirit that was pleasantly refreshing, and I was surprised that people that nice, were the first ones I encountered, in a place I expected to be cold and unfriendly.

As I went into the office, I remembered that the Scotsman

had warned me, to purchase a chart for the Hudson River before I ventured too far north on it. He said there were dangerous shoals and sand bars, sometimes right in the middle of the river.

The only furnishings inside the small empty office were a desk and a filing cabinet, so I knew they didn't sell boating supplies or charts there. When the manager told me he didn't know of a place nearby where I could get one, I decided to ask some of the boaters for directions and info. As I came back down the steps, I noticed a man and a woman sitting on a cabin cruiser sipping bottles of beer, so I walked toward their boat. "Hi, beautiful night," I began pleasantly. "I'm heading all the way up to Albany; do you know where I can buy a chart for the Hudson River?" I asked politely. The large, bleached blonde woman was taller than her stocky, dark haired husband, who wore a leather jacket and gold jewelry. Their thick New York City accents were classic, and sounded like they had come right out of a movie. They were friendly and tried to be helpful, but they hadn't been very far north on the Hudson, so they couldn't tell me much. I told them about my trip, as I pointed out my boat across the way. "I named it 'God Speed' because the Good Lord gave it to me almost for free," I said. They smiled and nodded politely, saying that God had also been very good to them. Sensing the conversation was over, I bid them good night, and "God bless you", as I turned to walk back to the boat.

I stopped walking, when my eyes caught a movement in the water next to the dock. At the base of the cliff, a black crowned night heron was wading among the rocks in the shallows. As I paused, the majestic bird froze and stared at me from just a few feet away. "O Lord," I whispered, "Here he is again, your bird with your crown. It couldn't possibly be the same one, is it, Father?" I asked. I was happy to see a night heron again, and greeted him, as if I was greeting an old friend. Maybe the three sightings were completely random events, but I wanted to believe that the Lord sent those three white birds to remind me of his presence.

Back in the boat, I cooked hot dogs and baked beans. I was starving after my long day of fighting the Atlantic, so they really hit the spot. After I ate, I washed my pan and utensils under a faucet on the dock and stowed them away. It was very nice to be on the water on such a calm moonlit night, so I strolled down the dock to unwind before turning in. A short distance down the dock, I heard the sound of a New York Yankee game, coming from a radio on a large power boat. A man was sitting in a captain's chair, listening to the game and reading the paper in the moonlight. "Good Evening," said a gentle, pleasant voice as I approached. As soon as I heard it, I knew it belonged to the father of that young family that passed me on the stairs. "Are the Yanks winning?" I asked, not surprised to find a Yankee fan in New York City. "No, they're having a bad year, but they always seem to perk up right around play off time," the man replied laughing. The thin young black man was intelligent, soft spoken and very friendly. He was eager to talk, and just as eager to listen. We hit it off well, and I got into a lengthy conversation with him there on his boat. I told him all about my trip, and how God had blessed my voyage and my life. I also told him about my videos, my ministry to outdoorsmen and my job at the Christian school. He was employed by the city of New York as a community youth services director. Part of his job was to organize and run a large youth summer camp in the New York City Area. His boat was his outlet for stress relief from that demanding position. When I asked where I could purchase a navigational chart of the Hudson, he went below and brought his out. Then he gave it to me, saying that he rarely used it. When I offered to mail it back to him, he insisted that I keep it, saying that he would pick up another one sometime.

Right about then, a cute little voice piped up from the cabin below. "Daddy, who are you talking to?" His daughter asked sweetly. "Just the neighbor honey, go back to sleep," was his gentle reply. "Just the neighbor", I thought to myself, as I reflected on his choice of words. Not a man from another boat, or a man I just met, but "the neighbor". I could see why his daughter was such a sweet little girl. The man had a heart of gold and a sweet, unselfish spirit that I admired, and I found myself wishing I could be more like him. I sensed that he was someone very special in God's plan, with a warmth and sincerity that set him apart from anyone else I had met. He didn't say he was a Christian, but he reacted very favorably to the name on my boat, and the fact that my voyage was partly a missionary trip. Almost reluctant to leave, I thanked him very much for the chart, and said that I thoroughly enjoyed meeting and talking to him. I told him that he had a beautiful family and was very blessed, as I shook his hand firmly and said goodbye.

As I lay on my cushion in the cabin that night, I praised the Lord for giving me a free waterproof chart of the Hudson River without having to make a stop. I prayed that God would touch and bless the life of that gentle, sweet man, and I asked the Lord to use him, to impact the lives of thousands of young people in the New York City area, for many years to come.

Voyage of the Heart

1871

Chapter 36

Guiding Angels on the Hudson

The next morning I was on my way down the inlet at first light and soon found myself passing under the Verrazano Narrows Bridge. As the gigantic steel structure loomed above me, I felt so tiny that it was almost depressing, until I remembered how big and important each one of us is in God's eyes. I was glad that I decided to pass through that busy seaport so early in the morning. Even at that early hour, several tug boats and the Staten Island Ferry, passed me at close quarters, leaving me rocking and rolling helplessly in their wake. The boats that seemed to churn up the water the most were the fast ferries lettered with the words: "New York Waterways". I quickly learned to give those boats a wide berth, and was very careful when the large wake they produced came my way. Halfway between Battery Park and the Statue of Liberty, a Coast Guard cutter was anchored, guarding the harbor. As I passed it, two young crewmen at the rail waved at me, and gave me a thumbs up. I went in very close to the Statue of Liberty and slowed almost to a stop as I snapped numerous photos. I wanted to get at least one "post card" quality picture of it, as a memento of the trip. Many people had pictures of that Statue, but very few had one that was taken from their own boat. Farther up river, there was a small side canal on the Jersey side, with a sign that indicated a marina. I turned in there and topped off all three tanks while I was still in "civilization". I didn't need gas badly right then, but I had no idea what facilities I would find as I headed north.

It was a cloudy overcast day, as I made my way north along the docks of Manhattan's west side. The river looked gray and cold, and the city skyline bleak and unfriendly under the dark threatening skies. I stayed as close to shore as possible, to take in the sights of the city from a perspective few people ever got to see. I passed dirty loading docks and rows of ferry boats. Then I passed an aircraft carrier with older style jet fighters displayed on the deck. I felt very sad as I passed the former site of the twin towers, but I could not see it well from the river. I went by a couple of docks where tourist boats were tied up, and then passed some private yachts so big they had to belong to billionaires. After being underway for two and a half hours, I finally passed the Empire State Building, and was glad I hadn't tried to make it that far up the river the night before. After so many weeks of worry and anticipation, it was hard to believe that I was actually passing under the George Washington Bridge, so I kept looking up in awe, to make sure I was really there.

The farther north I went, the narrower the river got, and once I was beyond the waves from ferries and other boat traffic, I rode into smooth, calm water. The skyscrapers, the concrete and the graffiti, gradually gave way to shorter buildings and trees as I cruised beyond Manhattan and the Bronx and into the suburbs. After I passed Yonkers and went under the Tappan Zee Bridge, there wasn't much scenery, so I turned on the TV to pass the time. Steering was effortless, so I sat where I could see the small screen inside the cabin, and also keep one eye on the water ahead.

I was amazed to see that the water was over one hundred feet deep, and I smiled as I thought about winding my way through the shallow swamps of New Jersey while Marty looked like he was dead. It was a beautiful day, and it felt good to have a time of relaxation and solitude as I cruised for hours on the glassy river without seeing another boat. Near Peekskill, I passed a large ocean going cargo ship that was headed for New York. The name and lettering on it looked like Russian, and an old timer waved down to me from the deck as it rumbled slowly down the river. Still farther north, the river got narrower but much more scenic. Rugged cliffs and steep wooded hills rose sharply from the river on both sides, as I passed through water that was one hundred and fifty feet deep. The hills were littered with huge boulders, and I was fascinated by the rock formations and exposed granite faces. It was on that stretch of the river that the US Military Academy or "West Point" was located. Large, impressive looking buildings were built into the cliffs and loomed above me. I could almost feel the history and tradition of that respected institution, as I passed below the stately, well maintained brick structures. I was surprised to see that the cadets and officers at West Point had their own "fleet" of small sailboats, and a few powerboats anchored below the campus for their use. Farther down the river and around the bend I passed a large stadium and wondered if it was the site of some of the Army - Navy football games.

As evening approached, I pulled up next to a man who was fishing from a small boat to ask directions. He told me there were several marinas in the area where I could spend the night. After pointing them out, he said the yacht club three miles up the river was probably my best bet, because there were lots of sailboats there. As I motored up the east side of the river looking for the yacht club, I passed a small sailboat anchored close to shore. A deeply tanned older man with no shirt waved at me so I went over to see if he needed help. The lone sailor was traveling from Albany to New York, in an older boat the size of mine. He had anchored there for the night so he didn't have to pay for a dock spot. I told him briefly about my trip, and how with God's help, I had miraculously gotten that far. Nodding thoughtfully, he said I had a very nice looking boat, as he studied the name and emblem on it. Since he had come from there, and seemed budget conscious, I asked him which marina near Albany would be the easiest and least expensive place, to have my mast taken down. He said there were a couple of marinas in Kingston that did that for people all the time. They were quite a few miles before Albany, but the Albany marinas were usually busier and more expensive. (I would need to lay it down and strap it to the top of the cabin before I entered the New York State Barge Canal. I had traveled the canal many times, and knew that I couldn't pass under the low fixed bridges that spanned it with my mast up). I thanked him very much, wished him a safe voyage, and called out a loud "God bless you", as I sped away down the shoreline in the direction of the yacht club.

The Riverside Yacht Club looked like a small, rural, member run facility for working class people who owned a sailboat. About thirty average looking boats, some bigger than mine and some smaller were anchored there and pointed up the river. Each vessel was attached to a discolored, algae covered mooring buoy, and a few of the buoys had no boat on them. The small "flotilla" rode peacefully near a wide grassy point of land, and colored markers that flashed all night marked the two outermost corners of the "fleet". There was a small clubhouse, with an older red car and a few boat trailers in the parking lot. As I pulled in against the wooden break wall, the place seemed to be deserted, but as I stepped ashore and started to look around, a heavy set young man with long hair approached me smiling. "I'm on a sailing trip, from Florida to New York, and I need a place to spend the night," I began. "Would it be possible to stay here?" I asked politely. "You came all the way from Florida in that boat?" he asked in amazement. "Well, there were some scary moments, but the Good Lord was with me and got me through them," I said smiling. "We'd be honored to have you here, at our little club for the night." he answered, as if I was some type of celebrity.

The young man introduced himself as Danny, and pointed down the shore to a tall girl fishing in the river. He said that he and his girl friend were club members, and just happened to be there fishing. As we talked, he pointed proudly to a blue catamaran among the anchored boats, saying that one was his. He said I could take any one of the moorings that was vacant, and when I asked him the cost, he said there would be no charge. I gave him a couple of tracts, and said that it looked like the Lord was still blessing my trip. He helped me cast off, and I thanked him very much as I motored toward the nearest open buoy.

The free mooring in that safe calm spot was a nice blessing. But I slept very little, as noisy freight trains roared up and down that side of the river, blowing their whistles loudly throughout the night. The next morning I was underway just before it got light, praising the Lord for another early start. Checking my New York State road map and Hudson River chart, I saw that I spent the night near Chelsea. That meant I wasn't even half way between New York and Albany yet. I was hoping to do the entire Hudson River in two days. My daughter Nicole and her husband Eric lived in a small town near Albany. When I arrived there, I was hoping they could pick me up and I could spend the night at their house. They were recently married, and I hadn't gone to visit them yet in their new location. Since I would be near their home, I wanted to arrive early that night, so I could spend some time with them. As I studied the map, I realized how far away Albany was, and I knew that the marina stop to lay the mast down could take hours, so I opened the motor to full throttle, hoping I could make it to the state capital before dark.

Soon after the sun rose, I was greeted by a very unique point of interest that I found fascinating. On a tiny island in the middle of the river, there stood a miniature two story brick home, with a matching brick light house tower. It was a beautifully preserved replica of a house from colonial America, with a real working light house beacon. It was stately and impressive looking, but just a little too small for people to really go inside. As I made my way up the river, I discovered several more of the miniature houses that were light houses. Each one was completely different, and each one was modeled after a classic colonial home. I learned later that the quaint little houses were famous landmarks and tourist attractions of the Hudson River. They had been standing there for generations, marking dangerous shoals, and the entrance channels to cities and harbors.

As I approached Kingston, I called directory assistance on my cell phone and wrote down the number of every marina and boat yard in that city. The more marinas I called, the more disappointed I got. One was too busy to do it that day, and two more didn't have a crane to put down a mast. A couple of them weren't even open yet, but one man said that Jack, over at Jack's Marina would do it for me, if I could get a hold of him. Trying that number, I got an answering machine at Jack's Marina, with the actual voice of Jack himself telling me to leave a message. Explaining my situation and my tight time schedule, I gave him my number and told him I would be passing the entrance channel for Kingston around nine o'clock. I would only pull in there, if I found someone willing to do it that morning, otherwise I would keep going and take my chances in Albany or Troy. It was 9:01 as I approached the small lighthouse that marked the channel to Kingston, and my heart sank, because no one had returned my call. Thinking I wouldn't get my mast down there, I prayed that the Lord would provide a place farther up the river that would do it for me quickly. As I passed the entry channel, the thought occurred to me to try Jack's marina one last time, just in case he opened at nine. To my delight he answered the phone. "Yea Dave, I just walked in and got your message," he explained. Then he said: "I can get your mast down this morning, but only if you can come in right now, because I have an appointment at eleven." I was just past the small lighthouse, but when I heard those words, I shouted: "Thank you Lord", and pushed the tiller hard over. As I circled back and headed eagerly up the channel, Jack gave me some directions, and in fifteen minutes I was tied to his dock underneath the mast crane. After he introduced himself and put a sling around the mast to support it, he told me to disconnect everything, and call him when I was ready to lay it down. Knowing how precious every minute of daylight was, I worked as quickly and efficiently as I could. In twenty minutes, I went inside to tell him that I was ready, and he came out and climbed up into the crane. Then he lifted the mast straight up off the boat and gently lowered one end to me. I rested that end on the stern pulpit, and then he eased it down until it was laying right down the middle of the boat, with the other end resting on the bow pulpit. Once it was down, he went back inside, while I put blocks of wood on the cabin top to support the weight of the mast. Then I lashed it down securely to the pulpits and cabin top, using several more bungees than I needed. As I worked and sweated in the August sun, a round faced man came to the end of the next dock and watched me for a few minutes. He struck up a conversation with me, saying that I had a pretty interesting name on my boat. Without missing a beat, I told him about my trip from Florida and how the Lord had blessed me, and even given me that boat. Taking in the whole story, he smiled, nodded, and shook his head, saying that God **had** to be with me, to make that trip, in that boat.

Once the mast was secured, I went inside to pay Jack and thank him for working me in that morning. I said that it had to be God's timing, because I was just passing the channel when I finally got him. Then I told him how God's hand and his timing had saved me many times on that trip. As I said goodbye, I shook his hand and voiced a sincere "God bless you", as I headed for the dock.

When I turned left into the Hudson, I was overjoyed as I passed the small lighthouse. I had pulled in there at 9:05 and at 10:30 I was back in the main river with my mast down, heading north again. I had a chance to witness to two men, and putting my mast down had only cost me sixty dollars. I praised the Lord as I opened the motor to full throttle and tried to steer the straightest course possible.

Without a mast I was no longer able to fly my Christian Flag, but when I thought about how many people I would pass on the barge canal, I figured out a way to do it. I had an aluminum whisker pole aboard that was sometimes used for the jib. Steering with my legs, I neatly attached the flag to the end of it using string and duct tape. Then I fastened the aluminum pole to one of the stainless steel uprights on the stern pulpit with several bungees. It wasn't pretty, but it was rugged and functional. The Christian Flag now floated proudly off the back as I sped along positioned like an American Flag on the back of a power boat.

I called Nicole and Eric and found out they had a church function that night. That meant the best they could do, was come to get me after church. I knew that could be as late as ten o'clock, so I had to make it to a marina or well lit dock so they could find me. I would reach Albany first, and I was sure there would be several marinas and some public docking facilities there. If things went well, and time allowed, I could go seven more miles into Troy. Troy was closer to Eric and Nicole's house. It was the starting point for the barge canal, and home of the first lock. I knew that each lock was surrounded by well lit, concrete docking areas, provided by the state for boaters to spend the night.

The trip from Kingston to Albany seemed to take forever. I kept calculating and recalculating how many miles I had to go, and how many hours of daylight were still left. During that stretch it always seemed to take much longer to cover the distance between two points on the chart than it should have. Puzzled, I thought it had something to do with the strong current of the Hudson, since I was cruising steadily upstream against the current. Then I realized that I had made a big and very stupid mistake. The scale of miles on the chart of the Hudson River was printed in nautical miles, not regular miles. All the way from Florida I covered seven miles in about an hour, but all of those charts were printed in regular miles. Since a nautical mile is longer than a regular mile, it takes much longer to go seven nautical miles, than it does to go seven miles. My heart sank, as I caught my mistake and realized how many hours I still had to travel to get to Albany.

Fortunately, I do have one positive memory from that never ending stretch of the Hudson. As I raced against the sun and the clock, trying to get to a place that was farther away than I thought, I had a close encounter with an eagle. In a wild, uninhabited stretch of the river, I passed very close to a mature bald eagle. It was fishing in the shallows, and as I approached, it flew down the river right in front of my boat for quite a distance.

As I passed a boat launching ramp on the right side, I could tell that dusk was approaching. I was desperate, because I really wasn't sure how many miles I still had to go. Worse yet, I had forgotten what time it got dark the night before. A tall man, wearing glasses and a baseball hat, came cruising slowly toward me in a blue runabout. He had a little girl with him and they waved at me politely. Blowing my whistle, I motioned for them to come over so I could talk to them. Without hesitation, they turned and came close to my port side, eager to help. "Could you tell me how far it is to Albany and to Troy from this spot?" I asked politely, and then I asked if they knew what time it would get dark that night. I went on to say that I was trying to make it to Albany or Troy before it got dark. If that wasn't possible, I had to get to a marina or safe dock while it was still light enough to see. "Oh you're fine!" the friendly man boomed, trying to be helpful. "Albany's only a couple more miles down the river, you'll see it when you go around the bend," He stated confidently. "Troy is about seven more miles from here, but it won't be dark until eight thirty. It's only seven thirty now, so you should be able to make either one of them before dark." He assured me, with a confident smile.

His words encouraged me, but in my heart I knew the map and my calculations didn't agree with him. Thirty minutes later it was very dark, and I wasn't in Albany yet, but I could see the tower of the new state capital building in the sky ahead. *People are so used to zipping along in cars and fast boats; they have a false sense of time and distance,* I thought. The man was very nice, and tried hard to be helpful, but he had no concept of how long it took to get somewhere at seven miles per hour. Right about then, my friends in the power boat came sheepishly crawling up behind me in the darkness, and came abreast of me. I could tell that the guy felt really bad for giving me incorrect information, and that I was now plodding along through the darkness, still far from where I needed to be. "Follow us," he said cheerfully. "We'll lead you right to the public docks in Troy," he boomed, in a voice that sounded like Dudley Do Right of the Royal Canadian Mounted Police. I told them it would take quite a while to get there at sailboat speed, and I really didn't want them to give up their night just for me. He said they didn't have anything else to do, and it would be an adventure and a good lesson for his little girl about helping others. He told me that my front running lights were out, and that he would get in front of me and be my "front lights". He stayed in front of me for almost an hour, leading me through the city and past the port of Albany. At one point, a large paddle wheeler tour boat, filled with laughing, drinking young people and loud music came toward us. As it passed us at close quarters in the dark narrow river, I was very glad that I had a set of "front lights".

All of a sudden the runabout sped up, circled back toward me, and pulled up next to me again. "There on your right is the Capital City Yacht Club", the man said excitedly. "Are you a member of a yacht club back home?" he questioned, and then added: "If you are, you can stay there for free." He said that the docks in Troy were still an hour away at that speed, and that he would be happy to take me there. But if I stayed here, I would have full facilities tonight and in the morning. I was exhausted, and wanted to see him get his little girl home. I needed gas and a hot shower, and it did look like a very nice place, so I agreed to stay there. Before I left them, I gave them one of my brochures which had my phone number and web site address on it. I asked them to send me their name and address when they got home. If they did, I would send them one of my wildlife videos as a thank you gift for being my "guiding angels" that night. As I thanked them, I gave the little girl several children's tracts, and gave the dad one that was perfect for him. I told the little girl to take good care of her daddy because he was a very good man, and the dad to keep spending that kind of time with his little girl. After a final goodbye, and a hearty "God bless you", I headed toward the yacht club docks, as they disappeared down the river.

The long, well lit fuel dock was the easiest dock to come into, as it had been at so many other marinas. I tied up securely under a light at the end of it, hoping no one would mind, so I didn't have to move the boat again. As I walked down the dock toward the clubhouse, I encountered a very nice, soft spoken man, who happened to be the vice president of the club. When I explained my situation, he said it would be fine for me to stay right there at the end of the fuel dock for the night. He said I could pay for my slip in the morning, and the dock master would sell me fuel, ice, a pass for the barge canal and maybe even a running light bulb. As he showed me around the club, I told him that my daughter and her husband would be picking me up there. When he heard that, he explained how to get to the yacht club by car, and showed me a pay phone, where I called Nicole and Eric with the directions. After my phone call, I thanked the man for making me feel so welcome, saying that he was a true gentleman, and one of the nicest people I had encountered on my trip. He shook my hand warmly, saying he hoped I enjoyed my stay there and then headed off toward the parking lot.

I waited on the corner for Nicole and Eric and was thrilled to see them when they arrived. They told me my boat was fifty minutes from their house. That meant I couldn't spend the night with them, because they couldn't bring me back there the next morning. They decided instead to treat me to pizza at their favorite pizza parlor in Troy. We had a great time eating, drinking, laughing and catching up on the latest news in my life and theirs. I shared some of the amazing ways that God blessed me on my voyage, and I thoroughly enjoyed seeing them. I blinked back a tear, as I accepted the fact that my little girl was now a grown up, married woman. I wished with all my heart that I could be that man in the blue boat, and that Nicole could be the size of his daughter again for just one more cruise. I knew those days were gone forever, but I hoped that she treasured and held on to those memories, and that they were as precious to her as they were to me.

On the way back to the marina, we stopped at a convenience store so I could buy bottled water and a few other staples I needed on the boat. They helped me carry everything down the dock, and said they were impressed with my vessel as we stowed things aboard. I hugged them both tightly, told them I loved them and thanked them for coming. Then I said goodbye, and they turned and walked away. As I watched Nicole walk hand in hand down the dock with her husband, I realized **that** goodbye was not just for that night. But that it was a goodbye to a little girl and a time in her life and mine that would never come again.

27
SENECA
SKANEATELES, NY

Chapter 37

The New York State Barge Canal

When my eyes opened the next morning, the first thought that popped into my head was, the radio! With the mast disconnected from the boat and laid down, there was no longer an antenna for the boats ship to shore radio. The antenna was attached to a fitting at the very top of the mast, and the wire from it ran down through the mast to the bottom. When the mast was in place the antenna wire coming out of the bottom of the mast simply plugged into a fitting on top of the cabin. Right now, the base of the mast, and the antenna wire that came out of it, was hanging four feet off the back of the boat dangling above the motor. It was eighteen feet away from the plug on top of the cabin that it should plug into for the radio to work. I had cruised on the barge canal many times, and knew that the most important piece of equipment next to a dependable motor was a working radio. I would have to pass through thirty locks and a couple of lift bridges on this trip. I would need to contact each lock and bridge operator to let them know I was coming, what time I would arrive and which direction I was heading. As I lay there, my over active, creative mind, devised a plan that might work. Digging through the storage compartments, I found some long pieces of insulated wire that had at least two different wires inside. I plugged the two wires into the fitting on the cabin top where the mast antenna usually plugged in. Then I ran that long piece of wire down the horizontal mast to the bottom of it. I had to splice two wires together to reach the back of the boat, and I wrapped it around the mast as I went, to keep the wire out of the way. I then spliced my long wire to the antenna wire coming out of the base of the mast. I worked carefully and painstakingly, making sure that each splice was perfect and wrapping them heavily with electrical tape. I felt like McGyver, as I created a connection from the radio to the mast top antenna with scrap wire and tape.

After I finished, I headed for the club house to take a shower, but I passed an older gentleman on the dock that looked like he was headed for his boat. "Looks like another beautiful day," I began. "Yes it does," he answered smiling. "Taking the boat out this morning?" I asked. "Not right away, I'm just gonna sit on it and read the morning paper," was his reply. Then I explained: "I've been having problems with my radio, and I'm heading down the canal today. Would you mind if I gave you a call to see if it's working?" I asked politely. "Not at all, that would be fine," he responded, and then added: "Her name is the Misty Lady, call me in about five minutes on channel seventy-eight". I eagerly walked back to the boat, happy that the Lord had provided a way to test the radio. Climbing aboard, I powered up the radio and set it on channel seventy-eight. "God Speed calling the Misty Lady, God Speed calling the Misty Lady, come in Misty Lady, do you read me?" I barked into the microphone, but was greeted only by silence. "C'mon Lord . . . please let it work . . . I don't have the heart to re do all those connections . . . I was so careful with every one of the splices," I whispered to myself, as I waited desperately for a response. I checked all the settings to make sure I was on the right channel and that the volume was turned up. "Maybe he's not aboard yet . . . I hope he didn't forget about me . . . Maybe he doesn't have his radio turned on yet?" I thought nervously, frustrated by the silence. "God Speed calling Misty Lady, God Speed calling Misty Lady, how bout ya Misty Lady, can you read me?" I asked, even more urgently. I heard the loud electronic pop of a microphone button being pushed and then: "This is the Misty Lady, I read you loud and clear captain, in fact you're knocking my ear off, turn your volume down!" crackled his crystal clear reply. "God bless ya, sir, thanks for the radio check, and have a great day," I responded happily. "You do the same captain," he replied warmly as he signed off.

After I used the men's room and took a shower, I went to the office to settle up with the dock master and purchase the other items I needed. I was greeted by a thin young man with blonde hair, bright eyes and an eager smile named Mark. His crisp, short sleeved, white shirt and trousers looked like some type of nautical uniform. He was eager to please, and when I told him about my trip from Florida, I immediately became his hero and friend. He was so helpful and so nice to me, it almost got annoying, yet he wasn't the least bit phony. I said that my trip was partly a missionary trip to remind people about God and his love. I told him how the Lord had blessed and protected me along the way. I also told him about my ministry and my job at a Christian school. He had been in the Coast Guard for several years, and had taken the "temporary" position as dock master after his discharge. Working at the yacht club, he made so many friends and grew to love the job so much he stayed on, and had been there ever since. He said he had a "ministry" leading the people there to healing and wellness through diet, meditation and exercise. Apparently club members came to him for all kinds of help and advice, and he saw himself as a friend, advisor and counselor to many. He told me he didn't believe in any one "religion" or "god", but did believe there was a supreme being who created everything.

He seemed so sure of himself, that I didn't have the heart or the time to get into a long winded discussion with him. I decided the best approach was to keep witnessing to him in gentle, friendly ways with my words and my actions. I only hoped I could plant a seed, and that he would see something in me that he wanted. The blessings just kept coming. He gave me the yacht club members discount for my dock spot, and three bags of ice for free. Then I was able to purchase a seven day pass for the New York State Canal System right from him, so I wouldn't be held up entering the locks. He didn't have a running light bulb, but he called the auto parts store on the corner to make sure they were open and that they had one. After a five minute walk, I was back in his office with the bulb, and he came down to the dock to help me install it. Once the running light was fixed, he filled all three of my fuel tanks and gave me the yacht club members discount on the gas. As he handed the tanks aboard and helped me untie, he told me that I was one of the nicest and most unique men he had ever met. He urged me to call him if I ran into any trouble on the canal, so he could send someone to come and get me. I gave him one of my brochures and a couple of tracts to read that were perfect for someone with his mind set. Then I shook his hand, saying that I couldn't thank him enough for going so far above and beyond the call of duty to help me. After I started the motor, I looked him square in the eyes and said: "You are a truly outstanding young man, with a servant's heart, great people skills, and a sincere love for others. Let God take control of your life, Mark, and he will use you and bless you beyond your wildest dreams. God bless you man, thanks again for everything," I concluded. I almost sensed that he didn't want to let go of the ropes. It seemed like he was having trouble saying goodbye, as if I was a beloved family member, and I couldn't understand what I had done to make such an impact on him. As I motored away, he stood on the dock watching and waving until I was out of sight. I believe that Mark was the reason I wound up **there** that night. That young man had one of the best hearts for people I had ever seen, and as I headed north, I prayed that the Lord would use his gift to touch and bless the lives of thousands.

Once in the Barge Canal system, I was in familiar territory and felt very comfortable. Although I had never come that far east before, my children and I had great memories traveling up and down the canal and going through the locks. Going through a lock on the New York State Barge Canal was an adventure in itself, and my kids always seemed to get a big kick out of it. Huge, tall steel doors would open slowly to reveal a long narrow concrete chamber. As you pulled into the lock, high wet algae covered concrete walls rose straight from the water on both sides, towering high above your boat. Other giant steel doors at the far end were closed, holding back a wall of water as high as the concrete walls on both sides of you. You would need big cushy fenders on one side of your boat, because you would come against one of the concrete walls and grab a vertical pipe recessed in the concrete, or two fat ropes hanging down from above. The steel doors where you entered would close behind you with a loud ominous boom that echoed through the chamber. Then the lock operator would open underwater flood gates and the higher water from the river ahead would fill the lock chamber, bringing your boat up to the next level of the river. The water around you would boil and bubble wildly as your boat moved and rubbed against the wall in the strong current. You had to hang on to the ropes, or put your own rope around the recessed vertical pipe, to keep your boat against the wall as it rose to the top. Once your boat reached the top of the wall the steel doors would slowly open, and you could proceed on your way down the river.

I made an amazing discovery in one of the locks, but I wasn't sure if it made me feel very relieved, or very upset. As the water rushed in around me boiling and frothing, the normally green water in the lock was churned up into a muddy brown color. As the water got muddy, the reading on my depth finder changed from fifteen feet deep in the lock, to only four feet deep! The suspended sand, mud and sediment in the churning brown water triggered a false bottom reading, and the depth finder showed the water to be much shallower than it really was. I realized then, what had happened off the coast of New Jersey. The big ocean waves had churned up the sandy bottom and I had been panicked by shallow water readings for hours, even though I was in deep water all the time.

I cruised right through cities and villages, passed waterfront homes, and wound my way through farmland and forests. Motoring smoothly on the calm narrow waterway, I decided that the New York State Barge Canal had the best and widest variety of scenery I had passed on the entire trip. After making it through several locks, I began to think about where to spend the night. On the canal, there were well lit docking spots at the approach to every lock coming from either direction. Now that I was getting close to home, my goal was to go as far as I could each day, and every minute of daylight was very precious. It was getting light around six, every morning, but the locks didn't start to operate until seven. If I tied up on the east side of a lock, (for the night) and woke up at five forty-five, I would have to wait until seven for that lock to open to get underway. I would lose an hour of daylight and eight or ten miles of distance that day. But if I got through the lock first, and then tied up on the west side, (for the night) I could get underway the moment my eyes opened and travel the greatest possible distance that day.

The next lock was about five miles away, and there wasn't another one after that for quite a distance. If I could just get through that one, before I tied up that night, I wouldn't have to worry about what time they opened in the morning. I thought I had forty-five more minutes of daylight left. But on that cloudy night, as the days got shorter, it turned out that I had less than thirty. I found myself motoring through a wooded area in total darkness with no moon or stars and no street lights. Even with my spotlight, it was hard to see, and I prayed that the lights of that lock would materialize out of the blackness ahead of me soon. Calling the lock operator, I told him that I was coming from the east and would be there soon. I let him know that I wanted to go through tonight, and then spend the night on the docking wall on the west side of his lock. He said he would have the gates open when I arrived, but to watch out for several large logs and tree branches that were floating at the entrance to his lock. I was relieved when I rounded a bend and saw the lights of the lock ahead. Remembering the logs, I approached the open gates very slowly. The operator came out on the approach wall with a flashlight and long pole and shoved the big logs and other debris out of the way so I could enter the lock safely. I thanked him very much, and voiced a loud "God bless you", as I entered the lock.

I spent the night under a street light on a long, well lit concrete wall just beyond the lock. It looked like a perfect spot, but I soon learned that heavily used railroad tracks ran right along the canal there. Needless to say, I slept very little, and I kept dreaming that the boat was parked right on the tracks and was about to be smashed by a train. The next morning I awoke just before it got light, and was on my way as soon as I could see fifty yards ahead. When I bought my pass for the canal system, I received a map that showed the location of every lock and how far apart they were. That made it easy to calculate when I would arrive at each one. The map showed that if I pushed hard, I could make it all the way to Oneida Lake before dark. Located east of Syracuse, the short stubby lake was three or four miles wide. It was twenty nine miles long running east to west, so the builders of the canal used it as part of that waterway.

One summer twenty years ago, my children and I took a canal cruise to Oneida Lake to spend a few days at Sylvan Beach. On that trip, we entered the lake from the west near Brewerton, and cruised all the way to the eastern end, where the canal left the lake again at Sylvan Beach. I planned that adventure, because I fondly remembered renting a cabin there with my parents when I was a boy. The small resort village was known for its sandy beach and also had a small amusement park, making it the perfect place to take kids on a boat trip. Tears came to my eyes, as I remembered how the Lord had been with us, even on that trip so many years before. Crossing the lake from west to east, we were hit by a violent thunderstorm with heavy rain. The kids were huddled nervously together in the cabin, while I kept steering through the storm. We approached Sylvan Beach just as it was getting dark and the rain had finally stopped. It was the Fourth of July, and a large group of boats had gathered to watch the annual fireworks display at the amusement park. After surviving the scary crossing, it was fun to watch the kids ooh and aah over the fireworks as we sat there happily anchored among the other boats. After the grand finale, the other boaters dispersed quickly, leaving us alone as they went their separate ways. Being a novice, I couldn't find the entrance to the canal in the dark, and didn't know that area at all. I began to panic as we slowly groped our way through the darkness, afraid of getting too close to the big rocks we had seen earlier near shore. Suddenly the red and green front running light of a boat came out of the darkness on the deserted lake, heading straight at us.

"Are you lost?" called a mature male voice. "Yes, I'm afraid we are," I replied. "Follow us, we'll lead you in," the friendly man said calmly. The pleasant elderly couple in the small powerboat led us safely up the canal, where we were able to tie up just thirty feet from the merry go round. My kids were in heaven as we spent the next two days tied up in the middle of an amusement park, riding rides and enjoying the beach. It was hard to believe that those people had somehow spotted us way out there in the darkness and **knew** that we were lost. The only explanation was that God sent them to us, and maybe, just maybe they had been angels.

According to the map, there were two locks very close together just before the canal entered Oneida Lake. Lock twenty-one was located about three miles from the lake, and lock twenty-two was just a mile beyond it. If I made it through those two locks that night, I would be in great shape! The next day, I could start out as early as I wanted to, and wouldn't have to worry about another lock for almost thirty miles. Because Oneida Lake was wide and ran east to west, it had a bad reputation for strong winds and big waves. If I headed out there at first light, I had the greatest chance to cross the large lake while it was calm. I would need gas before I started across, so I planned to get it somewhere that night, to avoid being held up in the morning. Things went well that day and I made great time. As evening approached, it looked like I would easily make it through the two locks, and be able to get gas and tie up in Sylvan Beach before it got dark.

When I got within four miles of lock twenty-one, the sky got very dark all at once. Then the temperature dropped quickly as I felt a brisk cold wind in my face. A jagged lighting bolt sliced the sky ahead, followed a few seconds later by the low ominous rumble of thunder. I quickly closed the cabin and donned what was left of the tattered rain gear, just as the sky opened up. A vicious wind drove the large cold drops mercilessly into my face and my eyes, and I could barely see. Lightning flashed through the sky above me and then thunder boomed so close and so loud that it startled me. I saw a bright flash, and heard a loud crack at the same instant, as lightning struck the transformer on a power pole less than a hundred yards away. A shower of sparks cascaded down the pole as smoke rose from the discolored metal canister. I decided that it was no longer a good idea, to rest my free hand on the horizontal aluminum mast above my shoulder, as I had done all day. It was a horribly unpleasant moment, but I kept going, determined to make it through those two locks that night, so I could cross the lake in the morning. I opened the cabin door to get at the radio, and all the maps got soaked as I did. "Lock twenty-one, lock twenty-one, this is the sailboat "God Speed", I am approaching you from the east and I'm about three miles away," I shouted anxiously into the microphone. Although I tried hard to be polite, there was a deep sense of urgency in my voice as the cold water ran down my face. "I need to make it through your lock and the next one tonight. Is it possible to have the lock open for me when I arrive?" I asked respectfully. "I'm sorry captain, state regulations say that I cannot allow any boats in the lock, or operate the lock when lightning is visible. You'll have to tie up to the approach wall and wait until the storm passes," he said. His answer disappointed me, and I hoped the delay wouldn't prevent me from reaching my goal that night. But I reluctantly accepted the news, knowing that God had a reason, even for this.

As I approached the concrete wall at lock twenty-one, I knew that it would not be fun, trying to come in and get tied up in those conditions. The strong wind was pushing the boat hard, and the deck was slippery. My rain gear flapped wildly as I tried to control the boat and jump to the wall with the ropes. As the boat bobbed and moved against the concrete, the fenders slid up and out of position. Then, as I stood on the concrete wall, I saw that in my haste, I left the still running motor in gear, and the boat was pulling me along the wall. I had to jump onto the slippery deck again to kill the motor, and then back to the wall in the downpour. I was completely drenched and exhausted by the time I had the boat secured and headed up to the lock office. A thin young man with short hair greeted me at the door, and asked me to come in out of the rain. He introduced himself as Josh and said that he was the lock operator. At a small table against the far wall, a middle aged woman with glasses, and a heavy set teenage boy were eating Chinese food out of cardboard containers. The care worn blonde woman was Josh's mother; and she nodded and smiled politely with her mouth full as I introduced myself. She brought Chinese food to the lock office, to have dinner with her son that night. The teenage boy was a young friend, who rode his bicycle over to hang out at the lock before the storm

I told them about my trip, and how the Good Lord had blessed me again and again along the way. Then I told Josh that I needed to get going fast when the lightning stopped, so I could also get through the next lock that night. He assured me that would be easy, because it was so close, and said he would call his buddy who manned that lock to let him know I was coming. As I told them about my position at the Christian school, the woman became less afraid of the bedraggled, drenched stranger in the ripped rain suit. She began to smile a little and talked more openly. We shared small talk as we waited for the storm to pass, and I created a small puddle in the center of the floor. I learned that she was a believer, and that she was very active in her local church. As she started gathering up the empty containers and slipped on her coat to leave, I got an idea. Since we had to wait for the storm to pass anyway, that unexpected delay could turn into a big blessing if I used the time to fill my fuel tanks. I asked her if she was going near a gas station when she left, and if she would be willing to take me there and then bring me back. She said she would be happy to help a fellow believer, so I eagerly ran back to the boat to disconnect the tanks. She pulled her small car down an access road and right up to the boat, so it was an easy matter to load the tanks. As we drove, I learned that her name was Darlene and that she had just been through a painful divorce. Josh's father had recently left the home, wounding her and her son deeply. Since that happened, she was finding it hard to believe that God was really there. As we reached the gas station my heart sank and I felt embarrassed as I realized I had left my wallet with my money and credit card on the boat. Without hesitating she cheerfully headed back to the lock as I apologized up and down.

All at once I knew that **she** was the reason the Lord stopped me at **that** lock and had me go inside, and I shared that with her. I was sure he was using me that night, to encourage her, and show her that he had never left her, nor forsaken her. I shared my testimony with her, explaining how I had lost a wife in a tragic car accident when my children were little. I told her how that tragic loss, had been part of God's plan for my life, and how he used that tragedy, to send my life in a whole new direction. I also told her how much the Lord had blessed and used me since the loss of a spouse. I said that he would do the same for her, if she would just trust him; reminding her that if the weather had been fine, I would have passed quickly through that lock and would never have met her. Then I went on to say that I hadn't gone into the office of any other lock on the canal, or even gotten out of the boat at a lock on that trip. I knew that God wanted her to hear my story that day, and even allowed me to forget my wallet so I would have more time in the car with her to share it. Tears began to flow down both of her cheeks as she nodded eagerly and agreed with me. She said I was absolutely right. My unplanned stop there that day, and the opportunity to share that story, was too perfect and too unbelievable to have happened by chance. She jokingly asked if I was about to tell her, that I was an angel sent by God. We both laughed, as I assured her that I was just a tired, wet, old sinner that he seemed to use a lot. As we unloaded the tanks and put them aboard, I noticed that the lightning had stopped and Josh already had the doors of the lock open. Darlene shook my hand almost off, as she thanked me and praised the Lord for using me to strengthen her faith. I took her name and address, and promised to send her one of my wildlife videos that had uplifting scripture verses in it. I said goodbye to her and reminded her one more time to trust God, as I pushed away and headed into the lock.

As I came through the other side of the lock it was dark. Because it was a rainy night it was so dark you could hardly see your hand in front of your face. I knew that as soon as I got away from the lights of the lock, it would be so black I would not be able to tell water from land. Lock twenty-two was less than a mile away through the blackness, and it would be very well lit. But as much as I wanted to get there that night, I chickened out and pulled over to the approach wall. About thirty minutes later, as I was eating a sandwich a voice crackled through the radio. It was the lock operator from lock twenty-two. He got worried, because I wasn't there yet, and was calling to see if I was okay and was still coming. I told him that I decided against it, because it was raining hard and looked so black up the canal in his direction. The nice young man said that was too bad, because he had the lock doors open for me. He went on to say that it was a pretty straight shot down the canal, and if I went just a short distance I would see his lights. His friendly voice reassured me, and I had done far more dangerous things on that trip, so I untied and shoved off into the blackness. My spotlight was no help as it glared off the raindrops making it even harder to see. I stared ahead and tried to guess where the middle of the canal was by looking at the shiny blackness of the water and dull blackness of the land. I crawled slowly along; feeling like I was blind, but eventually I did see the bright green light of lock twenty-two, far off through the darkness and straight ahead. Heading slowly toward it, I finally approached the well lit area and entered the lock. The young lock operator was as pleasant and friendly in person as his voice sounded on the radio, and I shared a little bit about my trip with him. I also told him that I thought the Good Lord sent me to lock twenty-one that night, just to give a word of encouragement to Josh's mother. He smiled and said that was good, because right now she really needed it. I spent the night on the approach wall just beyond his lock and slept very well in the rainy darkness.

At first light, I was passing the amusement park where I stayed years before with my children, and soon I was gliding smoothly across the open waters of Oneida Lake. It was early morning on a calm summer day so the lake was like glass for the entire crossing. It was a relaxing easy morning as I followed the red and green buoys down the middle of the lake while I watched cartoons on TV. I had grown up in Auburn, NY, and my parents still lived there. Since I was going to pass very close to Auburn that afternoon, I called my parents to see if I could visit them and spend a night at their house. The canal map showed a public docking area in Weedsport, just seven miles from my parent's home. It looked like a safe spot to park and lock the boat, and leave it for one night. When I called my mom, she said they would love to see me, and would be happy to pick me up in Weedsport, so I gave her directions, and said that I would call again when I got there. Just minutes before I reached the spot where they would meet me, I rode into another torrential downpour. Once again I had the unpleasant job of bringing the boat in and tying it up in heavy rain, and I got soaked. I knew I was going to see my parents, take a hot shower, eat a home cooked meal and sleep in a real bed, so I didn't let it bother me too much.

The public docking wall was not far from a canal side restaurant, so I had them pick me up there. It was great to see them and we had a wonderful night together, having dinner in the kitchen and sharing old memories. I dried my clothes, watched TV with them and then turned in early. The next morning they took me back to the boat and my dad helped me cast off. Several miles down the canal I made a mistake that almost cost me the boat and ended the trip on a tragic note. All along the canal, I had passed under bridges that had a large center support made of steel, concrete or stone. The large central pier was a substantial structure that rose from the water in the middle of the river to support the center of the bridge. There were lights and red and green channel markers on the bridges to show boats that they could pass safely through the openings on either side of that center pier. Most vessels kept to the right like cars on a highway, and went through the opening on their side of the river. After three days of passing through the opening on the right side of all the bridges, I wasn't watching the markers closely and almost wrecked the boat. One of the bridges looked just like all the others, but the red and green markers showed that the deep channel was only under the left side of the bridge and not both sides. The opening under the right side of **that** bridge was shallow water and **not** a boat channel. Daydreaming as I cruised smoothly along at full speed, I went under the right side of that bridge and into very shallow water. The depth alarm began to beep, but before I could even react there was a loud bang and the boat rose up and stopped dead. Horrified as I saw my mistake, I couldn't believe I had done something so stupid so close to home. As I looked down into the partially clear green water, I saw big rocks and boulders just below the surface. This was a little different than running aground in sand and mud. I could have sunk the boat, or done extensive damage to the keel and rudder. Revving the motor to full throttle in reverse I rocked the boat back and forth and after a few minutes, it miraculously came free. Backing quickly out of that dangerous area, I promised myself I would watch the channel markers carefully.

Somewhere around Lyons, I pulled into a run down little marina to get gas one last time. The place was back off the main canal in a small swampy bay. The fuel dock was hard to get to with a sailboat, so I nosed up to an old rickety wooden dock section along the canal. I figured it would be easier to carry the tanks than to maneuver in such tight quarters. As I tied up, a short, heavy set dark haired man came out of the office and yelled at me for docking there. I told him I was coming in to buy gas, and he pointed to the fuel dock as if I was stupid. I told him I couldn't get in there and I would carry my tanks over, so he shrugged indifferently. After he filled the tanks, I handed him my credit card because by that time I had used up all the cash. He got very upset, ranting and raving that they did not take credit cards there. Apparently there was a small faded sign on the fuel dock that said "cash only" but since I hadn't pulled in there, I hadn't seen it. Since the gas was already in my tanks, he said we would have to go talk to the owner. As we walked through the boat yard, I knew the place had seen better days. Grubby old time boats sat on rusty trailers and one of the storage buildings looked like it was ready to fall down. A couple of huge wooden boats that looked like they hadn't seen water since the fifties sat on cradles rotting, and the place looked like the marina that time forgot. In the midst of all the rust and decay, a thin red haired man was swearing at two other men, while the threesome tried to lower a beat up boat onto a cradle with an old forklift that barely ran. The red haired man appeared to be the "boss" and as he yelled at his helpers, every other word was a cuss word. When they finished the job, the dark haired man introduced me to the boss, saying that I tried to buy gas with a credit card, and that it was already in my tanks. He said it with the same tone that he would have used to tell him that he caught me **stealing** gas from their pumps.

The man was very upset when I told him I had no cash with me. He said he would have to drop everything and take me to the bank, so I could get a cash advance on my credit card and pay him for the gas. As we walked to his car he asked me where my boat was. When I pointed to it, he sneered and grunted, saying: "Ooh, you've got a blow boat." I tried to be nice, and I apologized up and down for my mistake and any inconvenience it had caused him. As we drove into town, I told him about my trip and how the Lord had blessed me and protected me along the way. He must have figured I was some kind of priest or minister, because he softened a little and began to talk to me, rather than yell at me. I saw that he wasn't a horrible mean man, just a hurting little boy. He had a very successful business in the southern part of the state, but sold everything to move here and buy that marina. After years of headaches and hard work he realized it wasn't a good decision. As it became more run down and fell into disrepair he became burned out, bitter and angry. I didn't have much time with him, but I tried to be sympathetic, encouraging, and a good listener. I told him to trust God, treat others the way he would want to be treated, and his business would be blessed. After I got the cash advance, we headed back to his marina and he was listening more than talking. I said that before I knew God, the "World's Biggest Loser" TV show should have been about **me,** but ever since I invited Jesus into my heart, I had led a blessed life. Back at the marina, I paid him and thanked him for the ride, saying that I enjoyed talking to him. I shook his hand and said that God would bless his life, if he would just trust him. Then I offered him a sincere "God bless you", as I picked up the tanks and walked toward my boat.

Soon after I got going again it began to rain, and it stayed rainy and drizzly the rest of the day. I picked up a traveling companion that afternoon. An authentic looking replica of a historic Erie Canal packet boat, caught up to me as I waited in one of the locks. Apparently someone had built and owned a fleet of the large, classic looking wooden vessels. People who loved nostalgia and history could actually rent one, to take a scenic cruise along the barge canal. The packet boat "Seneca" was behind me the rest of the day. I was moving faster than it was, but each time I was going to lose it, I came to a lock or lift bridge and it caught up to me again.

Soon after I exited lock number thirty in Macedon, I spotted an attractive marina tucked into a bay on the left side. It looked almost brand new, but what really caught my attention was a large blue travel lift, exactly like the one they used to lower my boat into the water in Florida. I would need a marina that had one of those, to put my boat back on its trailer at the end of the trip. My plan was to pull the boat out of the water somewhere near Rochester. In two days, the staff at our Christian school had faculty meetings all day to get things ready for the start of the new school year. As I thought about the trip coming to an end, I looked at the map and began to weigh my options. If I kept going one more day, I would be in the heart of Rochester, but had no idea who had a travel lift there. It was rainy, dreary, cold and windy, and I had been steering the boat for over a month. Eight miles away, the canal passed through the heart of downtown Fairport. The center of that town focused on the canal and was a boater's paradise. There was a well maintained boardwalk along both sides of the canal, with ample public docking facilities, in a high class, upscale environment. In fact I couldn't think of a prettier or classier spot to end my trip. Fairport was an eastern suburb of Rochester, so if I ended my trip there, I would have made it from Florida to the Rochester area. By ending my trip **that** night, I could see my wife, sleep in my own bed, and have the whole day tomorrow to rest and get things ready for the teacher's meetings the next day. I could tie her up in Fairport, and come back in a day or two to cruise her back to that nice marina in Macedon that had a travel lift. Maybe I could even talk my wife into coming on a short canal cruise with me if it was a nice day, just to get the boat back there. As I thought about the pros and cons, I looked straight up into the dreary gray sky. Cold rain drops drizzled on my face, running down my cheeks and under my clothing. "Well Lord, I guess the time has come to call it a trip," I said, with a mixture of sadness and joy. "Thanks for being with me all the way, and thanks for getting me here." I concluded.

With that I picked up the cell phone and called my wife. I told her my voyage was over, and that she could pick up a tired, cold, wet, lonely old sailor anytime after seven on the canal boardwalk in Fairport (if she wanted to). She said that sounded like a pretty good offer, and she might just be there. As I cruised into the center of Fairport past the expensive boats on both sides I spotted a long open spot on the left. I made a U turn, and pulled in there so smoothly you might have thought I had done it a few times. As I tied up, a pleasant older gentleman came over and introduced himself as the dock master. I told him my plans to leave the boat for a day or two until I could bring it to the marina in Macedon, and he said that would be fine. As we talked, I shared my adventure with him, and told him that I was a teacher at Lima Christian School. He was fascinated that I had come so far and he loved the name of my boat. He said he was a retired teacher himself, and he graciously helped me lift the bad motor from the cabin, up onto the dock and carry it into the parking lot behind the shops. I paid him the fee for one night, but he said I could leave the boat until I made connections with the marina, and pay the balance when I came back. I took only the clothing and personal items I would need for the next couple of days, because I was too cold, wet and tired to deal with very much right then.

I was just locking the cabin, when my wife Mary came down the board walk. She was really a sight for sore eyes, as she walked toward me smiling. Glancing at the boat, she asked me simply: "Are you ready to go home?" I hugged her tightly, looked her in the eyes and sighed: ***"Yes . . . I am ready to go home . . . very ready."*** Her car was already in the parking lot behind the shops, so I had her back up to the outboard that I had waiting there on a blanket. Once we loaded the motor and I threw my duffle bag in the back seat, we pulled out of the parking lot and headed for home.

THE END

After The Voyage

» Two days after I parked the boat in Fairport, my wife and I took a canal cruise after our teacher's meetings, and we brought my mother in law with us. ***(. . . A Calm Sea Never Made A Skillful Mariner . . .)*** It was a beautiful sunny afternoon as we brought the boat from Fairport, down to the marina in Macedon that had the travel lift.

» I found out the name and phone number of that marina from the lock operator in Macedon and had already contacted them. They were happy to pull the boat out of the water, set it on its trailer, and pressure wash it for me. They were very gracious and did everything at a reasonable cost.

» The following spring, I spent over three hundred dollars to have the original motor restored to like-new condition. Then I sold "God Speed" in order to get the money I would need to publish this book. The boat was purchased by a young pastor from Minnesota, who always dreamed of owning a boat that big. He and his family have kept the name and emblem on the boat. As a memento, they mailed me the Christian flag that flew at the top of the mast during this trip.

» The summer after I sold my cruising sailboat, I purchased a used sixteen foot day sailor. It has the name "God Speed" and a Christian fish emblem on it.

» I sold the motor I purchased in New Jersey on eBay for one hundred dollars less than I paid for it. I felt that was a very reasonable "rental fee" to use a brand new outboard for one week. The people at "Surf and Off Shore" were so nice and gave me such a great deal; I bought a 50HP Honda outboard from them for a fishing boat I refurbished. I drove all the way to New Jersey to have them install it on the boat in the spring of 2006. The name of the fishing boat is "Fisher Of Men" and it has the same Christian fish emblem on it as my sailboat.

» I mailed a touching video to Darlene and her son Josh soon after the trip, but I never heard from the tall man and little girl who were my "guiding angels" in Albany.

» If I ever took this trip again, I would want a much larger boat and at least twice as much time. I would want one other person with me at all times, and I would watch the weather closely and stay in the ocean for the entire state of New Jersey.

» All of the people, places and events in this book are real. The actual names of some of the people and businesses have been changed for their protection.

» A dramatic reading of this book, read by the author,

is available on audio tape and CD through my web site: www.myfathersworld.com. Autographed copies of this book and my wildlife and outdoor videos are also available there.

Dave Tripiciano is a lifetime sailor, outdoorsman and the founder of "My Father's World" Ministries. He is an award winning wildlife photographer and videographer. In addition to this book, he has filmed and produced eight wildlife and outdoor videos. These unique films, and autographed copies of this book are available through his web site: www.myfathersworld.com. He is a sought after Christian speaker and has been a school band director for thirty two years. He is currently serving as the director of bands at Lima Christian School in upstate New York. During the summer of 2004 he fulfilled a lifelong dream by sailing from Florida to Rochester, New York in his twenty five foot "Hunter" sailboat. When he planned the trip, he never imagined how many life threatening situations he would face, or how many lives he would have the chance to touch along the way.

Tate Publishing & *Enterprises*

Tate Publishing is committed to excellence in the publishing industry. Our staff of highly trained professionals, including editors, graphic designers, and marketing personnel, work together to produce the very finest books available. The company reflects the philosophy established by the founders, based on Psalms 68:11,

"THE LORD GAVE THE WORD AND GREAT WAS THE COMPANY OF THOSE WHO PUBLISHED IT."

If you would like further information, please call
1.888.361.9473
or visit our website
www.tatepublishing.com

Tate Publishing & *Enterprises*, LLC
127 E. Trade Center Terrace
Mustang, Oklahoma 73064 USA